This beautiful book shows that we can offer hope to women considering abortion, compassion to women who have an abortion, and love to those who work in the abortion industry. Read this, be inspired, and be part of the beginning of the end of abortion.

—**Governor Mike Huckabee,** Fox News host,
New York Times bestselling author

When we truly step out in faith, life does not get easier. It does, though, certainly get better and richer and more full of true living. Such is the reality reflected in these moving and encouraging stories brought to us by these dedicated and brave spiritual warriors. If you love life, read and be encouraged, and step out again in faith to be part of the Lord's plan for a new culture of life!

—**The Most Reverend Thomas Olmsted,** Bishop of Phoenix,
author of *Catholics in the Public Square* and *Into the Breach*

This book reminds me of what I told the 40 Days for Life founders when they came to me at the very beginning: Once this starts, it will ignite beyond our imagination. The ground is fertile! And now all these stories show how that has come to pass.

—**Fr. Frank Pavone,** National Director, Priests for Life;
President, National Pro-Life Religious Council

Shawn's book vividly weaves his own story with so many faithful and fruitful friends who compassionately responded to the call to help. These stories will fill every reader with confidence, faith, hope, and certainty that life will triumph through acts of selfless love and kind compassion.

—**Jor-El Godsey,** President, Heartbeat International

A must read. Be inspired by the prayers, fasting, and courage of everyday saints who inspire and challenge us to unite for the sanctity of life and family.

—**Alveda C. King,** Evangelist, Civil Rights for The Unborn;
niece of Martin Luther King Jr.

These stories share the very best of America and of how we can use our freedoms to offer genuine hope to those in need. The true stories in this book are living proof that the tide has turned on the abortion crisis.

—**Eric Metaxas,** *New York Times* bestselling author
of *Bonhoeffer: Pastor, Martyr, Prophet, Spy*

The book you hold in your hands tells amazing stories of courage, dedication, perseverance, trust and godly love in a dark cultural war. There is a hideous plan from the enemy to rob our nation of a generation through abortion. But 40 Days for Life confronts it the way Jesus would: tenderly, without condemnation—by his redeeming presence. Shawn's stories are amazing God-stories. I dare you to read this book without weeping!

—**Ruth Graham,** author of *In Every Pew Sits a Broken Heart*

These stories represent the often unreported hope that we see in America and beyond. The written word and the movie screen are powerful ways to bring truth, love and mercy into a culture of death.

—**Cary Solomon and Chuck Konzelman,**
writer and producers of *God's Not Dead*; screen writers,
producers, and directors of *Unplanned*

This powerful and inspiring book shows us what can happen when ordinary people courageously bring hope to the darkest corners of our culture.

—**Catherine Glenn Foster,** JD, President and CEO,
Americans United for Life

THE
BEGINNING
OF THE
END OF ABORTION

THE
BEGINNING
OF THE
END OF ABORTION

**40 INSPIRING STORIES OF GOD
CHANGING HEARTS AND SAVING LIVES**

SHAWN D. CARNEY
WITH CINDY LAMBERT

Cappella
Books
Nashville, Tennessee

ISBN 978-0-9882870-9-9

Unless otherwise identified, all Scripture quotations in this publication
are taken from the *Holy Bible, New International Version*® (NIV®).
Copyright © 1973, 1978, 1984, 2011 by International Bible Society.
Used by permission of Zondervan. All rights reserved.

Scripture quotations marked NASB are taken from
the *New American Standard Bible*. Copyright © 1960, 1962, 1963, 1968,
1971, 1972, 1973, 1975, 1977, 1995 by The Lockman Foundation.
Used by permission.

Scripture quotations marked NLT are taken from
the *Holy Bible, New Living Translation*, copyright © 1996, 2004.
Used by permission of Tyndale House Publishers, Inc., Wheaton, Illinois.
All rights reserved.

Insert photos provided by the 40 Days for Life organization unless otherwise indicated.
Insert background image by Paco Ayala / 123RF Stock Photo
Chapter opener image by Serg_v / 123RF Stock Photo

Cover design by Jeanette Gillespie
Author photos by Susan Soriano Photography
Edited by David Lambert for Somersault

Manufactured in the United States of America

18 19 20 21 22 • 19 18 17 16 15 14 13 12 11 10 9 8 7 6 5 4 3 2 1

For my beautiful bride, Marilisa.

*Your daily labor of love for me
and our children
points everyone around you
to the Author of Life.*

∽

Contents

We must be ready to allow ourselves
to be interrupted by God.

—DIETRICH BONHOEFFER in *Life Together*
Martyred on April 9, 1945, in Flossenburg, Germany

∼

Foreword

~

MORE ABORTION FACILITIES PER CAPITA THAN ANY OTHER STATE in the union. That was Iowa's claim to fame in 2011. But that was before 40 Days for Life stormed across the state … and everything changed.

For seventeen years I was the center manager of the Storm Lake, Iowa, Planned Parenthood facility. Like so many other abortion workers, I thought I was helping women. But God had so much more in store for me. Deeply troubled by the start of webcam abortions, I began seeking out pro-life organizations.

Jim Sedlak of American Life League described webcam abortions:

> For a webcam abortion, Planned Parenthood has a building, but no abortionist on site. A mother goes into these locations, talks with an abortionist over the Internet, and is then given the two pills needed to murder her child. She takes one pill in the Planned Parenthood office and then takes the second pill at home. If she has any problems at home, she is instructed to go to an emergency room and tell the staff that she is having a miscarriage.[1]

Around that same time, I left the church I'd attended my whole life and landed in a wonderful Bible-believing, Christ-centered fellowship. They loved me despite where I worked. I discovered

Christian radio and was constantly steeped in the Word. My heart softened, and I knew my days at Planned Parenthood were numbered. The decision was taken out of my hands: Citing downsizing, my bosses fired me. It was a tremendous relief.

The "ostrich syndrome" set in, where you do your best to ignore something you don't want to face. I avoided the street where I had previously worked, where Planned Parenthood was killing babies using drugs and an Internet connection. But when someone asked point blank about my former job and what they do there, and I saw the shock on several faces while I explained the horrific act of webcam abortion, my heart was convicted and I was spurred to action.

From my days with the abortion giant, I knew how much Planned Parenthood despises 40 Days For Life—"40 Days of Torture," they would call it. Or worse. But I had witnessed firsthand the chaos and struggle inside the clinic whenever someone was outside praying. I knew it moved hearts.

Registration for the 40 Days for Life Campaign of fall 2011 was closing soon, and without hesitation, I registered Storm Lake. There I was, a former Planned Parenthood manager who was now leading a 40 Days for Life campaign. It was both God's grace and his sense of humor as well. Our rural town had lots of great churches, but as far as doing events together, no way. So began the uphill battle of recruiting prayer volunteers:

What would I pray about for an hour?

What if it's snowing?

I'm not sure I want people to see me doing that!

Those were all common concerns of potential volunteers.

But somehow, over the brief time we had to prepare before the start of 40 Days, God worked another miracle. Our small team kept meeting, and I continued to share the facts of webcam abortion and that it was happening right here in our little town. Word spread. At the kickoff rally, seventy-five people showed up—a huge crowd for our little town! We sang, we prayed, we lit candles, and by the end of the rally, I thought maybe, just maybe, this might work. Though we still had many openings in our vigil schedule, time slots were indeed filling up.

The next morning, I pulled into my old usual parking spot—the one I had used for all those years of employment. Nervous about facing my former coworkers, I decided to just pray from my car. After all, it was a little chilly and I had my one-year-old with me. I rationalized that God hears our prayers no matter where we are, right? But I felt convicted for my timidity, and I got out of the safety of my car and stood in front of my former clinic for what would be the first of many hours.

There are no words to fully explain the blessings of that 40 Days for Life campaign. I faced my former coworkers, and yes, they ridiculed me. But I believe that deep down they knew I was standing for truth. I saw many former clients, some of whom were angry and others who immediately left once they realized that abortions were being done there. Some of the people driving by would offer a friendly wave; others, not so friendly. But even on our worst days, everyone who saw us knew we cared enough to be out there in the snow, sleet, or rain. Our prayers mattered.

Who was most blessed of all? That would be me. As a single mom with a never-ending to-do list, how did I have time to lead our community's first-ever 40 Days for Life? How could I bring together a town divided by denominations and different beliefs? Easy answer—I didn't. It was all about God. The Healer. The Redeemer. He is also the one who closed our abortion facility just three months after our 480 hours of prayer. Storm Lake, Iowa, was the first of twenty abortion facilities in Iowa to close!

There is indescribable power in every prayer. God hears and he cares. The blessing that 40 Days for Life brings is beyond what we can even imagine. My friend, you are called. Get out of your car and take a stand. If I can do it, you can. Pray with courage, believing and not doubting. For nothing—*nothing*—is too hard for our God.

Sue Thayer
Former Planned Parenthood Center Manager
40 Days for Life Campaign Leader

First Things First

~

We have a God who knew his way out of the grave.
—G. K. CHESTERTON

"Lots of people rise from the dead. It happens all the time."

I had taken courses from this history professor before and knew what I was in for. He had lost his faith and now considered himself agnostic. I perked up when, in a discussion of the resurrection and the events recounted in the Acts of the Apostles, he uttered those words.

My youth and Irish temperament kicked in, and I raised my hand because I wanted to say, "That's the dumbest statement I've ever heard in my entire life." He called on me and instead I said, "Name one."

"Pardon?" he replied.

I continued, "If 'lots' of people have risen from the dead, then name one, besides Jesus Christ."

Shaking his head, he looked at the ground and replied, "Well, like Jesus, many people claimed to have risen from the dead. It was a common claim and myth."

I said, "But they didn't."

He said, "They didn't what?"

"They didn't rise from the dead. They're crazy or dishonest."

"I'm sorry?"

"That's the difference between them and Jesus. And that's *the* difference that separates Christianity from other religions. That's why most people, when they hear Jesus' name, either bow their heads or roll their eyes. From the time he claimed to have risen from the dead, centuries of people have believed it happened. That's why, over those centuries, thousands have been willing to be martyred rather than deny him. Is that true of any of the others who have claimed to have risen from the dead?"

That was when I realized I was the only one talking—the entire class had gone silent.

"What's your point?" the professor asked.

"My point is, if he is merely one of many who claimed to rise from the dead, why do you know his name but can't name any of the others who claimed to rise from the dead?"

He didn't offer much of a response. He just continued on about how it was a common claim. As he droned on, I found it notable that the professor would not deny that Jesus rose from the dead and claim that therefore Christianity is false, nor would he acknowledge that Jesus *could* have risen from the dead or even that he *did* rise from the dead. He just left the matter undefined; he expressed no passion in any direction. This professor was an Italian who often cited his ethnic heritage. But he was an Italian without passion—which is both rare and somewhat unbearable. It's like an Irishman who takes himself seriously.

But we don't get to set passion aside with Jesus.

St. Augustine and C. S. Lewis articulated this point better than anyone—Christ must be either lunatic, liar, or Lord. If he's a lunatic, we must disregard him and his followers. If he's a liar, we must fight him and his followers. But if he's Lord, then we must follow the same orders that the waiters at the wedding feast of Cana received from Mary: "Do whatever he tells you" (John 2:5).

The entire sum of Christianity depends on life—life conquering death. Not symbolically conquering death, but literally rising from the dead in bodily form. As Christians we hang our faith and our lives on the fact that Jesus Christ died, was buried, and rose again. This is the most dramatic claim and occurrence in all human history. And most likely you have already based your hope in that truth, and you struggle to shape your entire life around it.

If we find the bones of Jesus, proving that he did not rise from the dead and ascend into heaven as the Bible tells us, then all is for nothing. We are fools and have been living a pious lie. We would indeed be, as one atheist told me, adults who discovered we still believed in Santa Claus.

But if he did rise from the dead, that makes him the conqueror of death. It also means we can *never* despair in the face of death or the culture of death. As G. K. Chesterton put it, "We have a God who knew his way out of the grave."[2]

And there is no room for despair in a life spent following Christ, no matter what is happening in the culture around us. Despair is for those who believe it is up to them to fix everything. Christians don't live in that world. We live as soldiers serving our victorious Master.

I mentioned that my professor had no passion when he discussed whether Christ was God or not. He would have had more passion debating whether college football was better than pro football.

But I did see passion from him once. And I'll never forget it.

It was at the height of the Iraq war, and our class was discussing global terrorism. It was also the fall of the first-ever 40 Days for Life campaign. In the middle of our class discussion, he abruptly cut the conversation short and said, "If you want to see real terrorism at work, drive by Planned Parenthood and look at the people standing outside praying."

He was dispassionate about the resurrection of Christ but not about abortion. For him, the line in the sand that ignited his passion concerned "terrorists" versus women.

Ironically, just before class I had dropped off my new wife, Marilisa, at Planned Parenthood for her 7:00 a.m. to 3:00 p.m. shift to pray on the sidewalk before I went to class. I was offended by his comment at first, but then I had to laugh inwardly, thinking, *I know we don't see eye to eye on everything, but I never thought he'd call my wife a terrorist.*

His comment was telling and points to one of the reasons you are holding this book right now. The abortion issue pierces the heart like no other issue, despite nearly five decades of legalization. It is anything but a settled issue because of what it does and who it does it to. We haven't gotten over abortion, even if some claim to have gotten over the resurrection.

We take abortion personally—and we should, because these are our sisters going in for abortions. These are our brothers and sisters being aborted, and these are our brothers and sisters doing the abortions. And with nearly 56 million abortions happening worldwide *every year,*[3] abortion is like no other issue in all human history.

Those staggering numbers may tempt us to throw our hands up in despair and resignation that abortion is here to stay. But the resurrection doesn't allow that. The resurrection of Christ is why you are holding this book in your hand. Without the resurrection, this book is pointless, and we might as well leave the fate of abortion in the hands of the pollsters.

The resurrection is what led to that first-ever 40 Days for Life campaign. I was in college and we had many reasons to despair. Abortion numbers were up at the Planned Parenthood abortion facility in College Station, Texas. On average, one in four women will have an abortion in college, and Texas A&M is home to over sixty thousand college students. You do the math.

After an hour of prayer with just four members of a local pro-life organization, the Coalition for Life, we decided to do forty days of prayer and fasting, community outreach, and nonstop peaceful vigil outside our Planned Parenthood abortion facility. That first campaign occurred in the fall of 2004, and since then God has responded and the world has come knocking.

This simple campaign has now spread to nearly eight hundred

cities in fifty countries. There have been thousands of lives saved from abortion, hundreds of workers who have had a conversion and left their jobs, and an ever-increasing number of abortion facilities that have closed—including the facility that was the site of the first-ever 40 Days for Life campaign in College Station. That former Planned Parenthood abortion facility now serves as the headquarters for 40 Days for Life.

The road to ending abortion doesn't start with a list of accomplishments, however. It starts with prayer. And that prayer must start today. Abortion has been legal in the United States since January 22, 1973, and what a long road it has been. God inspired us to use the same time period he uses throughout Scripture—forty days—perhaps because it's a short enough period to show us how quickly and miraculously his power can transform us and our circumstances, and it's a long enough period to remind us of our own frailty. We needed a roadmap, and he gave us one in the forty-day timeframe. And each time a new forty-day campaign begins, we start again to put one foot in front of the other to end abortion.

As we embark together on the forty-day journey of this book, let's put first things first. Our hope is in the Lord—the Lord who lived, worked, laughed, sweated, bled, suffered, died, and came back to life. The Lord who came into the world through the womb. The Lord whose mom was turned away from the inn. The Lord whose birthday was spent fleeing persecution. The Lord who loves us more than we love ourselves. That is where our hope is, and this hope strengthens us to face a culture in need of him and of his mercy, his tenderness, his fortitude, and his love.

Then let's look at our culture to see where we are and where we aren't. Fortunately, we can also look at the body of Christ—his people—and see how he is moving among our brothers and sisters to bring an end to abortion in their communities all across the globe. People, for instance, like Susie Calvey, whom you will meet in the next chapter.

~

Let us run with perseverance the race marked out for us, fixing our eyes on Jesus, the pioneer and perfecter of faith. For the joy set before him he endured the cross, scorning its shame, and sat down at the right hand of the throne of God. Consider him who endured such opposition from sinners, so that you will not grow weary and lose heart.

HEBREWS 12:1–3

Dear Lord Jesus, as I begin my journey through this book, focus my attention on you and the truth and power of your resurrection. Fill me with hope and expectation of what you will accomplish in the next forty days. Give me an open and tender heart, and influence my thinking and behavior in ways that only you can. I offer myself, Lord, to you. Amen.

Never Too Early ...
Or Too Late

~

It is better to be young in your failures
than old in your successes.

—FLANNERY O'CONNOR

"SO, YOU GUYS ARE GOING TO BE OUT THERE TWENTY-FOUR HOURS a day for forty days straight?" the college freshman asked, her face lit with a beautiful smile.

"Yes," Marilisa replied. "And we want to have more than one person out there at any given time, around the clock, so we need lots of volunteers."

"This is awesome! I'm in," the freshman said.

Marilisa and I hadn't been married even a year yet, and we were doing what we had done since we began dating—recruiting volunteers to pray outside the local Planned Parenthood abortion facility in the town where we went to school—College Station, Texas. That fall of 2004, we were helping launch the first-ever 40 Days for Life campaign. Marilisa had committed to be out there from 7:00 a.m. to 3:00 p.m. every day, and the Knights of Columbus, led by fearless, cowboy-hat-wearing David Arabie, had committed to cover the infamous "Knight" shift from 11:00 p.m. to 7:00 a.m.

Although many of the hours were covered, there were still some gaps. A forty-day, twenty-four-hour vigil meant a total of 960 hours, and we needed at least two people per hour. We needed all the help we could get.

The enthusiasm of this freshman recruit was refreshing. As she signed her name to the list, she said, "This so good. I've never done anything like this before, but I *am* pro-life, and I need to be more involved."

She put down the pen, smiled at Marilisa, and went on her way. Marilisa looked at the form and read, "Susie Calvey."

I replied, "No hesitation—I like that. I think we'll see a lot of her. She would make an awesome sidewalk counselor."

Marilisa said, "No kidding! Who wouldn't want to talk to her?"

We quickly learned that when Susie Calvey said, "I'm in," she meant it. She showed up for her hours to pray—and then some. It wasn't long before she became president of the on-campus student group Aggies for Life. Then she decided she wanted to become a sidewalk counselor. The counselors are volunteers who courageously and gently approach women and men going in for abortion appointments and offer living alternatives. Marilisa was the best sidewalk counselor I have ever seen in action. Susie quickly established herself as the second best. She was kind, joyful, and direct. She was also fearless—something I didn't expect.

During that first campaign, Marilisa and I became friends with Susie. She had a great sense of humor. She took abortion seriously but not herself—and that is a required trait for every good sidewalk counselor.

Susie's boyfriend, Andrew, joined her on the sidewalks. When Susie and Andrew weren't praying in front of the Planned Parenthood facility, they were in the Coalition for Life office helping wherever needed.

Andrew was a proud member of the Texas A&M Corps of Cadets, the largest ROTC program in America, so he was often in uniform. If you saw him at football games or church, Susie was right there with him. They were made for each other, and we were excited when they got engaged.

One day Susie came into the office and did something she had never done—complained. She escaped from the sun for a few moments, sat down in our office, and said, "It's so hot. And I'm *tired.*"

"Yeah." I replied, "it's brutal out there today. Plus, you've been out there a lot. Take a break. This work can wear on you, not just because of the heat but spiritually as well. It's a dark place. We need to remember that and know when we need some rest."

"Yeah, you're right. But it's not that." She slumped a little in her chair. "I'm really tired. I've had this weird pain in my neck, and I've just been feeling wiped out. Anyway, sorry to complain."

"Hey, there's firsts for everything," I said.

Susie slapped her hands on her thighs and said, "Well, guess it's time for me to get back out there," and left the office.

Marilisa said, "She does seem unusually tired."

"Yeah. She wasn't herself."

When Susie first signed up, she wanted to make a difference and maybe even help save a life from abortion. And she did exactly that. Her work as a sidewalk counselor saved six babies from abortion that we know of. But Susie wouldn't be there to see 40 Days for Life spread from that first campaign to over 750 cities worldwide. The pain in her neck turned out to be a tumor—a cancer so rare her doctors struggled to diagnose it. She was given just a few months to live. Her next few weeks and months were brutal, and yet Susie's faith in God was unwavering. She put all her trust in him and wanted to live what remained of her life just as she had planned. She continued to go to class, was always at church, and remained faithful to her commitment to go out to pray and sidewalk counsel—while wearing a neck brace and sitting in a wheelchair.

The one thing Susie adjusted in her life to accommodate her cancer was her wedding date. She and Andrew married sooner than planned. Andrew looked sharp in his tuxedo and Susie looking radiant in her beautiful wedding dress as she took her vows while lying in her hospital bed, smiling.

Two weeks after her wedding, Susie Calvey Martin passed away at the age of twenty-two.

> *If we live, we live for the Lord;*
> *and if we die, we die for the Lord.*
> *So, whether we live or die,*
> *we belong to the Lord.*
>
> ROMANS 14:8

∼

Susie had often said she got her energy and initiative from her dad. When I met Joe Calvey, I knew what she meant. There's no manual for what you're supposed to say to a parent who has lost a child. But meeting Joe at Susie's funeral is something Marilisa and I will never forget. We had gone to the funeral hoping to provide support and comfort for her parents and her siblings, but Joe Calvey beat us to it. Certainly, it was a sad funeral—but Joe turned it into a celebration as well. A dad who was always looking for a reason to brag on his children, he talked with gratitude and thanksgiving about his daughter's life—her faith, her struggle with cancer, her joy—and made her life and death seem part of God's plan.

Joe and I stayed in contact, getting together when possible. An outgoing guy, Joe owns multiple small businesses in San Antonio, has Spurs season tickets, and seems to know and care for everyone he meets. Every time Marilisa had another baby (we've had seven!), he would send us a note of congratulations. He even took me to a Spurs versus Lakers game, and his tickets were as good as advertised. I thought Kobe Bryant would be the best-known man in the building, but it seemed like Joe was. On our way to our seats, every few steps he was stopped or he stopped others, talking to them about their families and life.

One day Joe called and said he wanted to carry out something Susie had wanted to do. "You know how she was, Shawn. If she had her mind set on doing something, she was going to do it." Before I could answer, he rushed on. "She wanted to establish a scholarship for Aggies active in the pro-life movement. She didn't get to it, but I will. What do you think?"

"Let's do it! I can't think of a better way to honor Susie." The idea excited me, and names of potential scholarship recipients began popping into my head. "We have tons of volunteers who would be worthy applicants."

Joe established a scholarship at Texas A&M, given to five students each year. In the early days of the scholarship, we announced the awards in Susie's honor at our benefit dinner with over 1,500 people in attendance. We've had some prominent speakers at this event, including Laura Ingraham, Colonel Oliver North, Jeb Bush, Rick Santorum, Mike Huckabee, and Michelle Malkin. All of them were deeply moved by Susie's example and life. After every benefit dinner, despite the high-profile speakers, what everyone remembered was Joe Calvey handing out the five scholarships to grateful students.

Joe's passion for the scholarship inspired me to start a national scholarship for students involved in the pro-life movement and 40 Days for Life. The 4040 Scholarship is $4,040 and has been a great way to honor and recognize the future of the pro-life movement by encouraging worthy students. When I launched the scholarship, I called Joe for some technical advice on how to set it up, since he had years of experience. Before I could finish, he interrupted and said, "I'm sponsoring the first year. Where do I mail the check?" Susie was right—she got her "go-getter" personality from her dad.

Susie Calvey got involved in the pro-life movement because we invited her, and she was open to what God had in store. Joe Calvey got involved through the inspiration of his daughter, whom he loved and lost to cancer. After she passed away, Joe learned about all his daughter had done for the pro-life movement at Texas A&M. He also learned about the six babies who were alive because of his daughter. Joe Calvey had always been pro-life, but when he lost his daughter and looked at what she had done in her short life, it was the lives of those six babies that summed up his daughter's love of God and love of life and encouraged him to carry on the work she had begun. He dove into the pro-life movement.

The mothers of those six babies don't know Susie or Joe or you or me. They don't know her story or your story. But God does. And when we step out in faith to end abortion where we live, he will use our stories as well.

Although Susie died at only twenty-two, her early death didn't prevent God from using what time she had to help end abortion. Her beautiful life shows that you're never too young to say, "I'm in," and Joe's response shows that it's never too late to be part of the beginning of the end of abortion.

Don't let the overwhelming crisis of abortion paralyze you. Don't think that because you haven't done enough so far, you can't begin now. And if you're concerned that you're too old or too young or too tired, remember Susie and Joe Calvey. Get away from the noise of the world and be silent, pray, and don't be afraid to say, "I'm in."

∽

The LORD is my light and my salvation—
whom shall I fear?
The LORD is the stronghold of my life—
of whom shall I be afraid?
PSALM 27:1

Holy God, you and you alone know the number of the days we will spend here on earth. Help me, Lord, to spend my time and my efforts on the things that matter most, the things of eternal significance to you. Give me the courage, Lord, to live an "I'm in" kind of life. Amen.

The Invoice

~

Courage is not simply one of the virtues,
but the form of every virtue at the testing point.
—C. S. LEWIS

I couldn't sleep. The woman's words kept eating at me.

I had asked her *why* she got involved in the pro-life movement. I have yet to learn that there are no limits to the answers to that question.

The atmosphere had been cheerful. I had just spoken at a banquet for a pregnancy center and was visiting with some of their employees and volunteers as the hotel crew stacked chairs and cleaned up the room. I had been enjoying a lighthearted chat with several of their team when I asked that question of one the pregnancy center's employees. The look on her sweet and joyful face faded. Her eyes intensified as her tone softened. Her answer gave me a gut check about why we are all in the pro-life movement.

She explained that she had worked at a very large Planned Parenthood abortion facility near a major city. At the time, she justified her job because it was restricted to bookkeeping and other business tasks that were separate (she thought) from what went on in the rooms next door where the abortions were done.

"But one day," she said, "that all changed in an instant while I was sitting at my desk opening the mail." Her expression became more and more troubled as she continued. "I opened an invoice from the local morgue. It was for $350."

It was while she scanned the invoice that the reality of abortion hit her. "The service, listed in bold letters, pierced my heart: CREMATION SERVICE FOR 150 POUNDS OF MEDICAL WASTE."

My heart sank.

She looked me in the eye and said, "Shawn, I asked myself a question as I stared at that invoice, and the answer was what first got me involved in the pro-life movement."

I was certain it was the same question I was asking myself as I listened to her, a knot forming in my gut.

"The question that pierced my heart," she said, "was, *How many babies have to be aborted to add up to 150 pounds of 'medical waste'?*"

I didn't know the answer, and neither did she.

She told me how that question triggered her resignation from the abortion industry. She began working for a local pregnancy center to help women in need and to welcome babies into the world. She went all in to help preserve life.

Lying awake that night, I kept thinking about that question and how it ties back to the fundamental reason we pray, hold vigil, and persevere in this work: because abortion kills a baby. And once you kill that baby, you must professionally dispense of the remains.

I often think of that woman when I hear a Planned Parenthood advertisement or see their well-designed promotional materials. They are produced by skyscraper marketing firms, so they look and sound professional and positive.

But the Planned Parenthood staff sees what is really happening from the inside, and the world inside an abortion facility cannot be a vague world such as Planned Parenthood presents outside. Outside there are rhetoric, talking points, and shiny brochures, but inside there is the reality of carrying out the gruesome work required for abortion providers to be abortion providers.

Broad terms like "choice" and "healthcare" and "privacy" are not found on invoices like this one.

I travel a lot, and on those travels I hear many stories from salt-of-the-earth people who are working to end abortion. I have now added this woman's story to theirs. Her witness reminds us that no matter how cleverly you spin the "choice" for abortion, or how professional the wording seems, or how much you believe those words, the reality of what abortion actually is eventually seeps in. We can avoid it or we acknowledge it as this woman did as she nervously stared at the invoice in her hands. For her, that sheet of paper broke through the facade.

Many who support abortion rights, including many who have worked in the abortion industry, are turning away from that industry because they've had to live in its filth. This may be a hard chapter to read, but imagine living it. Imagine waking up to the reality of playing a personal part in the discarding of those tiny human remains. Our movement of converts swings in only one direction. It swings away from the facade, away from the darkness, and toward the light.

It's interesting that no one is likely to feel uneasy hearing about the work of a pregnancy center, including the one where this woman now works. Who gets distressed or feels attacked when free ultrasounds or free diapers are offered? The nature of this work is pure— and it has to be, to be successful. On the other hand, the nature of abortion, despite the attempts of the advertising agencies working on behalf of the abortion industry to make the industry appear smooth and attractive and compassionate, is in reality graphically ugly because it has to kill a baby in order to be successful.

Holding a pro-life position, as much sense at it makes, can still be the hardest position to live out. It will garner opposition and requires *courage* because abortion is a mighty foe. Abortion isn't a distant memory in our history books; rather, it's a huge, profitable industry happening right now all over the planet. But we can respond to that foe within our own neighborhoods and communities.

That's why many of those who leave the abortion industry (like the woman in this chapter) get busy in the pro-life movement. They go to work because they know better than anyone that abortion kills babies. And we know we can trust God and do something about it.

When I first realized the reality of abortion as a teenager, I was convicted to do something about it. Doing something may include being ridiculed or enduring an awkward moment of silence when you invite friends to participate in a pro-life activity. Your pro-life position may even cause a little tension at Thanksgiving dinner. Even greater, it may cost you something important. But the awkwardness, the tension, and even the cost are worth it. The cost was worth it for this woman. She overcame any hesitation, got up from her desk, spoke to her boss, and quit a secure job. And all it took was looking at one of the bills she needed to pay that day. She had the courage to respond to the challenge that abortion gives us to speak up for those who cannot speak for themselves.

I believe that invoice changed her life because it showed her what mankind is capable of without God. When we give ourselves license over the rights of others, there is no limit to the evil we can commit. Societies that remove the rights of individuals usually do so in the name of good. The problem is that without God, they use their autonomy to define "good" for everyone else and use force, verbally or physically, to carry it out. As Flannery O'Connor put it, "In the absence of faith we govern by tenderness. And tenderness leads to the gas chamber."

I never have trouble sleeping. I am very much a morning person and get up early—not because I'm disciplined but because I love coffee. Getting up early means that I'm usually dozing off by 9:30 p.m. But the night after my conversation with the woman who'd seen the invoice, I couldn't sleep, thinking about that "medical waste." It was shocking. It broke my heart. It led me to think about my wife and kids. It made me want to be a better husband and father. It motivated me to spend more time in prayer.

Our culture needs healing and love, and that starts in our families. We can't allow the graphic nature of abortion to be something that *distracts* us from our families; rather, it should point us to them and cause us to recommit ourselves to their welfare. Then with that priority straight, we need to grasp the reality of abortion and do something about it.

Nearly 56 million abortions take place around the world every year,[4] and it may feel as if whatever pro-life work you do doesn't make a dent in that. But as you will discover through the stories in this book, lives can be saved one at a time. You can pray, draw your family closer to God, and be willing to step out in faith if God calls you to do something in the pro-life movement. This woman did.

Abortion will end if we persevere—persevere in prayer, persevere in fortitude, and persevere in reminding ourselves of the great evil that abortion is. We must know who our enemy is and not forget that it is evil we are battling. This clarity of darkness should send us closer to the Light, the Author of Life. That's what it did with this worker and with hundreds of others who have left the abortion industry.

The invoice for disposal of "medical waste" does not reflect despair but shows what Christ can overcome. An unexpected encounter reminded me of what—*and whom*—we are fighting for.

So today I ask you the same question: What got *you* into the pro-life movement? If you haven't yet made that step, what question would help you past that final barrier? Take that question to silent prayer, and answer or reanswer it in the presence of God.

≈

One thing I do:
forgetting what lies behind and
reaching forward to what lies ahead,
I press on toward the goal
for the prize of the upward call
of God in Christ Jesus.
PHILIPPIANS 3:13–14 NASB

God, you are able to speak to us in so many ways. Ways we might never expect. I ask that you speak to me through whatever method you choose that will help me overcome whatever barriers are keeping me from serving you and the lives of the unborn. Help me to not be afraid to leave that which is secure and comfortable in order that I may serve you. Don't let awkwardness or tension keep me from standing for what is right. Amen.

A Movement of Converts

~

They continue to do these
40-day harassment protests.
It seems kind of silly.

—ABBY JOHNSON,
former Planned Parenthood Director

OUR CULTURE IS OBSESSED WITH LABELS. WE HAVE LABEL FEVER.
If you advocate for any cause, you'll be labeled by those who disagree with you or by the media. You may even be told that you hate another group of people and must be stopped. (This will be news to you.) This walk-on-eggshells approach to life has silenced some and exhausted others. But much worse, it has limited the human heart and mind to a mere accusatory shouting match.

It also eliminates the possibility of another wonderful human experience: being *wrong*.

Being wrong is underrated these days. We are all wrong, for we are all sinners. God can work with wrong. God changes the world with those who acknowledge they are wrong. If we are not allowed to be revealed as wrong, not allowed to see ourselves for the sinners we are, then no level of political correctness or labeling will ever satisfy us—and sadly, our own wrongness will always be "someone else's fault."

I was once in a conversation in San Francisco with a woman who supported abortion. (There are more than a few out there who do).

She told me I had no right to oppose abortion because I was a man and, furthermore, was white. There wasn't much I could do about either of those two things. I asked her what exactly I *should* believe about abortion. She said, "Nothing. You're a gender supremacist. What you say or believe doesn't matter."

"I'm a gender what?" I asked.

She calmly repeated, "A gender supremacist."

I put my head down in defeat and said, "You know, you're right. I am a gender supremacist—it's actually the title on my business card. Do you want to see it?"

She looked at me silently, and then we both burst into laughter. She could tell I was trying to lighten the mood.

"Gender supremacist" is, after all, just another label, and all these labels have caused us to be far too polarized. As a result, we don't engage in meaningful dialogue about the points, pro and con, of an issue. Instead we make everything personal—we trade insults and labels.

The stereotype is that pro-life people are self-righteous Christians trying to force their religion on others and tell them how to live. But the pro-life people I know don't fit that description. We are a movement not of saints but of sinners. Our movement doesn't have a distant ivory-tower, holier-than-thou relationship with abortion. Quite the opposite. The most powerful voices for life are women who have lain on that table and had an abortion. They are the voices of men who have pressured, persuaded, and paid for an abortion. They are abortion facility workers who have counseled, sold, and advocated abortion, and even doctors who have done abortions. These are the voices of the pro-life movement. Not self-righteous Christians but professed sinners. We are a movement of converts.

And a movement of converts can only be a movement of hope.

I learned this firsthand as a freshman in high school. I had wonderful Irish priests in my Catholic school who urged me to go to a pro-life event at the largest Baptist church in my town of Tyler,

Texas—Green Acres Baptist. I had never been to a Baptist church before, and as a Catholic this was my first exposure to the powerful Christian unity in the pro-life movement.

In that Baptist church I listened closely to the guest speaker, Carol Everett.

Carol had run four abortion facilities in the Dallas area before her conversion. As a teenager, I was struck by the honesty with which she described how she carried out this evil work. She openly talked about lying to women, making money, and hiding any woman who chose life from those who were outside praying. She wanted to crush the morale of the praying pro-lifers.

As I listened to Carol, a convert to the pro-life cause, little did I know that one day I would have another Planned Parenthood director walk into my office with a change of heart—another convert. It was the pro-abortion, preconversion Abby Johnson who said the words in the quote at the top of this chapter. I had watched Abby go in and out of her facility for eight years before she unexpectedly walked into our office next door. She sat down, cried about finally seeing the truth of the work she had been part of—and resigned from her job the next day. Today Abby Johnson is one of the most powerful voices for the unborn. (More about her later in the book.)

While in high school, I also saw a video about the conversion of Norma McCorvey, who, prior to becoming pro-life, represented abortion rights for women as the "Roe" of the infamous Roe v. Wade case. Later, at Texas A&M, I was afraid to become a sidewalk counselor until I heard five post-abortive women share their powerful testimonies. Their stories emboldened me to serve on the sidewalk.

Dr. Bernard Nathenson, founder of NARAL Pro-Choice America, the oldest abortion advocacy group in the country, was one of the first abortion doctors to have a conversion, subsequent to his filming a live abortion with his ultrasound machine.

Sue Thayer, Jewels Green, Ramona Trevino ... the list of converts goes on and on and on.

The pro-life movement, because it is a movement of converts, is a movement of hope. That is why, despite decades of legalization, there is more momentum in the pro-life movement than ever before.

From women who have been through an abortion, to men who encouraged abortions, to doctors who have done abortions, to people who at one point supported abortion rights—the conversion gate seems to swing in only one direction. I haven't heard of women who get married, have children, run a pro-life group, and then decide they should be running a Planned Parenthood abortion facility. I haven't met doctors who regret not going back and doing abortions instead of oncology, radiology, or another field of medicine. "I regret my abortion" is one of the most frequent signs you will see at 40 Days for Life vigils. I have been to over 450 of our locations worldwide and have yet to see or hear, "I regret not having an abortion."

The change in hearts and minds is moving in only one direction because it is God who opens the floodgates for us to change and be made new. Jesus' words are simply "Repent and believe" (Mark 1:15). The pro-life movement reflects that beautiful reality like no other movement in our culture, and that should give us great hope.

About a quarter of 40 Days for Life local campaign leaders are women who've had an abortion. Sometimes the vigils they lead are in front of the very abortion facility where they had that abortion years before. Their leadership reflects the mercy of God and the very reasons we go out to pray. Their presence reminds us why it is so important that we be there after a woman has an abortion to offer comfort and counsel. That's the hope that can only be found in a movement of converts.

Our presence on the sidewalk represents the last sign of hope for the baby and the first sign of mercy for the woman. Our body language, our comforting words, our silence when they expect judgment are things they will remember forever. If we have learned one thing, it is that women never forget the day of their abortion. They will remember it just as they will remember our being there. Our presence may not save the baby, but it can serve as a gateway to healing for that woman who had the abortion five, ten, or even thirty years down the road. I know this because post-abortive women have told me so time and time again.

The most effective tool the devil uses to attack us is discouragement. I admit that I have fallen into this trap many times. The Irish cynic in me sometimes feels that when it comes to ending abortion, Good Fridays outnumber Easter Sundays. But Good Friday is where the work gets done. It's where our Lord saves us from ourselves by giving up himself. And Easter Sunday always follows.

Even at his weakest moment, Jesus converted a criminal. He could barely breathe, yet he opened the gates of eternity to a man condemned to die. He gives us hope because he came "not to call the righteous, but sinners" (Matthew 9:13). The repentant thief on Calvary reminds us that we must have a zeal for souls, no matter how tired or discouraged we may feel. Having zeal does not make you a radical or a fanatic; it makes you different in a culture that walks on eggshells. And different—honest and kind—is often what so many who have had an abortion or who work in the abortion industry are truly looking for.

When we seek the mercy of God, we don't use rhetoric or justification—we just look at our sins. We see them for what they are, ask for forgiveness, and resolve to change. That change comes from Christ, and that change makes us free.

That freedom can be seen in the thousands of pro-life converts who lead our movement—a movement rooted in hope.

G. K. Chesterton said, "It is only ten minutes after all hope seems lost that hope first begins to dawn." We are seeing that dawn in the pro-life movement, and it's up to you to discern what your role is.

∼

Those who hope in the LORD
will renew their strength.
They will soar on wings like eagles;
they will run and not grow weary,
they will walk and not be faint.
ISAIAH 40:31

God of hope, thank you for the hope you give to all of us who repent and trust in you for our salvation. Thank you that the pro-life movement is filled with so many who at one time participated in abortion but who now are advocates for life. Make me an instrument of your hope in this broken world, Lord. Amen.

Lunches with a Wildcatter

~

America was not built on fear.
America was built on courage,
on imagination and an unbeatable
determination to do the job at hand.
—PRESIDENT HARRY TRUMAN

"HI, MR. OGDEN. I'M SHAWN CARNEY. I'M A SENIOR AT TEXAS A&M and just started part time at the Coalition for Life."

"Well, you've done that. Now what do you want?" Emil Ogden replied.

I couldn't help it—I busted out laughing at his response, even though he wasn't kidding.

"Carney is an Irish name," he said, as if that were tolerable but not great.

"Yes sir, it is. My middle name is Doyle—from my mother's side."

"Shawn Doyle Carney, mercy me," he said quietly. "What's your major?"

"History and philosophy."

"Now *that* I will talk to you about," he said.

"I plan on going to law school after I finish my undergrad degree. I'm twenty-one. I got married earlier this year, and we want a lot of kids."

"Well," he replied, "I can talk to you about that as well. All right. You don't seem so bad so far. Let's go to lunch."

That would be the first of my many lunches with the World War II veteran who would become a mentor and friend. It was July 2004.

Mr. Ogden seemed more like a character out of a novel than a real person. His kids often joked that his life was like Forrest Gump's—running from adventure to adventure. He grew up during the Depression. After his father abandoned the family, they struggled just to get by. When the Japanese attacked Pearl Harbor, Emil joined the navy.

After the war he focused on the things he loved—providing for his new wife, Clementine, and their young family, and playing baseball. A great athlete, Emil played in the minor leagues. It required lots of travel but didn't pay well. After an away game, God gave Emil clear direction during a phone call to Clementine. She had German roots, and it was in her blood to get to the point. "You can be a husband or a baseball player, Emil. But you need to pick one."

"That was the end of my baseball career," Mr. Ogden said, laughing.

He went home to Clementine. Over the years they were blessed with six children. He struggled to succeed in the oil business, even going from one small country house to the next trying to sell small oil leases.

Mr. Ogden considered himself an expert on failure. He drilled for oil fourteen times and hit a dry well every time. Many of his friends told him he needed to consider a different kind of work. But Emil would not give up. He was halfway through life before he struck oil—on his fifteenth attempt.

Perseverance was the theme of his life. He never gave up on himself or others. He always put his faith in God as the ultimate guide of his life. When he did well, he gave his money away, and when he failed he remembered where he came from.

"I'm a wildcatter," Mr. Ogden said during that first lunch. He tapped the table once. "In the oil business, being a wildcatter means I drill for oil where others won't, where there is no known oil field."

"So, what do you do when you drill and there's no oil?" I asked.

"Lose a heck of a lot of money!" he said with a laugh.

"So if you strike, you eat, and if you don't, you starve."

"You got it," he said. "That's why I'm still working. I call it 'work' but others call it professional gambling. The truth is that in this country if you work hard, trust God, and love your family you can do anything. That's why abortion is such a scourge on this great nation. It removes all hope and opportunity. It breaks my heart every day. Despite what any politician says, it's the defining moral issue of my and your generation."

〜

That first lunch with Emil was a week after I transitioned from being a volunteer at the local pro-life organization, the Coalition for Life, to being a part-time employee. My bride, Marilisa, also worked there.

After my lunch with Mr. Ogden, I went back to the office, where I found Marilisa looking over abortion statistics. She pointed out the increase of abortions in 2004 at the local Planned Parenthood facility. We knew that students would soon be coming back from summer break, and it seemed inevitable that the abortion numbers would increase even more. David Bereit, our inspiring leader, called a staff meeting to discuss what we could do that fall to stave off the increase. He mentioned the biblical significance of doing something for forty days straight. It's a time period that pops up over and over again in Scripture, Old Testament and New. David wondered aloud what would happen if we gave everything to God to end abortion for that period of time.

Sitting around an old wooden table, we prayed. Based on that hour of prayer, David, Marilisa, one other person, and I decided we would commit to a twenty-four-hour-a-day 40 Days for Life campaign built upon prayer, fasting, community outreach, and peaceful vigil. You can read the story of God's work in launching that first 40 Days for Life campaign in our book *40 Days for Life.*

That first campaign was a huge success and helped lower local abortion numbers by 28 percent. But when it was done, it was done—or so we thought. We never imagined we'd hear the term 40 Days for Life again. We were so surprised when 40 Days for Life campaigns popped up in Dallas, Texas, and in Green Bay and Madison, Wisconsin. After that we watched as God used 40 Days for Life in seven cities. Marilisa put together campaign training packets to answer the requests for help we began to receive from all over. I spoke at a few of their kickoff events; they were using the fliers we had given them, removing our name and putting in their own city and identifying the local abortion facility where their vigil would take place. I was beginning to see that when Americans take abortion personally, they do something about it at the local level.

God opened our eyes to a new pro-life opportunity: recruiting local leaders and training them online. For months, David and I discussed the possibilities of launching 40 Days for Life nationally in the fall of 2007, agreeing with each other and our wives that we would take this leap of faith and do one national campaign. We didn't know how many cities would sign up; we were hoping for at least twenty across the United States. In preparation, we looked at logos, website options, and other logistics. I produced and hosted a show on EWTN to help launch the campaign. Because we didn't expect 40 Days for Life to continue beyond this one event, we didn't hold a fundraiser, nor did we file for 501(c)(3) status, but I did work with an attorney to incorporate 40 Days for Life for legal protection.

We were surprised at the response. People from one end of the country to the other were interested. Coalition for Life had agreed to cover many of the expenses of the campaign, and we had already personally covered others, but we knew that was just the start—this would be expensive. One of my jobs was to help raise funds. I started by making two phone calls. The first gentleman committed to give

$5,000 but couldn't give it until the campaign started. That was generous, but it wouldn't help with things we needed to pay for before the campaign.

My second call was to Emil Ogden. I said, "We need to go to lunch, and I'm going to ask you for money."

He laughed and said, "Let's do tomorrow."

"Good," I replied. "Things are moving fast, and it's about time I let you in on it."

I got to lunch way too early and was way too nervous. By this time I knew Emil well, yet we hardly ever talked about money because there was no need to. He had always been generous to the Coalition for Life. And I had certainly never asked him for an amount like this—an amount great enough to cover the estimated costs of running the campaign.

At one of our earlier lunches, Mr. Ogden told me to get over my reluctance to ask him for money. "These babies are dying, and we need the best for them. You can't run a company poorly, and we certainly shouldn't run Coalition for Life poorly. I have money, and I expect people to ask for it. It's my duty to God to give it away. If I can't, then I won't, but it's their job to ask, and it's my job to say yes or no. So don't be ashamed to ask."

I remembered that invitation as I watched him walk into the restaurant. He was dressed, as always, in a coat, tie, and cowboy hat and wearing his classic smile. I reminded myself that whether he gave or not, this was in God's hands.

After I asked him for $57,000 he said, "I can't give you that much right now, Shawn—I wish I could. Things are a bit tight. But I can get you off the ground." He told me the amount he would give and said, "I'm in a few tough spots and can't make that commitment. Believe me, I would if I could. You need this right away, don't you? OK, I'll drop off a check later today."

True to his word, Mr. Ogden walked into the office later that blistering July afternoon and gave 40 Days for Life's national effort our first donation. It was for $5,000 more than he had promised. As he had done with the $10,000 check he had given us three years earlier when we launched the first 40 Days for Life campaign in College Station, he looked up, smiled with eyebrows raised, and said, "Good luck."

Prayers had been said, and the pieces were assembled.

That fall of 2007, we saw God take 40 Days for Life to eighty-nine cities in thirty-three states. From there, God used that money to take the campaign—and us—to places we never imagined. Eleven years later, the vigils take place in over 750 cities in over fifty countries with over 750,000 participants worldwide, in part because a faithful wildcatter took a risk and made a sacrifice.

Over the twelve years Emil and I had lunch together, we discussed religion, politics, philosophy, raising children, history, and sports. We shared memories, stories, and possibilities. He always asked about Marilisa and the kids, and I often told him that another baby was on the way. "Dang you, Carney," he would say, "you're gonna end up passing me and Clementine. That's good! We need bigger families these days."

He insisted on working every day, even into his late eighties, accompanied by his faithful assistant, Liz, who cared for and watched out for him.

In July of 2017, when I heard that he wasn't doing well, I rushed home from a California trip so I could say goodbye in person. But when I called Clementine, she said he was too weak. She and I talked and laughed as I shared what Emil meant to Marilisa and me. He had taught me so much about faith, family, and sacrifice. He was my friend, and I loved him dearly.

He passed away the next day at the age of eighty-nine, nearly ten years to the day after he handed me the first check made out to 40 Days for Life.

Marilisa and I loaded the kids into the car and drove from our house in Houston to College Station for the funeral. I took advantage of the driving time to tell my kids many of the stories and memories I had of Mr. Ogden. I told them all about this smiling World War II veteran who grew up during the Depression, played professional baseball, struck oil in his midfifties after failing fourteen times, met six US presidents during his long life, had been married for sixty-nine years to his sweetheart, and was grandfather to twenty-three and great-grandfather to twelve. I shared with them how Mr. Ogden was always trying to bring those around him closer to Christ. And observing him in many social and professional situations, I had seen him bring up the topic of the dignity of human life to everyone he encountered.

At the funeral I saw the many lives he had impacted, from people without a home, to the Knights of Columbus, to abandoned children he put through college, to those at the sheriff's office where he had been a volunteer deputy. He had a deep love for Christians in the Holy Land, expressed through his work as a Knight of the Holy Sepulcher.

Mr. Ogden was involved in many things, but his heart was with the unborn. Anytime he heard of a baby being saved or a mom getting back on her feet, he would tear up. Although his pro-life work happened behind the scenes, he had a hand in every one of the babies saved at 40 Days for Life vigils. "Best investment I ever made," he said to me, laughing.

Mr. Ogden represents so many of the wonderful people who pray and work to end abortion where they live. He is an example for all of us that we should spend our days speaking up for those who cannot speak for themselves.

It would be a mistake to look at the state of our society and think that the time for the Emil Ogdens of the world has passed. There are still many selfless servants who put God first across America and around the world. The media doesn't talk about them, but they are there and their trust in God is the beginning of the end of abortion.

Because 40 Days for Life focuses on the local level, you can do something to end abortion where *you* live. You can trust that God will help your community, and in doing so, will heal our land.

∽

Let us not become weary in doing good,
for at the proper time we will reap a harvest
if we do not give up.
GALATIANS 6:9

God, I want to thank you for the life of Emil Ogden and the many others like him whose names I do not know—people who have given sacrificially to save the unborn. I thank you for the example he sets for all of us. I pray that I will trust you and sacrifice in order for lives to be saved, because every life is precious to you. Amen.

A Few Good Men

~

Brave men are all vertebrates;
they have their softness on the surface
and their toughness in the middle.
—G. K. CHESTERTON

I HUNG UP THE PHONE WITH JIM FRUEND IN GREEN BAY, WISCON-
sin, stuck my head out my office door, and yelled to the Coalition for
Life staff (only two other people at the time), "Awesome! Green Bay,
Wisconsin, is going to do a 40 Days for Life campaign!"

It was spring of 2006.

We had already helped Dallas and Houston begin campaigns,
but Green Bay might as well have been the North Pole to me. I knew
nothing about Green Bay except cheese, and because we kids grew
up Cowboy fans, we hated the Packers. Jim Fruend, a man of Jew-
ish faith, was all in. He saw abortion as today's greatest attack on
the human person. Although he was determined to organize the
campaign alone if necessary, he had found many Christians to work
with him.

I couldn't wait to get home and share the news with Marilisa
that another city had not only asked about 40 Days for Life but was
committed to doing it. Flying to their kickoff event, as they had
requested, would be my first trip away from my wife since our first
baby, Bridget, eight weeks old, had been born.

I walked into the bedroom to share the news and was surprised to see Marilisa looking back at me smiling, her eyes wide with excitement. "What's going on?" I asked.

She opened her mouth to tell me and then started to laugh; she couldn't get the words out. She seemed to be somewhere between disbelief and elation. Her laughter was contagious. I started laughing too, still having no idea what we were laughing at. I tried to get her to stop laughing so she could tell me, but that's pretty hard when you're laughing yourself. Finally, we stopped, and I said, "What is it?"

She held up a positive pregnancy test.

"Awesome!" I shouted. I turned to eight-week-old Bridget and said, "Congratulations sweetie, you're a big sister!" Bridget stared at us with big eyes, and Marilisa broke into laughter once again.

"What if we have another girl?" I said. "They could actually end up in the same grade. They could get married on the same day! Think of the money we would save!"

Marilisa was still laughing. I was one year out of college, twenty-three, married, and now had a second baby on the way. Life was good, and I hadn't even gotten a chance to tell her the Green Bay news yet.

∼

A few weeks later I landed at the Green Bay airport, walked out, and saw Jim Fruend holding a sign that said, "Shawn Carney."

"Hello, Jim, I'm Shawn. Great to meet you."

He was silent for a moment and then said, "You're Shawn?"

"Yes sir. It's cold here!"

He quietly led me to his car and drove me past Lambeau Field (which I had to admit was awesome).

I could tell something was on Jim's mind, but I decided to let him work up to it. As we sat at a red light and Jim thumped on the steering wheel, staring straight ahead, I asked him about the hospital that does abortions in Green Bay. He didn't respond. Eventually he looked at me and said, "Shawn, I need to ask you something, and I don't want you to be offended." (Which, of course, is what we say to people before we offend them). "How old are you?" he said.

Of course. All our communications up to this point had been via phone and email; this was our first face-to-face meeting. I said, "No big deal, Jim. People ask this a lot. I may look young for my age, but I graduate from high school later this year."

I could tell his heart nearly stopped.

"I'm kidding!" I said. "I'm twenty-three, and my wife and I have a second baby on the way."

He laughed and said, "Congratulations!"

Jim took me to a meeting where I spoke to pastors about what 40 Days for Life was and what it wasn't. I talked about the 40 Days for Life campaigns in College Station, Dallas, Kitsap County, Washington, DC, and Houston. I didn't speak about future plans because at that time 40 Days for Life was a small endeavor with no real future planned. God had not yet shown what he was going to do with 40 Days for Life.

Then Mark, a pastor from one of the local evangelical churches, got up to speak. He looked like he could play linebacker for the Packers. In his deep voice, he powerfully exhorted the rest of the pastors: "Look, this is Green Bay. This is our home. We hunt, we ice fish, we take our kids to church, and we watch the Packers in the fall. We take care of one another, and abortion is a threat to our way of life. You need to get in the game! I'm all in with this thing. Some of us are Catholic; some of us are Protestant. I don't care which you are. Heaven and hell are full of both. What matters is that we defend these babies. So please—let's do this!"

Mark had me so pumped up I was ready to head for the sidewalk that minute.

And that wasn't the only thing that made Jim's kickoff event fantastic. After the closing prayer, the crowd poured out of the church with a plan for everyone to proceed to the hospital where the abortions in Green Bay were done. As the church emptied, the local bishop, Bishop Zubik, grabbed me and said, "May God bless your apostolate."

All I could think is, *I don't have an apostolate.*

He looked at me and said, "This must go on. This must grow. Safe travels back to Texas." It was a short and impactful conversation.

On the flight home, as I watched Green Bay getting smaller and smaller through my airplane window, I couldn't believe that 40 Days for Life had come here, and I began to imagine what our little dream could be. Where was God taking this effort? I had no idea at the time, but that trip was a pivotal moment for me and was the start of a long relationship between 40 Days for Life and Green Bay, Wisconsin.

Later that year, Marilisa delivered a beautiful baby girl three weeks early—which meant that my two oldest girls, Bridget and Bailey, are ten and a half months apart, and yes, they are best friends. The year 2006 was a good one and the start of many things—a rapidly growing family and a new swelling of momentum for 40 Days for Life.

∼

I can't figure out what's going on, Jim Ball thought as he drove past the hospital complex and saw a man walking while trying to hold up a sign in the blistering wind and driving rain. Jim's work brought him past this hospital and adjacent medical arts building frequently. Finally he pulled over, approached the man, and asked him in the direct fashion that's customary with Jim, "What the heck is going on out here?"

The man who answered was Jim Fruend. "40 Days for Life," he said. "We're praying for an end to abortion."

That was Jim Ball's introduction to 40 Days for Life and a bad day for the abortion industry in Green Bay.

A year later in 2007, when we launched 40 Days for Life nationally, a courageous woman named Lori Koschnick signed up to lead the Green Bay campaign, and Jim Ball was quick to offer his help. His eagerness was prompted by one sentence spoken to him during the 2006 campaign. A woman had driven up to him, rolled down her car window, and said, "I just wanted to tell you how great it is to see men out here on the sidewalk praying."

Her comment made Jim not just think about abortion but think about it as a man, and that lit a fire in him. *We're the cause of all of this,* he thought. *We've slept through this whole abortion thing. We get women pregnant and then forego all responsibility. This is our fault. We get our faces painted and go out to bars to cheer for our sports team, and we get women pregnant and leave them with the problem. I, for one, am sick of it.*

From 2007 on, he had one mission in mind—to get more men taking responsibility for abortion, defending women, and praying on the sidewalks. In the fall of 2008, Jim Ball's desire for big challenges was combined with his big heart, and he took over leadership of the Green Bay campaign. After filling out the online application, his finger hovered over the send button for some time. When he finally hit send, he became campaign leader for the next ten years.

Jim implemented a call to men he named "Sleep No More." His challenge was for men to come pray all through the night during their twenty-four-hour vigils. Over time, it went viral.

"You don't defeat the dark side by sitting in an easy chair," Jim said. "If you can sit in a deer stand for twelve hours, don't tell me you can't get out on the sidewalk. If you can go watch a Packers game for four hours and sit at Lambeau Field when it's below zero and drink beer, don't tell me you can't pray on the sidewalk."

He doesn't claim it's easy, but he does have ways of getting himself moving. "Every time I feel sorry for myself when the alarm goes off at 11:30 at night and I've got to get dressed, and I can hear the wind blowing or the rain falling, I think of Deacon Dave. He has five kids. He's got a lot of responsibilities at his job. Yet Monday through Friday he's on the sidewalk for two hours a day."

Jim's commitment to challenge men is always applied first and foremost to himself, and the men follow. Here's an example:

One night a nasty winter storm blew in. (You don't need me to tell you that it can get bitterly cold in Green Bay.) Jim had the midnight to 2:00 a.m. shift that morning and was on his way to pray when the guy who was scheduled to take the next watch called—"Jim, they haven't plowed my road. I can't get out."

"That's all right. I'll stay out there."

After a few phone calls, he was able to find someone to split the shift with him. Even though the icy snow and brutal wind kept blowing, there was Jim Ball extending his shift. A few weeks later, they heard from a woman who had been scheduled to have an abortion that night. But she had seen a man with ice hanging from his hat and holding his sign that read simply, "Pray to End Abortion." That stormy, snowy night, she decided, *I'm keeping my baby.*

∼

The volunteers on the sidewalks praying through the campaign had no way of knowing what the hospital was fighting behind the scenes. There were doctors who didn't want abortions performed there. Representatives from 40 Days for Life had tried a number of times to arrange a meeting with any of the hospital executives but had never been successful. Then a doctor from the hospital asked for a meeting with Jim Ball.

Jim says, "I came to the hospital at 4:00 in the afternoon on a gray February day. When I sat down in his office, I could see my dedicated vigil volunteers outside."

The executive settled into his expensive chair and looked at Jim. "I think this is going to be your last vigil out here." he said. "The abortions in the OB/GYN are shutting down."

Jim wanted this to be true more than anything. "What do you mean exactly?" Jim asked.

The doctor explained that the OB-GYN Group was in the red

and business was nearly nonexistent. The only abortionist left was in financial straits too. The hospital offered him a contract that would have him work for the hospital, but contract language completely restricted him from doing abortions even in his off hours. The OB-GYN group was to close its doors, and with no abortionist available, abortions at the Medical Arts building were to end. Which officially happened on July 31, 2013.

As Jim heard these beautiful words, he looked out the window and saw the volunteers who had no idea how their prayers were being answered at that moment. Then he turned back toward the doctor. "I've got to ask one thing," Jim said. "Did our presence and our prayers impact this closing at all?"

The question transformed him from a soft-spoken man, weary to the bone at the end of a long day's work, into one who practically bolted out of his chair. As Jim described it, the doctor shot out of his chair "like he just had three cups of coffee infused into his heart."

"Absolutely!" he said. "Tell those people that if you hadn't been out there, we wouldn't be having this conversation."

Green Bay will always be a special place because of the faith, commitment, and sense of duty I saw in the people there—especially the men led by the two Jims.

Jim Ball was always pro-life, but he had never really done anything about it until he saw a dedicated man, another Jim, standing in the wind holding a sign in front of a hospital. The two Jims responded as too few men do. They knew that, as men, they had to defend women and life, and they did something about it.

Jim Fruend and Jim Ball allowed their hearts to take charge of their hands and feet. They went to work and trusted God with the results. And God delivered results through the hands, feet, and fortitude of a few good men.

～

When I was a child, I talked like a child,
I thought like a child, I reasoned like a child.
When I became a man,
I put the ways of childhood behind me.
1 CORINTHIANS 13:11

Dear Jesus, we are instructed to be like you—and you were a defender of women. I pray that we who love you would stand strong, becoming men and women who will put life before our own comfort. May we take responsibility for our actions and challenge others to do the same. And may these choices save more lives. Amen.

The Challenge of Mercy

~

Death is always important for it seals a destiny.
Any dying man is a scene.
Any dying scene is a sacred place.
—ARCHBISHOP FULTON J. SHEEN

HEIDI IS IN FOR THE ENCOUNTER OF HER LIFE, AND SHE HAS NO idea.

She is a nurse—not an easy job, but she's good at it. She works in intensive care and has seen thousands of patients. Still, there's something different about the one who requested that she come see him just before her late-night shift ended.

Heidi believes in the power of prayer and participated in her local 40 Days for Life campaign. Like most volunteers, she would spend an hour a week outside—sometimes more—praying for an end to abortion. Her local campaign saved lives from abortion, and the presence of the praying volunteers on the sidewalk hurt the business of their local abortion facility.

Heidi saw the fruit of her prayers when that abortion facility announced that they were going out of business and closed their doors for good. Her community was now abortion free, and she was glad she'd had a role in ending abortion where she lived.

One of Heidi's gifts is comforting her patients, especially the ones just hours from death. The man Heidi had cared for on this night had very little time left, and he knew it. The two of them had spoken about many things over the past few days, but tonight was different. He beckoned her nearer to his bed and, in a different tone of voice from their previous discussions, he said, "I have done some very bad things." He paused, as if thinking how best to continue, and then said, "Years ago there was an abortion facility here."

Time stopped. Heidi remembered. She recognized this man—he was the abortionist who had run the abortion facility where she had prayed all those years.

The man confirmed it. "I was the doctor who did the abortions here in town. I was a different man then. I was lost. I didn't know God. Over time, I realized the evil I was doing and closed my office. But here I am about to face judgment for all those abortions. Please pray for me. Pray that I receive God's mercy, and that I can trust in the mercy of God in my remaining hours on earth, so that I can find peace."

Tears came to Heidi's eyes as she gathered her thoughts on what to say at this sacred moment. "God is merciful," she said at last. "Christ came for sinners, not for the righteous. God loves you, whatever you have done." And with that she began to pray with the man until he passed away.

God's mercy is real.

The beautiful reality of his forgiveness is that we really do need it. We are all sinners in need of his grace. He came because we are sinners, and he wanted to set us free from our sin.

Heidi's experience reminded me of a conversation I had with another former abortion doctor, my friend Dr. Haywood Robinson.

"You see, Shawn," Haywood started in his characteristically pleasant but direct way. "As an abortionist, to confront what you've done, the sins you've committed, you have to go to a very dark place. And it's not easy. The forgiveness of Jesus Christ can be reached through the grace of God, but first you must acknowledge the gravity of what you have done."

I've known Dr. Haywood Robinson for seventeen years. From

my early days of praying in front of Planned Parenthood while struggling to determine whether our effort was doing any good, to being overwhelmed when the world came knocking and 40 Days for Life spread to fifty countries, Haywood has always been there as a partner, a friend, and a mentor.

Haywood was there when Planned Parenthood announced they were building the first-ever abortion facility in Bryan/College Station, Texas, where he and his wife practiced medicine. Haywood was there when the Planned Parenthood Federation of America sent their national CEO to College Station and labeled it "the most anti-choice place in America."[5]

Haywood was there at midnight of the first hour of the first day of the first-ever 40 Days for Life campaign. Haywood picked up his phone when the director of our local Planned Parenthood, Abby Johnson, walked into my office after witnessing an abortion for the first time and wanted out of the abortion business. Haywood was there when we launched 40 Days for Life as a national and then international movement.

And Haywood was there when the newly closed Planned Parenthood in Bryan, Texas, the site of the first-ever 40 Days for Life campaign, became the headquarters of 40 Days for Life. Haywood and his wife, Noreen, are both former abortionists who went to that dark place and, recognizing the evil they were doing, accepted the saving grace of Christ. The suffering, crucifixion, and death of Christ was brutal. It was bloody, sweaty, and violent. What Christ endured was due to our sins, but he did it out of love for us which fuels his deep desire to forgive our gravest sins when we repent. "No one takes [my life] from me," he said, "but I lay it down of my own accord. I have authority to lay it down and authority to take it up again" (John 10:18).

I've been around Haywood now for countless professional and social situations, and every time I realize what a walking billboard he is for God's sweet and consoling mercy. Haywood has been there for more of our events than I can count, from the smallest to the largest. From the first time I started praying in front of an abortion facility, to the birth and growth of 40 Days for Life, to the closing of abortion facilities, to the conversion of abortion workers, to the countless meetings, conferences, and speeches, Haywood has been there.

No one ever forgets Haywood. He has a joyful nature, a classic smile, and he really does look like a younger version of Morgan Freeman. It doesn't hurt that sometimes being with him in the trenches of this work can feel like *The Shawshank Redemption*. I wrote about Haywood in the book *40 Days for Life*, and former Planned Parenthood director Abby Johnson wrote about him in her book, *Unplanned*. Haywood has shared his testimony and been a voice for the unborn around the world.

But Haywood never forgets where he came from. He also never loses perspective on what abortion is. *Never.*

I've worked with many former abortion workers and doctors, and there is a significant gap between your relative or coworker who supports "reproductive rights" and those who actually do the abortions. Many who advocate for abortion but don't actually do them want no data, pictures, or details. Not because of cowardice but because of revulsion. Current abortionist Warren Hern was open about this during his interview with *The Guardian*: "The pro-choice people don't like it when you talk about how it really feels to do this work."[6]

The catchy slogans that Madison Avenue public relations firms come up with to justify abortion are nowhere to be found inside an abortion facility. That's where it becomes real and final. The doctor who does the abortion must dismember, tear, pry apart, and force his will onto a smaller, weaker human being that he can often see on an ultrasound monitor.

Warren Hern has been doing abortions for over four decades,

"We have reached a point in this particular technology where there is no possibility of denying an act of destruction," he says. "It is before one's eyes. The sensations of dismemberment flow through the forceps like an electric current."[7]

The babies have no idea what is happening to them, but the abortionist does. Abortion is fueled by the evil philosophy that might makes right. Nothing displays that more than the brutal reality of the surgery itself.

By the grace of God, Haywood, his wife Noreen, and many other abortion doctors have found a path out of that living hell, and that path was God. But they have done more than that. They have allowed God to use them to shine light into the darkness. That's not easy. It takes humility, courage, and the willingness to go back to your darkest sins with a flashlight for the world to see.

I've seen Haywood share his testimony many times and discuss his past. More than any former abortion worker or doctor I know, he has been healed and rejuvenated to the point that he is able to directly share his past role in abortion. His honesty and acceptance of God's mercy is evident.

God shook Haywood and called him to repentance, and Haywood trusted the mercy of God.

I have seen many active abortionists. I even sat between one and his wife on a plane. I have also talked to many former abortion doctors and clinic workers. And I ask this question of myself and all 40 Days for Life participants: If abortionists can, for years, do this barbaric act on God's most precious and innocent children; if they can fly to different locations and use their medical expertise to kill babies; if after all of that, some of them can get to a place where they can trust God's mercy—then shouldn't we place our hope in God's mercy *before they convert, as we see them walking in and out of their abortion facility?*

Trusting the mercy of God gives us peace when we pray at an abortion facility. It reminds us that we are not there for ourselves but for him. He is in charge, and any anger we have about the reality of abortion should be channeled into a zeal for souls.

Heidi didn't expect to find a repentant abortionist that day when she went to work. I didn't expect Abby Johnson to walk into my office and have change of heart. And I'm sure many of the women Haywood did abortions on did not expect him to become a pro-life advocate. I promise you that if I could get into a DeLorean and go back in time and pray in front of Haywood's office when he was doing abortions, I would not have imagined that one day this man, this horrible man doing abortions, would be a traveler with me on this pro-life journey.

We often hear stories of radical conversions and praise God for them after the fact. But we need to trust God's mercy and use it as a driving force to pray and witness to those who are actively doing abortions today. Just as they are the future of abortion in our country, they are also the future converts. They are the future Haywoods. They are the future Abby Johnsons.

Perhaps God is calling you to be a future Heidi?

Stop and take to prayer the possibility that one day your local abortion doctor will look you in the eye and ask you to pray for God's mercy with him.

∼

Let us then approach God's throne of grace
with confidence, so that we may
receive mercy and find grace
to help us in our time of need.
HEBREWS 4:16

Amazing Lord, I confess that when I think of an abortion doctor, I think of him as a villain. Help me to see him instead as a potential recipient of your awesome mercy. Thank you for having mercy on me, a sinner. Now enlarge my understanding of how great your mercy is. Forgive my lack of trust in your mercy for these who commit these horrific acts. Plant in me compassion and hope and grace toward all abortion workers. Use my voice in this world, Lord, to call others to join me in prayer for those who perform abortions and those who support abortion. I want to rise to the challenge of mercy. Amen.

A Tale of Two Abortion Doctors

~

The nearer Christ comes to a heart, the more it becomes conscious of its guilt; it will then either ask for his mercy and find peace, or else it will turn against Him because it is not yet ready to give up its sinfulness. Thus He will separate the good from the bad, the wheat from the chaff. Man's reaction to this Divine Presence will be the test: either it will call out all the opposition of egotistic natures, or else galvanize them into a regeneration and a resurrection.

—ARCHBISHOP FULTON J. SHEEN

GOD'S MERCY IS REAL. AND WE REALLY DO NEED IT. WE ARE ALL sinners in need of his grace. He did not come to save us because we are all nice people—he came because we are sinners, helpless in our sin, and he wants to set us free.

That hit me in a new way during one of many conversations with my friend Dr. Haywood Robinson. We were discussing former abortion doctors, and, since he is one, he had much to say. He was speaking of hitting rock bottom when he was going through his initial healing process, and said, "I had to look at myself in the mirror and acknowledge that I was no different than the Nazis.

Haywood and all the courageous former abortion doctors need prayer. Spiritual warfare always follows a repentant abortionist.

Haywood has been in the trenches doing pro-life work for decades. He went to Cal Tech, is highly intelligent, and is twice my age, but that didn't stop me from worrying about him on our trip to England in 2016.

I called our general counsel, Matt Britton, who was also going to England for a conference and to train our international leaders. Matt answered his phone after one ring. (Very typical.)

"We need to pray for Haywood," I said. In an unprecedented opportunity, Robert Colquhoun, our international campaign director who lives in London, had arranged for Haywood to debate an abortion doctor on the radio. Haywood had agreed, and the event had been added to our trip. I really wanted to be there to support Haywood, but my flight would arrive too late, so Matt would go with Haywood to the debate for support, prayer, and when needed, humor. Matt takes God, duty, and his family seriously but himself not too seriously. He was the perfect person to accompany Haywood. As a veteran prosecutor he has seen and heard it all. Still I reminded Matt over the phone, "Try not to interrupt the interview, take the abortionist to court, put her on the stand, and ask the judge for sentencing."

In his typical sarcastic tone, he replied, "Fat chance. That is my exact plan."

I laughed.

Matt said, "I'm going to sit in silence behind Haywood in the radio studio and pray. It's an abortion doctor talking to a repentant abortion doctor. The rest we're leaving to God."

So with Matt behind him in prayer, Haywood entered into a debate with British abortionist Wendy Savage on the Premiere Christian Radio Network:[8]

Justin Brierley, Premier Christian Radio host: [It's] extraordinary to think [you've performed] somewhere over ten thousand [abortions]. [Does this number cover all] reasons that a woman might be looking to end a pregnancy?

Dr. Wendy Savage, Doctors for a Woman's Choice on Abortion:
Very few are due because of a risk to a woman's health.
About 1 percent are done because of fetal abnormality.
The rest are women who just do not want to continue
with a pregnancy....

Justin: Haywood ... tell us how you first began to get into ...
abortion....

Dr. Haywood Robinson, 40 Days for Life: During residency
training, I spent time [in] obstetrics. That residency is
where I learned to do abortions. We have a saying in
medicine: "You see one, you do one, and then you teach
one." I've found the first step in dehumanizing the child
is seeing one. I remember my first abortion that I saw,
you know, it didn't feel quite right. But then again, you go
back the next day, you're not quite as disturbed. And in
just a few weeks you're desensitized.

Justin: What made that change [from you performing abortions
to becoming pro-life]?

Haywood: Well, I did become a Christian. I started to see life
from God's point of view. God is the author of life. One of
the first things after becoming a Christian that the Lord
did was convict my wife and [me] of our participation
with abortion. When you see things from God's point
of view, you become sensitized to [the fact that] we're ...
not just some protoplasm that we can take out of another
person and call it medicine.

Justin: What kind of procedures ... were you [performing]
earlier in your career?

Haywood: I was doing what we call first-trimester abortions.
Abortions on women thirteen weeks pregnant and less.

Justin: What ... does that type of abortion involve?

Haywood: Well, the mother is put on the table. She's put
in position and speculum is put in. You give some

anesthesia. You dilate or open up the cervix, which allows you to put in a tube or curette that is going to tear the baby up and suck it up out of the uterus. In seven to ten minutes, you've terminated a human life and you send the woman on.

Justin: To what extent would you say the woman in these cases was familiar with what was going to happen?

Haywood: Unless you're going to show them a video, I don't think you can verbally tell them exactly what's going to happen at an abortion because it's such a traumatic experience.

Justin: Do you regard it just the same as any other medical procedure ...?

Wendy: Lots of medical procedures are quite unpleasant ... but I mean, it's the use of language. At the point you're doing a first-trimester abortion, you're dealing with a fetus. You are not dealing with a baby.

Justin: Do you put a time, though ... when you would classify the ... fetus, becoming a baby ...?

Wendy: I think it becomes a baby when it's born.

Justin: And you would always call it a fetus even up to, you know, thirty-nine weeks of gestation?

Wendy: Yeah. We call it fetal monitoring when we are looking after the woman in labor.... We don't call it electronic baby monitoring. Whilst it's connected to the mother and doesn't have an independent existence, then it's still a fetus. Once the baby is born, then that's different.

Justin: Obviously when you're dealing with something that looks a lot more like a full-grown baby, it's more disturbing.

Wendy: I mean, the vacuum extraction, you know, a little fetus comes down in a tube. You don't have to look at it. I always used to look to make sure we've got everything out so the woman doesn't come back with bleeding afterwards. ... But the later abortions are done by dilation and evacuation, so the fetal parts are too big to go down the tube, so you have to take them out with forceps. You're so busy concentrating on making sure you got everything out....

Justin: Would you say you've gone through that sort of desensitization process that Haywood described?

Wendy: I don't think I'm desensitized. I'm always aware ... that this is a potential human life that you are destroying. But when you've spoken to the woman, you understand why she wants it, what the depth of her feelings are, and see her ... relief at not being pregnant. You know, it makes it worthwhile doing something which isn't exactly pleasant.

Justin: Why does the fetus become a person precisely at the moment of birth?

Wendy: Because it's separated from the mother. Until that time, it's dependent on the mother for its nutrition.

Justin: I guess I'm just wondering why that specific definition of personhood.

Wendy: Well you've got to start somewhere, haven't you? And it seems that birth is a reasonable place to start.

Justin: Do you think it's a doctor's place ... to encourage a woman to ... at least seek an alternative point of view before making a final decision?

Wendy: Women aren't stupid. If you are pregnant and you don't want to be, you can either have the child and keep it, ... have it adopted, or have an abortion. The majority of women don't take very long to decide which of those options.... A woman usually gets to the doctor knowing what it is she wants to do. All right, you can tell her all the pros and cons of having an abortion, what the side effects are, etcetera, but basically the woman—if she has made up her mind—she's going to go and do it anyway.

Haywood: That's really not true. When a woman has an unexpected pregnancy, the first thing is usually shock, fear, parents are going to find out, not going to finish school. When you expose the woman to rational discussion and the options and give them some time, they start to think more rationally. One of the things about the business of abortion is that you want to get a woman in and get it done. Because the longer you wait, the more likely [it is that] the woman may change her mind. If you're in the business of selling abortions, you don't want the women to change their minds.

Justin: In your experience, Haywood, does it make any difference to a woman's choice whether she sees a sonogram?

Haywood: Absolutely. We found the ultrasound has been the most powerful baby saver that we have in our pregnancy help centers.

Justin: What do you say to someone like Wendy who simply disagrees that you're dealing with a human life here?

Haywood: I don't look at it as my personal view. Chapter one, paragraph one of my embryology book said that human life begins at conception. There's no question. Biology 101 tells you when the sperm and ovum come together to make one cell that then becomes two cells, then becomes four cells, you're dealing with a separate individual from the mother. You're not "potentially" this. You're not "almost" this. You're 100 percent human at the time the sperm and the egg come together. That's basic embryology.

Justin: Wendy, you obviously disagree. If Haywood could persuade you that you're dealing with a human, would that still not for you trump a woman's rights to her own body?

Wendy: A potential human life is not the same as actual human life. I'm not going to change my mind on that.

This historic interview is another testimony that we cannot live in fear. We must be a voice for the unborn. That day Haywood had no fear of defending children to a pro-abortion doctor whom he could relate to more than anyone. He handled himself with the love and mercy of Christ. And as always, he didn't forget where he came from.

Wendy Savage had no fear either. She unapologetically defended the dehumanization of the most innocent human beings and has personally killed ten thousand of them in the name of freedom. We who are pro-life sometimes find it a serious challenge to interact with Wendy Savage or any other abortionist without anger. It is hard for us to hear them strip away the dignity of unborn boys and girls, but they have no choice if, indeed, they are to abort those same children. How else could they bear the work that they do?

The unborn have no voice but yours. They cannot defend themselves. There is no place for fear or timidity or straddling the fence on abortion. If Haywood can walk into that room and do that interview, then you can speak on behalf of the unborn at work, church, or a dinner table. This doesn't mean we run around all day talking about abortion like some kind of weirdo. It does mean that we don't cower or fear ridicule when defending the most basic and beautiful right—the right to life. When we do speak up, God works miracles, and those who compared themselves to Nazis can be transformed into ambassadors for the gospel.

It happened to Haywood. It can happen to anyone we encounter.

~

In your hearts revere Christ as Lord.
Always be prepared to give an answer
to everyone who asks you to give
the reason for the hope that you have.
But do this with gentleness and respect.
1 PETER 3:15

Dear Father, it is hard sometimes to speak up about my faith in you, my respect for human life, and my heart for the unborn. At other times, it is hard to speak gently and with respect when confronted by those who disrespect you and the life you give. Help me to live out 1 Peter 3:15—to be prepared to give an answer for the hope I have in you and to speak with gentleness and respect to those with whom I differ. Thank you, Lord. Amen.

I Was Also an Unborn Baby

~

*Freedom is the right to question and
change the established way of doing things.
It is the understanding that allows us
to recognize shortcomings and seek solutions.
It is the right to put forth an idea, scoffed at by the experts,
and watch it catch fire among the people.*

—PRESIDENT RONALD REAGAN at Moscow State University

AFTER SIXTEEN HOURS ON A PLANE, ANTE (PRONOUNCED ON-TAY)
Caljkušić arrived in the United States of America for the first time
in his life.

I met him outside security, and together we maneuvered through
the extremely crowded international terminal at Bush airport
in Houston. As people hustled around us to pick up their loved
ones from the airport, Ante yelled enthusiastically with his arms
extended, "I am finally here! I am in America! May God bless this
beautiful country!"

I laughed at his joy and at the looks of those hurriedly moving
past us. He was like a kid on Christmas morning. I said to him,
"America is happy to have you, Ante. Now let's go eat and I'll teach
you what a real hamburger tastes like."

I had invited Ante to the United States from his home country of
Croatia for him to share at our 40 Days for Life dinner in Texas how
God had used 40 Days for Life in his nation.

Ante's journey had been lengthy. Not long ago, Croatia was still under Communist rule. From the time he courageously brought 40 Days for Life to Croatia in 2014 until now, he has spread the campaign from his home city of Zagreb to nearly thirty more cities. Very impressive, especially considering there are only thirty-six cities in the entire country.

Ante recalls his first encounter with the abortion issue:

There were a few situations in my youth where God was preparing me for the work I am doing today. These situations are nothing spectacular, but to me they were something powerful and important, something stored deep in my heart. The first was a simple pro-life photo shown in the religious education classroom, in my second or third grade of elementary school. I set my eyes on a photo of a happy, smiling little girl carrying a sign in her hands reading, "I was also an unborn baby."

Two months before Christmas of 2013, I started praying to the Lord to use me in some way to spread the good word. I felt a strong encouragement in my heart to do something more for Croatian society. I told my wife, Sara, about my prayer and I asked the Lord to respond, if it was according to His will, by Christmas. If it was not, it would only mean for me to carry on as before.

However, there was no reply, so I told Sara, "Sara, it's two weeks until Christmas. The Lord hasn't responded to my prayer yet. If he responds or not, I leave it all to him."

At the very Christmas of 2013, during the evening Mass, Sara and I met common friends of ours and we invited them to our place. This was a really spontaneous and touching meeting. Somewhere during the dinner, my friend suggested that I start 40 Days for Life.

I asked, "What is 40 Days for Life?" Suddenly I remembered my prayer to God which, interestingly enough, I had forgotten about! I told my friend that his suggestion to me was quite a big project and that I would have to quit my job as a professor in order to dedicate myself to it fully. The friend responded, "Ante, if this is God's calling for you, you need not worry. He will provide everything."

I suggested that we say a prayer. So all four of us sat under the Christmas tree, in front of the manger, and went into a deep prayer. We all felt deep peace and the presence of the Holy Spirit. Being inspired by the Holy Spirit, I told my friend, "Here, open the Holy Scripture. Let's see what God wants to tell us." This was not a sheer opening of the Bible due to some sensation. I felt very encouraged in the deepest moment of the prayer. The friend opened the Holy Scripture to Second Chronicles, chapter 7, verse 12, saying, "I have heard your prayer and have chosen this place for myself as a temple for sacrifices." He read verse 14 as well, emphasizing, "If my people, who are called by my name, will humble themselves and pray and seek my face and turn from their wicked ways, then I will hear from heaven, and I will forgive their sin and will heal their land."

All right, I thought, this is not anything connected with abortion. However, since it contained some kind of promise, we decided to start with serious work on this the next day. We wanted to give our best. We did not want to "slack" if this was God's will.

The following day the friend called me, absolutely thrilled, asking me to look up quickly my email containing a promo video of "40 Days for Life" which he had sent me. I opened up my email—I always get goose bumps when I talk about this— opened the video, and in its very beginning I recognized the quote which we had opened: Second Chronicles, chapter 7, line 14! We found out that this quote was the guiding Scripture for 40 Days for Life.

As a result, in 2014 Ante brought the first-ever 40 Days for Life campaign to Croatia. He used his endless joy and his gifts as a speaker to get city after city throughout the country involved in 40

Days for Life. There had never been such a large-scale, organized pro-life effort in Croatia before. In the capital, Zagreb, they began seeing the results—saved babies—immediately. Women were choosing life. Requests to bring 40 Days for Life to different parts of the country increased.

Ante recalls:

I especially remember one older woman from the town of Križevci. I came to this town to speak, desiring to motivate the people to start 40 Days for Life in their own town. After my speech a lady approached me, deeply touched, and said, "This thing you do, this is great. Thank God you're here. I did my abortion thirty years ago, and I still remember, every time there is a piece of bread left on the table, my own child to whom I did not grant life. I will come to the vigil every day."

This woman became a regular volunteer in front of the local health center and is actively involved in the activities of 40 Days for Life.

Another volunteer, named Ivana, was very nervous. She said, "Although I feel great fear when I need to pray in public, my boyfriend persuaded me to be a shift leader in an autumn campaign and the recently finished Lent campaign. I simply said, 'God, You know of all my weaknesses and fears, but I know that you need me. With your help I will be brave, and you can use me as a means of your love. Even if I experience something uncomfortable, let it be for your glory.' I took a morning time slot before going to work.

"It happened often that I was left alone in front of the hospital while praying. I would stand alone with my rosary while the people were passing. I have to admit I wasn't feeling comfortable, but what is that in comparison to what God had suffered for us? There were various reactions, and when it came to the unpleasant ones, I was carried ahead by the thought that I knew for whom I was fighting and who was always with me.

"One day a lady passed me by and stopped shortly. It seemed

as if she was thinking about something. I waited, not knowing what to do. She came back, and with tears in her eyes she told me her story. The niece living with her had gotten pregnant and the woman did not know how she was going to help her and the child financially. Her niece Viktorija ran away to her in Zagreb because the father of the baby and her mother were persuading her to do the abortion. I was overwhelmed by the feeling of gratitude because she had come right at the time when I was standing in front of the hospital. We talked, and I encouraged her to fight for the child. I also gave her contacts that would help them both financially and spiritually. With the help of God, the little baby was saved."

After hearing her story, Ante said, "My dear Ivana, can you see that the Lord can do wonders through only one person? God answered you in the most beautiful way possible."

The growth of 40 Days for Life in Croatia is one of many instances of the world knocking on our door, saying, "Help us bring what God is using in the United States to our country, to end abortion where we live."

Ante was moving fast. A young husband and father, he had a stable career with excellent pay and benefits. But he decided to quit his job as a theology professor in order to dedicate all his energy to ending abortion in Croatia. He started Croatia for Life, which would include 40 Days for Life campaigns. He used his many gifts to raise money for Croatia for Life and launched the first-ever national march for life in Croatia!

Ante also worked on a documentary to highlight the 40 Days for Life campaign in Croatia and recruit volunteers. In order to get more Croatians involved in the fight for life, he thought, *Why not ask Pope Francis to meet us and give us his support?* In a country that is 95 percent Catholic, that would go a long way.

Despite the fact that Pope Francis is busy and the Vatican moves very slowly, Ante was determined to meet with him. Petra and his other coleaders said, "Ante, we do not have time for this. Pope Francis is not going to meet with us. We need to focus and get more people involved. Trying to get Pope Francis to meet with us will be a waste of time."

But Ante would not be deterred. He wrote a letter to Pope Francis anyway.

Three weeks later, the Croatian team was at the Vatican for a meeting with Pope Francis. They asked him to bless a mother and her baby saved from abortion. Pope Francis blessed them and Ante. At the end of the meeting, Pope Francis looked at Ante and said, "This is the most important work in the world." Then the Pope slowly made a fist. He looked at these brave Croatians and softly said, "Fight, fight, fight."

It was a long drive home from Rome, but Ante, Petra, and the rest of the Croatian team returned home rejuvenated.

Ante's joy and simple faith in God is contagious. Much of it springs from the experience described earlier, in which, as a student in elementary school, he saw a photo of a child holding a sign that said, "I was also an unborn baby."

Later, Ante asked his older sister, "Katarina, why does this sign say 'I was also an unborn baby'?" She thought about it and said, "Each and every one of us was once a small, unborn baby in the womb of our mother. You, me, this little girl—we all grew and lived in the womb of our mother."

Ante recalls:

As she was answering my question, she was looking at the photo sharply. Behind her sharp look there was hiding itself the reality of abortion, whose meaning I understand fully today. From that day I would remember this photo often. As 40 Days for Life grew, I wanted to find out who that girl in the picture was. After a couple of months, in a conversation with a good associate of mine, Dr. Antun Lisec, the representative of Human Life

International for Croatia, I found out that this was his niece. Today I carry the photo on the back of my cell phone, marking my first encounter with this important work.

Abortion attacks the most beautiful bond in all of humanity—the bond between a mother and a child. That message from the picture of a girl Ante carries on the back of his phone unifies us. She doesn't identify her politics, religion, or nationality. Her message is simply, *I was also an unborn baby.*

∽

When we first received the application from Ante to bring 40 Days for Life to Croatia, I had to look at a map to find the country. Despite the fact that we were worlds apart, God took Ante and us on a journey together.

May the message that hit Ante hit us as well. If it doesn't, then we will never take abortion personally. *I was also an unborn baby* was an invitation to Ante. May it be so to you as you read this chapter (and perhaps wonder exactly where Croatia is).

Ante responded to that invitation. As we sat eating our first meal together, I asked him what he had learned leading 40 Days for Life in his country. He took a break from saying how good the hamburgers were in America to lean across the table and say, "God uses the weak to do his work."

∽

If my people, who are called by my name,
will humble themselves and pray and seek
My face and turn from their wicked ways,
then I will hear from heaven,
and I will forgive their sin and will heal their land.
2 CHRONICLES 7:14

Great God, around the globe there are many who are working on behalf of saving children. I pray for our brothers and sisters in Christ who are praying in all kinds of weather, under all kinds of persecution, in all kinds of cultures, to have strength to remain faithful in their prayers and work on behalf of the unborn. Amen.

40 Days for Abortion

~

Imitation is the sincerest form of flattery.
—CHARLES CALEB COLTON

THERE IS A LOT OF PAIN INSIDE THE ABORTION INDUSTRY.

Not just the obvious pain felt by the babies who lose their lives or the mothers who lose their children. But because abortion requires constant internal justification, rationalization, and validation, there is also pain that extends through every level of those who work in the abortion process—from facility workers all the way to the corporate executives who market abortion.

Many former abortion workers say they dreaded being asked by family, friends, or in casual interactions where they worked. Do you find that strange? I do. Those who work to support a cause are usually eager to show their passion and discuss the specifics of what they stand for. Environmentalists talk about the environment; those working for organizations that provide aid to other countries speak about the people they desire to help. But the abortion workers I've spoken with said they avoided talking about abortion. They said they would deftly move the topic from the specific to the abstract and then breeze by the vague notion of choice.

It's true that when people are in pain or helping someone else who is in pain, it's easy to deny science, dismiss nature, and ignore God in an attempt to justify whatever they believe will stop that pain— including abortion. So when we're talking with people in pain, we need to rely on prayer and compassion—rather than arguments—to change hearts. Arguments aren't the answer to pain. Love is.

I'm not saying that reasoned arguments about the truth of abortion don't have a place in the pro-life movement. They are important in that they can help articulate the pro-life message. But we must remember that we are dealing primarily with *pain*. Arguments and logic are effective inside the head, but that doesn't always translate to the heart and the will—and that's where the pain of abortion lies.

Prayer is what causes thousands of women to turn around at the very last moment before their abortion. It's prayer that opens the hearts of abortion workers, and it's prayer that offers hope and healing to women as they leave the abortion facility post-abortion. It's prayer that sustains a discouraged volunteer or motivates a hopeful leader to bring this campaign to their community. Prayer can also help those who are tired of praying.

Prayer is our strongest weapon because it takes the focus off ourselves and places our hope in God and his holy will. Prayer prevents us from being overwhelmed. Prayer humbles us when God answers in his time, not ours.

As peaceful as the 40 Days for Life campaigns have been, as prayerful as the presence on the sidewalks are, as selfless and loving as the hundreds of thousands of participants have been, that does not mean that everyone feels warm and fuzzy about 40 Days for Life showing up on their doorstep. Let's look at a few examples.

Planned Parenthood's national president described the birthplace of 40 Days for Life, Bryan/College Station, Texas, as "the most anti-choice place in the nation."

Unwittingly, the abortion industry has made comments that show us that 40 Days for Life is effective at saving lives and changing hearts and minds. For instance, Pro-Choice Coalition of Canada said, "40 Days for Life has an impressive level of organization including coordinators, a user-friendly website, many participating churches and schools—each responsible for one day of harassment.

This ensures city-wide participation, meaning the organizers are able to produce a consistently high number of volunteers."

The CEO of Planned Parenthood of Western Washington, Chris Charbonneau, said, "We know from past experience that these rallies and prayer vigils create barriers that deter our patients."[9]

An ACLU spokesperson addressing a group of abortion advocates said that 40 Days for Life was "the greatest threat to choice" because it was "so highly organized and effective."[10] And a Planned Parenthood executive in Chicago said that eventually the 40 Days for Life volunteers will "give up and go back to their normal lives." That location is on their eleventh 40 Days for Life campaign.[11]

Honestly, though, we didn't expect the abortion industry to be supportive of 40 Days for Life.

The irony of the pro-choice movement is that during a 40 Days for Life campaign, the woman has no real choice once she arrives at the facility. Planned Parenthood escorts won't allow their clients to speak with volunteers or take information about local alternatives to abortion. Countless times I've witnessed escorts and Planned Parenthood employees in the parking lot rip up the information about adoption or help for unplanned pregnancies in the community.

But all the hostile, and sometimes just plain bizarre, reactions from the abortion industry I've heard over the years, added together, didn't hold a candle to the pro-abortion bluster I encountered when I landed in Omaha, Nebraska, to give a speech at Creighton University. The moment I powered up my phone while still on the runway, it began ringing and buzzing with texts and emails from media outlets wanting comments on the new campaign from Planned Parenthood.

What campaign? I wondered. Once I got to my hotel room and checked the calls and emails in detail, what I saw astounded me.

A Planned Parenthood affiliate in California had teamed up with Clergy for Choice and launched a mock 40 Days for Life campaign called "40 Days of Prayer." Their campaign featured daily devotionals and prayer requests to match the 40 Days for Life model! While they say that imitation is the sincerest form of flattery, this was appalling. Here are a few....

> DAY 1: Today we pray for women for whom pregnancy is not good news, that they may know they have choices.

> DAY 5: Today we pray for medical students who want to include abortion care in their practice. May they receive good training and find good mentors.

> DAY 7: Today we pray for the 45 million American women who have had safe, legal abortions. May they stand tall and refuse shame.

> DAY 14: Today we pray for Christians everywhere to embrace the loving model of Jesus in the way he refused to shame women.

> DAY 34: Today we give thanks for abortion escorts who guide women safely through hostile gauntlets of protesters.

> DAY 40: Today we give thanks and celebrate that abortion is still safe and legal.[12]

These sad and misguided daily prayers reveal the lengths to which the abortion industry will go in order to justify the unjustifiable. They also expose the huge disconnect between the talking points of the abortion industry and the pain and heartbreak I've witnessed in the women who seek abortions.

These prayers reveal a mindset that sees abortion as "sacred" and which would include "good training" in abortion for medical students. For women in developing countries, they put abortion in the same desirable category as employment or education.

The women seeking abortions are scared, they feel alone, and they see no other way out. That's not self-determination—that's fear.

And it's something they want to forget about the moment it's over. The disconnect couldn't be any stronger or sadder.

This disconnect increases with women who have already had abortions. In my view, Planned Parenthood has a history of being unable to connect with most women who have had abortions but then struggle, because Planned Parenthood's ideological view is that abortion empowers women. Thus, they believe that women who have had abortions should be proud that they are taking control of their own lives.

This was never more evident than in their failed 2004 campaign to push T-shirts that said, "I had an abortion." Their idea was that women who have had abortions would be proud enough of it to brag. Of course, very few bought the T-shirt, and the media had a field day with it. So Planned Parenthood stopped selling the T-shirt not long after it was released.

Planned Parenthood's campaign of daily prayers was another example of how out of touch they are with post-abortive women by praying that they "refuse shame." As though a woman is wrong to regret her abortion and should resist the way she feels. It is not unusual to feel shame after an abortion—just ask a woman who has had one. Ask members of groups like Silent No More Awareness or Rachel's Vineyard—who have reached out and helped hundreds of thousands of post-abortive women—if shame is something women can just "refuse." Because Planned Parenthood doesn't do follow-up appointments after an abortion, these groups step in and tirelessly help women find hope and healing. Planned Parenthood, on the other hand, expects them to move on like it's just another choice in their life.

This disconnect between Planned Parenthood's view of women and the human heart is scary. It seems that not only does Planned Parenthood sell the woman the abortion, but they want to control how she feels about it afterwards. Not only are they praying for these women to "refuse shame," but they encourage them to "know the blessing of choice." Perhaps there are women who feel this choice was a blessing. All I know is, of the hundreds of women I have met both inside and outside the pro-life movement who have had abortions, not one of them has considered her abortion a "blessing."

It was because of this disconnect that this mock prayer campaign became a public relations nightmare for Planned Parenthood as social media, radio, and blogs circulated the brochures that had the daily prayer intentions. In my hotel room in Omaha, I pulled up Foxnews.com, and there it was on the homepage!

Planned Parenthood's response from their California CEO, Denise Vanden Bos, was troubling. Vanden Bos said, "Clergy for Choice believe that human life is holy and believe in all parents choosing to be a parent or not."[13]

Human life is holy, but not as holy as the right to get rid of it?

While Planned Parenthood might have intended this as a campaign to mock 40 Days for Life—and with us, all people of faith who recognize the God-given dignity of every human life—it backfired, giving 40 Days for Life a massive publicity boost in more than 400 media outlets.

The whole fiasco pointed to one thing—prayer works.

It is in prayer, not abortion, that the real power lies. Planned Parenthood's mock 40 Days for Life campaign was simply an effort to make abortion appear godly. It is extremely encouraging to see that their efforts failed.

It is also encouraging to see that as frustrated as we may become with our secular culture, that culture still does not accept the idea that abortion is empowering, good, or from God. The very reason Planned Parenthood mocked us is that 40 Days for Life has an impact, and it has an impact because prayer works.

And prayer works because it addresses the pain.

When our culture turns its back on our Lord, it is still not content. It can kick and scream about the restraints of Christianity or rage about dated morality, but still it is not content. It wants either to mock religion or to use religion to justify itself. Neither of those approaches has anything to do with healthcare or women's rights or helping women in undeveloped nations. They have everything to do with pain. That's why we pray and entrust this work to the Great Healer.

~

This is the confidence
we have in approaching God:
that if we ask anything according
to his will, he hears us.
1 JOHN 5:14

We are warriors, Father; our weapon is prayer. I pray today that I will be able to keep my mind and heart on you, not on arguments. I pray that you will enlighten me to the pain in another's eyes. May I never forget the truth that the abortion industry is overflowing with pain, and thus have compassion on women and workers alike. Amen.

Fasting versus Bacon

~

Fasting cleanses the soul, raises the mind,
subjects one's flesh to the spirit, renders the heart contrite
and humble, scatters the clouds of concupiscence, quenches
the fire of lust, and kindles the true light of chastity.
—AUGUSTINE OF HIPPO

LITTLE THERESA[14] HAS NO IDEA SHE IS A WALKING MIRACLE, BUT her parents, Will and Carrie, never forget that if not for the fasting of their fellow 40 Days for Life volunteers, Theresa would have been another tragic statistic.

Carrie had participated in 40 Days for Life by standing in prayer outside a Planned Parenthood facility for several campaigns. Sometime later, she discovered that she was pregnant. Tragically, at the time of her pregnancy, Carrie was suffering from severe depression. Immersed in feelings of helplessness, she felt so desperate that she suggested to her husband, Will, that if she were to keep her baby she would take her own life. To Will's horror, Carrie then scheduled herself for an abortion at the very facility where she used to stand vigil.

Will was beside himself. No matter what he tried, he could not talk Carrie out of the abortion. He confided in Russell, another 40 Days for Life volunteer. Russell offered advice, gave abortion alternatives, shared names of some local pastors, and said everything he could think of to help Will break through to Carrie, but nothing dissuaded Carrie from her plans to go though with the abortion.

As the scheduled abortion drew closer, Will and Russell grew more alarmed by the day.

With time almost gone, one day as Russell fervently prayed for Carrie, Will, and their unborn child, he had an idea. He turned to the 40 Days for Life leadership team. With their help, he organized a special focused day of fasting among all the local volunteers. To protect Carrie's privacy, they gave no details of the identity or the circumstances in need of prayer. God knew and that was enough. They simply told the volunteers that an anonymous 40 Days for Life volunteer was in extreme need. They scheduled the day of fasting for the day of the abortion.

The volunteers responded. Even though they had no information about the need, they agreed to fast that day for their fellow volunteer. Imagine Russell's relief and the amazement of the leadership team when they learned that evening that Carrie had decided not to show up for her abortion!

Today, when Will and Carrie attend 40 Days for Life campaign events, they bring little Theresa with them. They know at those events that they are surrounded by fellow believers who blindly fasted on their behalf. Since the circumstances for which the volunteers fasted has never been revealed, only Russell and the small handful of leaders know that Theresa is a living testament to what God can do when we answer his call to fast.

∾

Have you ever gone on a fast—or even considered it—and then immediately begun thinking about food? If you've done this, or struggled with fasting in some other way, then congratulations. You're normal!

I love food. And I don't discriminate against any kind food. In fact, I have demonstrated many times that I am quite willing to eat even when I'm not hungry. Fried food, carbs, saturated fat—I pretty much like it all.

As a Texan I've always had access not just to food but to *good* food. Mexican food, BBQ, butter, and even vegetables that have been enriched and blessed by being lowered into a deep fryer. There are many great things to eat in the South, and many of them were walking around at one point.

If you can relate, then you know one reason God calls us to fast—the hunger for food drives us, powerfully, every single day. Fasting gives us the opportunity to intentionally replace our powerful hunger for food with an intentional hunger for God.

We have access to so much food and comfort today. We can eat our fill, yet our culture suffers from a great emptiness. Our lives are overflowing with daily comforts, yet our culture suffers from great longing. We need to fast, perhaps now more than ever.

Fasting, along with prayer, is the foundation of a 40 Days for Life campaign. Every campaign has three components: prayer and fasting, community outreach, and peaceful vigil. I can't tell you how many media interviews or speeches I've given where I mention this in passing and the reporter or someone from the audience comes to me with questions about fasting. For some, 40 Days for Life is an introduction to fasting; for others, it gives a most worthy intention to a discipline they have practiced for years.

Fasting is a powerful biblical practice that detaches our hearts and minds from ourselves and centers our lives more on God. Throughout Scripture—in both the Old and New Testaments—God's people deny themselves as they seek to reject sin and turn closer toward the Lord. Here are just a few examples.

Old Testament Fasting

Moses fasted forty days on behalf of Israel's sin: Deuteronomy 9:9, 18, 25–29; 10:10.

David fasted and mourned the death of Saul: 2 Samuel 1:12

Elijah fasted forty days after fleeing from Jezebel: 1 Kings 19:7–18.

Ahab fasted and humbled himself before God: 1 Kings 21:27–29.

Darius fasted in concern for Daniel: Daniel 6:18–24.

Daniel fasted on behalf of Judah's sin while reading Jeremiah's prophecy: Daniel 9:1–19.

Daniel fasted regarding a mysterious vision from God: Daniel 10:3–13.

Esther fasted on behalf of her people: Esther 4:13–16.

Ezra fasted and wept for the sins of the returning remnant: Ezra 10:6–17.

Nehemiah fasted and mourned over the broken walls of Jerusalem: Nehemiah 1:4–2:10.

The people of Nineveh fasted after hearing the message of Jonah: Jonah 3.

New Testament Fasting

Anna fasted for the redemption of Jerusalem through the coming Messiah: Luke 2:37.

Jesus fasted forty days before his temptation and the start of his ministry: Matthew 4:1–11.

The disciples of John the Baptist fasted: Matthew 9:14–15.

The elders in Antioch fasted before sending Paul and Barnabas: Acts 13:1–5.

Paul fasted three days after his conversion: Acts 9:9.

Paul fasted fourteen days while at sea on a sinking ship: Acts 27:21–34.

During 40 Days for Life campaigns, we have had people who are very disciplined in fasting, who struggle with fasting, and who have never fasted before. I have had countless people say that 40 Days for Life was the first time they ever considered doing a fast. They were drawn to do so because of the focus of the fast: unborn children in danger of abortion, their mothers and fathers, and those who work in the abortion industry.

Fasting is a powerful force against abortion because in it we deny ourselves what we desire so that we can draw closer to God. Abortion does the opposite. It encourages and gives the false promise that if you indulge in what you desire, there are no consequences.

There is no doubt that one great defense against abortion is virginity until marriage. The only better defense is the sacred bond we have with the one God has in mind for us. The reason this is completely countercultural is that sex has become more meaningless to people. Society has degraded women into objects, promising no consequences and then selling them an abortion as their way out. Both are lies. The devil is a liar before he is an accuser. He tempts and then prosecutes. In abortion the devil promises that a fifteen-minute surgery and $500 will make all your problems go away. It is very tempting, but the women driving away from the cold parking lots of abortion facilities realize they are paying a much higher price. They may at first think their problem has gone away, but once the abortion is over, so many experience remorse and guilt through which the enemy seeks to destroy the self-worth and value of the woman.

Since my early years of college, I have been honored, inspired, and challenged by hearing the testimonials of women who have had abortions. Their courage and burden often keep me going when this work gets difficult. They usually share that the toughest part of their healing is believing that they have been redeemed, accepting that their sin can be forgiven. This is a struggle for every Christian, but abortion is different. I've heard post-abortive women share how forgiveness is required to enjoy a birthday party for another child, or to see a newborn being pushed out of the hospital, or even passing the diaper aisle of the grocery store. The pain that abortion causes women, as well as men and abortion workers, can often lead to abusing alcohol, drugs, food, social media, or some other distraction. But fasting cuts out the temporal and refocuses us on Christ. Fasting pushes us to dependence upon God and his mercy.

Fasting is not dieting. Dieting, unless done for health concerns, is usually another experience about *us*—while fasting draws us out of ourselves. Fasting makes us more dependent on God rather than worried about hitting a goal next time we step on the scale. It is focused not on achievement but on love of God and stripping away our excess for him. Fasting helps us forget ourselves and seek humility, which we all need more of. The clearest definition of humility comes from Rick Warren: "True humility is not thinking less of yourself, it's thinking of yourself less."[15]

~

So what does a fast look like?

I hate this question and am asked it all the time. I'm not a fasting expert—I just confessed how much I love food. I never give a real answer to this question because fasting is personal, not social. At 40 Days for Life, we are not in the business of telling people what they need to give up, and those who choose to fast don't need to broadcast it to the world.

Jesus gives specific warning against this, in fact, when he tells us how do conduct ourselves during a fast:

"When you fast, do not look somber as the hypocrites do, for they disfigure their faces to show others they are fasting. Truly I tell you, they have received their reward in full. But when you fast, put oil on your head and wash your face, so that it will not be obvious to others that you are fasting, but only to your Father who is unseen; and your Father, who sees what is done in secret, will reward you." (Matthew 6:16–18)

I had a friend call me on Day 1 of the 40 Days for Life campaign a few years back and say, "Yeah, it's going great so far, except

I nearly died from all my fasting. Man, I'm committed." I cracked up. If someone around you is boasting about their fast, who cares. Don't let it rob you of the beautiful and freeing practice of fasting. Whatever we fast from or need to cut out of our lives will be obvious with prayer, an honest examination of our daily activities, or asking a good friend. If you're married, ask your spouse—they will know what you need to give up or do more of. It's the sign of a good marriage.

After years of 40 Days for Life campaigns, I have seen some people make tremendous sacrifices and others give up small things that remind them to pray for the victims of abortion and for those who are doing abortions. Here are some examples of common fasts during a 40 Days for Life campaign:

Decreasing food consumption at every meal

Giving up certain type of food (sweets, meat, snacks)

Abstaining from coffee

Not drinking coffee after 8:00 a.m.

Eating one meal per day

Giving up warm showers (taking cold showers instead)

Sleeping without a pillow (a reminder to pray every morning and night)

Abstaining from alcohol

Giving up soft drinks

Waking up an hour earlier for prayer

Cutting off TV entertainment and social media

No listening to the radio or music in the car

Limiting Internet use to one day per week

When considering all of these, remember these words of pastor and missionary David Peach: "While a fast, by nature, is inconvenient, it should be an inconvenience to you—not to those around you."[16] This quote is gold. If you're irritable or a pain in the rear to be around, then you will defeat the purpose of your fast. I have been guilty as charged. Nobody has any interest in being around a crazy, angry fasting person.

My grandfather on my mom's side was Irish, witty, and fought in World War II in the Pacific. We Irish are not a very humble people, and what little humility we do have, we are extremely proud of. As kids, every year my siblings and I would consider what to give up for Lent. We asked our grandfather what he was giving up, and every year he said strawberries and skydiving. He hated strawberries and didn't go skydiving.

He did actually give something up, though he never told us what. But his answer serves as a funny reminder that we need to do something. We can find something to forego on behalf of our love for God, his unborn children, and these women who lie on that table and have an abortion. Your fast will come and go, and you may even forget, years later, what it was you gave up this year. But abortion lasts forever.

Fasting is a beautiful opportunity to make a small sacrifice in this life for those who are robbed of their lives through abortion, for those who live with the regret, and for those who are doing abortions today and need repentance and the mercy of Jesus Christ. When they seek that mercy, he will respond.

∾

*This kind [of demon] does not go out
except by prayer and fasting.*
MATTHEW 17:21 NASB

Lord, I want to fast in order to intentionally replace my powerful hunger for food or some other comfort with an intentional hunger and desire for you. Help me now to consider what I might give up so that I may be drawn closer to you. Hear me, Lord, as I pray and fast for the protection of the unborn, for the hearts and hurts of women who have chosen or are choosing abortion, and for the workers in the abortion industry, that you might bring them to repentance and redemption. Amen.

Wrong Number

~

Coincidence is God's way
of remaining anonymous.
—ALBERT EINSTEIN

ERIN WOKE UP ONE MORNING, SAW HER TWO OLDER KIDS OFF TO school, and dropped off her preschoolers at a friend's house. Slipping into the car, she noticed the time. Her already racing heart stepped up a beat. She was going to be late for her appointment at Planned Parenthood.

She couldn't miss this abortion. She was desperate. She had four children and their father was in jail. On top of that, Erin had just lost her job, her electricity was about to be shut off, and she didn't have enough money to pay the rent.

Her mother and sister had insisted that, given the circumstances, an abortion was the best answer. They had told Erin that she just couldn't handle another child, and she knew they were right. Daily she struggled with the four she had now. How would she deal with another? She hated the thought of having an abortion, but what other choice did she have?

Hands trembling, Erin picked up her cellphone to call Planned Parenthood to see if she could still come in for the abortion. In her haste, though, she dialed a wrong number. Instead of Planned Parenthood, she got Joseph, a volunteer with the 40 Days for Life campaign who was at that moment standing in front of the Planned

Parenthood facility and who had been asked to answer the 40 Days cellphone.

"Hi. This is Erin. I have an appointment for an abortion. But I'm afraid I'm too late."

"Okay," Joseph said, realizing what must have happened. He took a deep breath and tried to be as calm as possible. "Give me your name and number and I'll have someone call you back." After taking her information, he immediately called Elizabeth, a counselor for 40 Days for Life. "You won't believe what just happened," he said. Then he passed along Erin's information.

Elizabeth called Erin. "Hi. Erin? Please don't hang up. You have not reached Planned Parenthood. You reached 40 Days for Life instead."

Erin pulled over to the side of the road, stunned.

"Are you a Christian?" Elizabeth asked her.

"Yes."

"Erin, I believe God's grace is at work here in this 'wrong number.' It's no accident that you called us." As she spoke, Elizabeth said a quick, silent prayer. "Why don't you tell me what's going on?"

Shaking and confused, Erin poured out her situation in a rush of words.

Elizabeth took notes and then said, "Erin, can you come to our office right now?"

Erin nodded, then realized Elizabeth could not see her. "Yes," she breathed.

The moment Elizabeth hung up, she spread the word about Erin's situation. Immediately ten volunteers who had gathered outside Planned Parenthood that morning to pray pooled their cash to pay her rent. Another volunteer offered to pay her electric bill.

When Erin reached the office and heard what had already transpired on her behalf, she reacted with both joy and disbelief that strangers would help her—especially strangers who were gathering outside Planned Parenthood, powerfully opposed to what she had planned to do. If she hadn't dialed the wrong number, Erin might have easily seen these newfound friends as enemies as she walked past them to keep her abortion appointment.

Erin did call Planned Parenthood later. She got the right number this time. She cancelled her abortion appointment and requested a refund. That was the last phone call Erin would make to them.

But that wasn't the end of the story. Eileen Hartman, a woman who left the corporate world years ago to dedicate her life to running a pregnancy center and the 40 Days for Life campaign in Indiana, reached out and helped Erin find a job. She believed that Erin had a lot of potential but needed support since her mother and sister were still encouraging her to abort the baby. She offered the support Erin needed.

When I think of the extremes the medical community will go to save the lives of premature babies, children with cancer, or victims of traumatic car accidents, I'm grieved that Erin's baby would not have benefited from any of that effort. Her baby was scheduled to be aborted and people were willing to help bring that about, ending that baby's life. Nothing but an act of God could have put Erin in the path of someone who would look out for her baby. It literally took a wrong number.

∽

You might think Erin's story is like a lightning strike. It couldn't happen again, right? Wrong.

This story takes place where 40 Days for Life first began—College Station, Texas. We had just bought the house next door to Planned Parenthood and were offering free pregnancy tests there. Our office had been set up for only a few days when the phone rang. The caller asked, "Is this Planned Parenthood?"

The staff member who answered quickly realized this was most likely an abortion-minded woman on the line. "No," she said, "but we can offer you a pregnancy test, a free ultrasound, and counseling."

"No thank you," the woman said. "I really just wanted to reach Planned Parenthood. I can get those things from them. So I don't think I need anything else."

"All right," the staff member hurried to say, "but you might like to know that our ultrasound will be free. If you go to Planned Parenthood, they will charge you for it."

There was silence on the line as the caller considered that. "Well, all right." She gave her number so that our staff member could call back with her appointment time.

When the 40 Days staff member called the pregnancy center to set up the ultrasound, the scheduler at the pregnancy center said that this same woman had mistakenly called them about a half hour earlier. "We've been praying that you guys would be able to speak to her before she reached Planned Parenthood," she said.

They marveled that this woman had called not just one wrong number, but two!

The pregnancy center was able to get an ultrasound appointment for her that day. But she didn't show up. The next day, she turned up unannounced at the Coalition for Life office, which is next door to the pregnancy center.

She sat down with our counselor and after some encouragement to tell her story, admitted that she'd had an abortion in the past and was considering another. She fiddled with a pen on the desk and said in a soft voice, "This isn't my husband's baby." She looked up quickly as if expecting a look of shock or disgust on the counselor's face. Instead, what she saw was compassionate acceptance. "We were separated and I met this man …" Her voice trailed off. She took a deep breath and fiddled with the pen on the desk some more.

The counselor gently encouraged her to continue. The more details the woman gave about her life, the worse the situation seemed to be.

The woman took another deep breath and said, "I don't think I have any other options except to get an abortion." She put both hands in her lap and said, "I need to know how far along I am so I can do it in time."

The counselor asked for details that might pinpoint the time of conception and then said, "I can show you about where you are in your pregnancy." She took out some materials to give the woman, including some illustrations of fetal development. She emphasized that there was already a living human being inside her, and that there had been from the moment of conception.

The woman looked at the drawings and photos carefully, laying each in a neat pile on the desk when she was done. After hearing about the baby's life inside the womb, she expressed sorrow. She told the counselor softly, "I murdered my last child."

The counselor waited silently.

"How could God ever accept me? I broke his commandment to not murder." The distress in her voice lead to quiet tears that slid down her cheeks.

The counselor leaned forward and told this sorrowful woman about the infinite mercy, freedom, and salvation that God offers through Jesus.

After she left the office, encouraged and with our reassurance that we would help her each step of the way, those of us in the office looked at each other, astounded. How could this woman have confused both a pro-life group and a pregnancy center with Planned Parenthood? How could Erin possibly have misdialed a number and ended up speaking to us? Coincidence? The only explanation is God's intervention and his answers to prayer! Because there are no coincidences ... and in these cases, no wrong numbers either.

∼

You can make many plans,
but the LORD's purpose will prevail.
PROVERBS 19:21 NLT

God, sometimes I can only sit back and look with awe at what you have done. How the impossible happened. How these impossible events can look like coincidence. Oh, but God, I am rejoicing in whatever you did to cause these women to end up in the care of those who loved them and their unborn children. Let me not forget these stories as I walk through each day wondering if our prayers have an impact. Bring them to mind on the days I feel my prayers don't make a difference. Today help me to remember and rejoice in the "coincidences" that have occurred in my life. Help me to always see the amazing guidance of your hand in these events. Amen.

The Night Shift in Prison

~

You can never learn that Christ is all you need,
until Christ is all you have.

—CORRIE TEN BOOM, Holocaust Survivor

As the day approached when she would begin leading her first-ever 40 Days for Life campaign, Christine grew increasingly nervous. But she knew God was calling her to do this. She had attended one of our regional training sessions and was plunging ahead in faith. I would have never guessed that she was about to open a new door for abortion ministry—one I'd never seen done before and that I never would have dreamt possible.

Christine wasn't ready to commit to a twenty-four-hour vigil so she planned for a twelve-hour vigil outside their abortion facility, from 7:00 a.m. to 7:00 p.m. Then it hit her—her parents were leaders for their local prison ministry. What if she asked the prisoners at the local prison to cover the night shift. from 7:00 p.m. until 7:00 a.m.? They wouldn't be able to pray on the sidewalks, of course, but they could pray from their cells.

It's not such a far-fetched connection. Many prisoners have a past touched by abortion. In a poll conducted by one international post-abortion healing ministry, Rachel's Vineyard, 90 percent of men in prison had a role in an abortion during their life. Perhaps a sister or a girlfriend had one, or perhaps just a close friend. Christine recognized that playing a part in a 40 Days for Life campaign was often healing for those with abortion in their past. Would some of the prisoners respond to this opportunity?

Christine anticipated that maybe five to ten men might volunteer. To her amazement, the prisoners recognized the correlation between the pain of abortion involvement and the healing power of prayer. Forty to fifty men volunteered to join the night prayer shift—ten times what she'd hoped! She had expected that the prisoners would sign up for an hour, say 9:00 p.m. to 10:00 p.m., for one day of the forty. But instead, they signed up from 9:00 until 10:00 *every* night for forty nights!

"We actually had so many signups that the prison ran out of signup slips and we had to send more," Christine said.

When she tallied all the sign-ups, she was overwhelmed to discover that all twelve hours of every night were covered! "Because they didn't have to get up and go to a job the next day, they were able to wake up in the middle of the night and do their hour of prayer," Christine said.

One prisoner was traumatized by the fact that he had paid for at least seven abortions before his incarceration. He thought there could be no healing, no forgiveness, for him—his sin was just too big, and he would have to carry the burden of what he had done forever. When 40 Days for Life came into the prison, he was one of the first people to volunteer. "This is giving me hope! It's something I can do, even from here. I can pray. And if I can pray, maybe I can be forgiven. Just being able to pray within the prison gives me hope that maybe that abortion clinic will shut down and nobody like me will ever pay for an abortion again."

He signed up to pray daily from 7:00 a.m. to 8:00 a.m.—he was the "last guy" of the night shift.

Another prisoner, Terrence, woke up early every morning. He considered himself the anchor to the start of every day. One of the major focuses of his prayers was to pray for the people who would be standing on the sidewalks that day in prayer outside the abortion facility.

Christine's team used a praying schedule card that the prisoners designed. The prisoners found an artist on the inside to design the front of the card—a gorgeous sunset with a dove flying across it. Then they sewed in four pages by hand so there would be enough room inside for all the different prisoners who were involved to sign.

"They put a lot of effort into designing the card," Christine said. "They even used colored pens and pencils. It took a lot of work to get all the different supplies together that they needed just to make the card. It even had glitter on it." Christine didn't know (and didn't ask) where they got the glitter. "It may not seem like much to us on the outside, but in prison it really showed how much they cared about 40 Days for Life."

There are multiple security levels at the prison, so the prisoners weren't all at lunch or recreation at the same time. "The prisoners really had to put some work into coordinating how to get this card passed back and forth through the different levels of security. They even passed it through some security guards and left it on a cafeteria table so that everybody was able to sign and then have it available the next time the prison ministry team came in so they could give it to them to get it back to the outside," Christine said.

Heading into a 40 Days for Life campaign, many leaders are looking forward to seeing the numbers—the number of women who walk away from abortion at the last moment, the number of lives saved, and the number of abortion workers who leave their jobs. The leaders are excited to share the victories of their location to encourage their own volunteers and other cities.

"Being involved in the prison ministry was a blessing that we never saw coming. We were anticipating the numbers. You want to save those lives. But the healing that could happen among a group of men that you had discounted, that you had never thought of including, was so powerful. The healing of the prisoners just brought so much more meaning to the campaign because this campaign also serves to heal after the abortion."

When abortion comes up in prison, it is usually because abortion advocates are fighting to get female prisoners more access to abortion. As one abortion advocate said in a Guttenmacher report, "The right to decide whether to have an abortion is not lost because of criminal punishment and incarceration."[17]

But thanks to 40 Days for Life, for some prisoners, their involvement meant penance and prayer for those being led to the slaughter, for the pregnant women and their men, and even for those standing vigil outside the abortion facility. They were using their incarceration time to pray for *us*. Jesus calls us to pray for and visit those in prison. But imagine prisoners praying for you as you stand vigil for the unborn! Would you ever have thought this possible? I hadn't.

Christine opened my world to the impact prison ministry can have on ending abortion. The pain of abortion inside prisons has always been there and is often buried and forgotten behind the crime that landed a person in prison. But imagine the power of giving that pain over to our Lord on the cross. Using the time—the night hours in prison—to pray for an end to abortion. I had never expected this would become part of a campaign, but God did because he knows the pain of abortion better than any of us. These are his children being aborted, these are his women and men seeking abortion, and these are his inmates—and he is reaching out for them just as he did before he took his last breath on the cross, when he opened the gate of heaven to a man condemned to die.

Jesus wants to reach the pain in the world—and abortion is the source of much pain. No one grows up wanting to go to prison, and no one grows up hoping to need an abortion someday. Sin leads us down roads that require our rescue. In Jesus' words, "I have not come to call the righteous, but sinners to repentance" (Luke 5:32).

Christine's heart connected with these prisoners, and she wanted the campaign to give them hope. "We bring hope to abortion facilities. I want hope for prisoners as well. I hope they feel God's love and they're able to heal from what they've done and what they've gone through."

The prisoners who prayed in Christine's 40 Days campaign didn't allow incarceration to prevent them from participating in ending abortion. They sacrificed their freedom for their crime, but even so they found a way to contribute. Most of us, on the other hand, still have our freedom. We are not incarcerated. There are no guards or fences or locked doors preventing us from peacefully standing vigil, using the rights those prisoners no longer have.

What do I do with my freedom? This is the question that challenged me when I heard Christine's story. I hope it challenges you as well. Today, tomorrow, and next week many people will use their freedom to rob the freedom of a defenseless baby who has no idea what is happening. Let us thank God for the freedom to be his hands and feet. Let us trust him with our liberty—for through him many are freed from the prison of abortion.

∾

Then he said, "Jesus, remember me
when you come into your kingdom."
Jesus answered him, "Truly I tell you,
today you will be with me in paradise.
LUKE 23:42–43

∾

Let us close today's chapter with the timeless prayer of Ignatius of Loyola:

"Take, Lord, and receive all my liberty, my memory, my
understanding, and my entire will, all I have and call my own.
You have given all to me. To you, Lord, I return it.
Everything is yours; do with it what you will. Give me only
your love and your grace, that is enough for me."[18]

Just a Simple Country Attorney

~

All men are afraid in battle. The coward
is the one who lets his fear overcome his sense of duty.
Duty is the essence of manhood.
—GENERAL GEORGE PATTON

MATT BRITTON, A COMMONWEALTH'S ATTORNEY FOR VIRGINIA, was tapping his finger on the table waiting for the judge to sentence the man he had just prosecuted.

It was quiet in the courtroom. This case involved the abuse of children. Every case mattered to Matt, but any case involving harm to a child was a case for which he spent many weeks and long nights preparing. Now he anxiously awaited the sentencing.

The judge knew Matt well and had seen his commitment and professionalism as a prosecutor many times. Matt also knew the judge and suspected he was leaning toward a lesser punishment than was deserved.

"You know there are a lot of options in this case," the judge began. Matt could feel a lesser sentence coming and, thinking of the victims and their families, felt as if his head was about to explode.

The judge continued in a casual tone: "You know the court can do many things today. For instance, we can give a stiff prison sentence, impose probation, or we can even do nothing."

With that statement Matt suddenly stood and did something he had never done before—he interrupted a judge.

"Judge, I'm sorry. I know that this courtroom is a dignified and special place, and my dad taught me to never interrupt a priest or a judge. But, excuse me. Is doing *nothing* really on the table?" His words bounced off the windows of the courtroom as he stared at the judge in disbelief.

Silence poured over the courtroom.

The judge's eyes widened in surprise. "No, counselor," he said. "I'm not saying that. I don't mean to minimize what happened here. I'm just saying there are options." He then handed down a lighter sentence than Matt wanted. To this day Matt believes the judge was going to let the guy off completely. He's glad he interrupted the judge. It was a risk, and he plans to never do it again, but he doesn't regret having done it.

I've come to know Matt Britton well. He is one of the most honest men I've ever met.

He loves God, loves his family, and has the greatest sense of duty of anyone I know.

He hunts, rides motorcycles, is a licensed pilot, doesn't drink alcohol, would never drive a truck with an automatic transmission, smokes cigars, and aggressively claims that he makes the best beef jerky in the world. As a proud Texan I arrogantly disputed this point only to be proven wrong when I consumed his tasty fare.

Matt was elected to four terms as a commonwealth's attorney in Virginia, and his talent as a litigator did not go unnoticed. He was courted by many corporations. Over time, he transitioned to representing global tech companies, and for years Matt traveled the world—especially Asia. He can converse in French and even order food and hire a taxi in Chinese.

Matt realized, however, that he wanted to use his experience for something greater. Often while in China or Japan, after completing his day's work, he would walk around town, find a church, and there ask God what he wanted him to do with all of this experience. From simple country attorney to legal representative of major corporations, Matt didn't believe he'd yet seen the pinnacle of his career.

Matt was pro-life, and he and his wife ran their own pro-life organization—their family of eight children! They also participated in 40 Days for Life and other pro-life causes. So we asked Matt to serve on our board of directors. He accepted and now cares for our organization's legal needs. He also assists local 40 Days for Life leaders with their legal needs.

Then we had an inquiry about doing the first-ever 40 Days for Life campaign in China.

Abortion and China are linked together in the most horrid of ways, more so than any other country in the world. China's "one-child" policy was implemented in 1979 to control population. The brutality of this policy was on full display in 2012 when Feng Jianmei of China's rural Shaanxi province was brutally forced to abort her seven-month-old unborn baby after failing to pay a hefty fine to family planning officials for being pregnant with her second child. NBC News reported:

> She [Feng] was blindfolded, thrown on a bed, and forced to sign a document that she couldn't read with the blindfold still on her eyes. Then two shots were injected into her belly. Thirty hours later she gave birth to a dead baby girl.[19]

The picture of this beautiful baby girl lying on a bed next to her mother after being brutally killed by the government went viral and raised even more questions about the practices there.

China may seem far away from the West geographically, but the atrocities of abortion there are not so far removed from our own. The cold mentality that limited the size of families due to "population control" was tied directly to the support and advocacy of the largest abortion provider in America—Planned Parenthood. The Planned Parenthood affiliate has been in China for over eighty years.

They started in 1936 after their founder, Margaret Sanger, traveled to China to inspire a eugenics movement in the 1920s.

Norman Fleishman, the former director of Planned Parenthood World Population in Los Angeles, supported China's one-child policy when he stated that the policy is just "a start" and that without action, "the world is doomed to strangle among coils of pitiless exponential growth."[20]

Unfortunately, China is another place where Planned Parenthood has not just talked about population control but practiced what they preach. International Planned Parenthood is a federation of member organizations, and China Family Planning Association (CFPA) has been a member for eighteen years.

When China Family Planning Association was created, the official communiqué announcing its creation stated clearly, "The association will implement government population control policies."[21] In a 1993 report, CFPA admitted that it had "participated and supervised that the awarding and punishing policies relating to family planning were properly executed."[22]

This assault on the unborn fueled our passion to have the first-ever 40 Days for Life campaign in China. No easy task. With the persecution of Christians in China and the restrictions on freedom of speech, it seemed impossible. But not to Joseph, an American missionary living in China, who applied to lead the first-ever campaign in Hong Kong.

Joseph spoke the language and felt God was calling him to do something about the atrocities happening there. "Sadly," he said, "churches have been almost entirely silent on this issue, and so I was inspired to begin the conversation about abortion and stir Christians to pray, speak, and respond."

The social and legal obstacles to publicly opposing abortion in China seemed astronomical. But God was way ahead of us in providing the perfect man to help us do just that—Matt Britton.

Matt immediately went to work. He had the legal expertise

and experience to explore how to do the campaign in Hong Kong. Slowly, obstacles began to slide away as Matt worked with Chinese attorneys, Joseph, and courageous local churches to hold the first-ever 40 Days for Life campaign.

Then we got our first report from Joseph of a baby saved in China. "For the first time," he enthusiastically wrote, "I saw a picture of a baby whose mother chose life because of the work of 40 Days for Life!"

The mom had booked an abortion at the China Family Planning Association. But before her appointment, she saw on Facebook a picture of two people praying at the abortion facility with the 40 Days for Life team.

Joseph wrote, "The mom changed her mind! Her son is now six months old."

God continued to use Joseph's courage and Matt's expertise in ways none of us would have imagined in a place like China. That first 40 Days for Life campaign in Hong Kong led Hong Kong's Catholic diocese to launch its first formal pro-life ministry. Also, a giant international marketing firm launched an educational campaign to address sex-selective abortion in China (which kills thousands of unborn girls every day). One of the highlights of their efforts was placing a billboard right by the Planned Parenthood in Hong Kong!

Judging from the pictures we've seen and reports we've heard or read of Chinese Christians coming to pray in the streets of China for an end to abortion, it seemed that Matt's many business trips to China had served the purpose for which he'd prayed in those late-night churches in China and Japan.

If abortion were measured by statistics, this chapter would be rather empty. China has claimed to prevent 400 million births since the 1970s through their one-child policy, yet we know of just one baby alive today due to the 40 Days for Life campaigns there. But we don't live for statistics. We live for faith, hope, and love. And China needs hope.

That one baby boy alive today represents the hope that even in the darkest of places where governments and organizations strip away people's dignity and weed out those deemed unwanted, God is at work. Though that baby boy does not represent the *end* of abortion in China, he shows us all that we are seeing the *beginning* of the end of abortion there.

Every so often on my travels I meet a talented, well-off executive who says he or she really wants to use their gifts to save unborn children. It always encourages me because babies and their mothers deserve gifted people in the world trying to help them. But Matt Britton didn't just say it. He did something. He made the jump and left hundreds of thousands of dollars behind so he could become general counsel for 40 Days for Life.

Having a full-time dedicated attorney for our local leaders is something we would never have dreamed of when we launched 40 Days for Life. But God provided the right man—a man who was listening for his call.

Matt and I were recently driving through the countryside of Virginia on our way to Washington, DC. Matt was reflecting on his days as a prosecutor and said, "I'm just a simple country attorney."

I suddenly felt as he had when he was listening to the judge hand down a sentence years ago. I interrupted him. "Look, I'm from east Texas and I know a lot of country attorneys. Country attorneys don't speak Chinese, know good sushi places in Tokyo, or know how to break down IT law in Asia off the top of their head. You're no simple country attorney, whether you want to be or not."

"Just a simple country attorney." That may be the only lie I've ever heard from the mouth of Matt Britton.

We need more Matt Brittons fighting for the unborn, no matter how large or small their role may be. We need more people to interrupt their lives and ask, "Is doing nothing on the table?" Asking such questions can lead to saving a baby who might otherwise become just another statistic in the eyes of the world.

～

If the watchman sees the sword coming
and does not blow the trumpet to warn the people
and the sword comes and takes someone's life,
that person's life will be taken because of their sin,
but I will hold the watchman accountable for their blood.

EZEKIEL 33:6

Dear Lord, give me the courage to interrupt my life. I'm asking now what Matt asked as he strolled the streets of China and Japan: Lord, what do you want me to do with all of my experience? *I'm ready to serve you. Let me hear your call and respond. Amen.*

It's Not Pie in the Sky

~

Pain is God's megaphone to rouse a deaf world.
You see, we are like blocks of stone out
of which the Sculptor carves the forms of men.
The blows of his chisel, which hurt us so much,
are what make us perfect.

—C. S. LEWIS

IT'S FOR GOOD REASON THAT PRO-LIFER JEFF NORMAN WAS SKEP-tical of 40 Days for Life coming to town. His community of Santa Cruz, California, is one of the most politically liberal places in America, and he was rightly concerned that carrying out pro-life activities on the street, besides being unsafe, would do more harm than good.

Jeff worked with a local pregnancy center. When he learned about our informational meeting, his response was, "I wouldn't be caught dead praying in public. Jesus said not to do it, and I'm not doing it."

Still, he went to the meeting to understand what 40 Days for Life was all about. He soon learned the vigils aren't a public protest but instead are a mission to peacefully reach those considering abortion and offer them alternatives. He noted the high standards that the vigil and its participants are held to. "About halfway through the informational meeting, I had to admit to myself that this could actually work here." He sat, he listened, he prayed. He respected what he heard. By the end of the meeting, Jeff Norman had volunteered to lead the campaign in Santa Cruz.

Jeff owned his own business and had built it up to the point that it could function without his daily involvement, so he elected to take forty days completely off, dedicating all of his time to the campaign. "I started to wonder what kind of shape my business would be in after the campaign, but I trusted God that I was doing the right thing." From the beginning, Jeff's message to himself and all of his volunteers was simple: "We walk by faith, not by sight."

Jeff attended the vigil leader training and carried out all the preparations we recommend, including meeting with the police to let them know what the campaign would be doing—which in Santa Cruz is a must. Not long after, Jeff cast his net into the deep—and the waters were as rough as he'd thought they would be.

On Day 1 of the vigil, Jeff arrived early, eager, and excited for the kickoff event. Such a large crowd had come! He'd spread the word and worked hard but wasn't sure how many people would actually show up. The large crowd excited him at first—but only moments later his heart sank as he realized that among the crowd was a group of about fifty people there not to participate in the vigil but to upset it. The presence of these protesters would be Jeff's first opportunity to walk by faith, not by sight.

It's important to note that nearly all 40 Days for Life vigils experience little in the way of hostility from opposition. This is one of the reasons over 750,000 people have participated. Rarely do we experience something we haven't seen before—mostly it's small things like someone driving by yelling or telling us that we're number 1—with their finger. But Santa Cruz was different from the get-go.

As the opening prayers started, the protesters interspersed among the volunteers. They shouted at the families and children praying. They held up vulgar signs, including one reading "God is gay." Moments later several homosexual protesters began to perform lewd acts. Jeff's response was not anger or hatred; he did not scream or shout. He displayed his unshakeable faith by, as he tells it, "simply continuing to pray and sing worship songs." In fact, the protesters' actions drew his heart to deeper compassion. "That impacted me because of the children who were there. It convicted me that we have a community that places no value on children. It showed me how badly we needed to be out there."

Eventually the press showed up and interviewed both sides. In Santa Cruz, the media coverage often seems predictably one-sided, but it wasn't on this occasion. Later that evening 40 Days for Life got very positive coverage on the 10:00 p.m. news program!

That turned out to be both good and bad news for Jeff and the vigil. Media attention meant more awareness, but more awareness brought more persecution.

For the next week, several protesters showed up in the afternoons wearing ghoul costumes and shouting at prayer volunteers. Throughout the vigil, volunteers were spat upon and had water bottles thrown at them and signs ripped out of their hands. One day a young woman drove by the vigil site, honked her horn to get the volunteers' attention, and then began a profanity-laced tirade. She lifted an expressive finger through her sunroof. As she drove off, the 40 Days for Life volunteers couldn't help but notice the bumper sticker on her car: "Tolerance." "I quickly learned that tolerance is a one-way street in Santa Cruz," Jeff said. "When we would ask for tolerance from a passerby, we were often called their insult du jour.

"We never knew what the next day would bring. But we can't ever predict if tomorrow is going to be a good day or a bad day. We are not the author of that story." Jeff maintained the outlook and attitude of a servant. "We are not here for a feel-good, pie-in-the-sky experience. We simply face every day with hope. And I've seen people walk away from our vigil with the hope of our Savior."

Jeff and his team continued to pray, knowing that the 40 Days for Life volunteers would not be viewed in Santa Cruz as being meek and loving. But they were.

Santa Cruz is a rare animal when it comes to 40 Days for Life campaigns. It represents two extremes—the extremists who oppose and harass peaceful volunteers in vulgar ways, and Jeff's faith in God when faced with persecution. How many of us could lead and still endure what he endured day after day, not just in that first campaign but in all the campaigns since? Think of the comments, doubts, and ridicule he has had to overcome to lead this effort. I asked him about that once, and he simply said, "But these instances and persecutions pale in comparison to the times that mothers have walked up to us to share a story where, in the midst of difficult circumstances, they chose life for their baby because of the peaceful vigil."

He then pointed to "real" persecution. "Pick up a paper and see what ISIS is doing to Christians in the Middle East. Look at what Christians living in China and under the regime in North Korea go through. Read about the gulag in the Soviet Union or what Hitler did to the Jews. Come on, this is America. You can curse at me or spit on and ridicule me. These things happen. But can you really call it persecution? I don't want to belittle any of the things we have gone through, but it is a small price to pay to see a child born and given a chance to reach his or her potential."

God had chosen the perfect man to lead the campaign in a very hostile environment. Through all the hardships, Jeff never saw himself as a victim. And his hope of witnessing the gift of children in a place so hostile toward them happened—women were choosing life.

This courageous Christian man who went to a meeting as a skeptic was changing his community when many—both inside and outside the church—said it couldn't be done.

Through all the victories and successes, Jeff remembers one face more than any other.

A volunteer approached Jeff at a vigil and said, "This couple just came out to smoke a cigarette before she has an abortion. Please go talk to them." Deep down, Jeff didn't want to. But it was rare to have such an opportunity. He approached them, praying for the right words to say.

Jeff could tell that the woman was conflicted. He said, "The decision you are about to make is your decision. But you should know that if you need help with anything at all, we are here for you."

The woman studied him as she sucked on her cigarette, then blew the smoke into the air. She began to share why she needed an abortion. When he responded to her comments, Jeff could see that she was listening and considering what he'd said. As she neared the end of her cigarette, Jeff knew he didn't have much time. "We can help you carry this child to term," he told her. "We can support you and offer you adoption opportunities. You could pick a great family for your baby."

He thought he saw something shift inside her. He sensed that she was going to choose life. Then a hardened look crossed her face. She stubbed out her cigarette and went inside for the abortion.

Frustrated, Jeff sat there praying she would come out. But she didn't; she had the abortion and that child was lost.

"That was a seminal moment for me. We helped so many moms who did take up our offers, but that one was a reminder of what we are up against. I hope to run into her one day. I have no animosity towards her, and I want to share that with her and to let her know we are still here for her after her abortion. We don't judge or condemn these ladies. We are truly there for them."

Jeff is a leader whose reason for getting involved was not simply to see results. But he has seen them. He has seen moms turn around. He has heard passersby stop and offer words of support. His theme of walking by faith and not by sight has helped him keep first things first.

One day a woman pulled up and rolled down her car window. Those praying thought she might yell something, so they calmly walked toward her. The young woman leaned toward them and said, "I came here for an abortion a year ago, and you were here. I saw you and just couldn't do it. Thank you for being here. Please look in the backseat. See my little boy? He is alive because of you."

Jeff has now led over sixteen campaigns in Santa Cruz and helped spread and support 40 Days for Life campaigns in the nearby cities of San Jose, Watsonville, Gilroy, and Monterey. As for the persecution, the hostile groups, and the costumed ghouls, Jeff said, "We haven't seen them in a while, but 40 Days for Life is still active in Santa Cruz, and God is still saving lives in the parking lot of Planned Parenthood."

Because I've known Jeff for many years (and have tremendous respect for him), I know that Jeff had personal hardships in his life during his many years of leading difficult 40 Days for Life campaigns. But he never complained. He has the perspective of the gospel, and it shows. He is always more concerned about how his volunteers are faring than he is about himself. For instance, when I asked him one day what he considered his greatest success from leading 40 Days for Life, it wasn't a mom or a baby or having endured all the garbage. It was his prayer partner, Rae Ellen.

Rae Ellen, confined to a wheelchair, had been a faithful volunteer since the first Santa Cruz campaign. She handed out literature and helped save many babies. Jeff said, "Being handicapped, she was the poster child for why so many feel we *need* abortion."

One day Rae Ellen went out to the sidewalk alone, without telling anyone she was going. While she was there, alone, someone came by and ridiculed her and spat in her face. It broke Jeff's heart to think about this young woman in a wheelchair, loading in and out of a handicap taxi to get to and from the vigil, and to then go through this. He was so upset that he urged her to never go out alone again, explaining that in a place like Santa Cruz it was too dangerous. Rae responded, "I knew I was doing right. The spit was like validation."

Another day, a couple went inside and saw, through the window, Rae holding her pro-life sign outside. Through the window, Rae could tell that as they talked, they were doubting their decision to abort. The boyfriend came outside and asked Rae if he could see the sign. He then held it up so his girlfriend could see it clearly. She came outside and joined him and Rae. The boyfriend handed the sign back to Rae and said, "Thank you for being out here." They chose life.

Rae Ellen will never read this chapter. God called her home before publication. But she didn't need to read it. She lived it, and so did so many others in Santa Cruz because of Jeff Norman's decision to walk by faith and not by sight. He simply went to a meeting, said yes, and meant it.

$\sim$

"If the world hates you,
keep in mind that it hated me first.
If you belonged to the world,
it would love you as its own.
As it is, you do not belong to the world,
but I have chosen you out of the world.
That is why the world hates you."
JOHN 15:18–19

Father, help me to walk by faith, not by sight, in this work. Help me to trust that even if I see no results, you are working behind the scenes, doing things I may never be aware of. Help me to walk by faith no matter what insults the world hurls at me. And help me to believe by faith that prayer is a powerful force beyond what I can imagine. Amen.

The Fugitive

~

Midway upon the journey of our life
I found myself within a forest dark,
for the straightforward pathway
had been lost.

—DANTE

WHAT IN THE WORLD IS GOING ON? EDWARD WONDERED AS HE tried to focus on his prayer. He was spending his scheduled hour at the 40 Days for Life vigil outside an abortion facility on a chilly November afternoon in London, England. It had been a quiet morning until a few minutes ago, and now there was some kind of disturbance near the front door of the facility. Several people had appeared there, shouting and gesturing, clearly angry, and now the police had arrived as well.

It was quite a mess, but he didn't think any of his fellow 40 Days for Life volunteers were involved, so he thought it best to continue praying. He shrugged it off, bowed his head …

Except—*now* what was going on?

What was that woman doing? At one of the front windows of the facility, a woman was jumping repeatedly, apparently in a frantic effort to get herself high enough to crawl out the open window. Edward stared, unable to look away. Each time, she came a little closer. He turned away to catch the attention of another volunteer, and by the time he looked back, the woman had made it out.

What should he do? And did this woman have anything to do with the disturbance at the facility's front door?

He watched as the woman sprinted through the parking lot. Edward couldn't imagine what would happen when she reached the fence—and then he watched her jump that fence and then two more to escape!

Edward later learned the rest of the story. The woman's family had driven her there to force her to have an abortion against her will. She had been there the day before and reluctantly taken the first abortion pill. (This was an abortion consisting of two pills—taken on two consecutive days—that cause contractions so the baby is eventually "passed," a euphemistic term for "aborted." It is a horrific process physically and extremely damaging psychologically and spiritually, since the woman often sees her tiny baby pass.) Now, on the second day when she was to take the final abortion pill, the woman refused. Her family, however, had made it clear that the abortion must happen. The woman felt trapped as her family drove her to her appointment and parked the car. As she passed a 40 Days for Life sidewalk counselor, she told him what was happening.

Then the family of this reluctant woman pushed her into the abortion facility. She felt like screaming as loudly on the outside as she was on the inside, but she couldn't bring herself to scream. The only people on her side, she assumed, were those 40 Days for Life vigil volunteers outside.

Sitting in the lobby, she was surrounded by family and many other women, yet she felt all alone. It was hell. She told the clinic staff that she didn't want to proceed with the second pill, but they told her that if she continued with the pregnancy at his point, after having taken the first pill, her baby would be deformed and she'd end up giving birth to a monster. No buts or maybes; they insisted she'd have a disabled baby. Now she saw no way to avoid taking the second pill that would end the life of her baby.

She sat in quiet desperation until the sound of her name—Julia—was called and broke the stillness. Julia stood slowly, her helplessness a sharp pain in her heart. There seemed to be nothing she could do. *I will remember this day forever,* she thought.

As she stood, something clicked inside her. She fully realized what was taking place. She suddenly felt empowered. Julia made a choice for freedom.

She looked at her family and said firmly, "I'm not taking that second pill. I'm not finishing the abortion. I want my baby."

Furious, they insisted that she *would* take the second pill.

She heard their words, but her own thoughts spoke more loudly: *The second pill makes it final. I'm not taking that second pill.* She considered her few options as her family surrounded her. One of her relatives shouted, "This is just because of those people outside! This is all in your head because you saw some religious nuts praying out front."

"I shouldn't be here. I don't *want* to be here," she said to everyone. "I'm not going to move unless it's to the parking lot to leave." She sat, arms crossed, not budging. She had been just moments from finalizing the abortion, but now she was making a stand for her baby.

Enraged, her family headed to the front door intending to confront the 40 Days for Life volunteers and the sidewalk counselor. As the front door opened and the family spilled out, the sidewalk counselor called the police because he could see this was a case of forced abortion. The police were very prompt but did not manage to see Julia because they were engaged with the threatening family. Meanwhile, Julia asked the abortion center staff if there was another exit and they said no.

With the police speaking to her family outside the front door, Julia, still inside, saw that this was her chance! But her way of escape—the front door—was blocked. So she began her determined jump to escape through the window of the bathroom.

As the cops listened to the family explain why they were there, Julia carried her baby to life by crawling out a window and jumping three fences. Now that's empowerment, freedom, and choice!

Julia's natural instincts as a mother had kicked in. She saved herself and her baby by escaping like Harrison Ford in *The Fugitive*. It was quite a scene. The sight of a mother defending her child is powerful—apparently even for those who had forced her to be there, because the family members changed their minds. The witness of the 40 Days for Life vigil had moved and empowered Julia, but it was her determination and drastic escape that eventually transformed the family.

Although she had taken the first pill, the baby not only lived but was perfectly healthy. Her family decided to support her pregnancy, and once born, the baby was dearly loved by the family.

Julia later said it was the power of those she had seen praying on the sidewalk that made the difference.

When, like Edward who witnessed much of Julia's story, we show up to pray against abortion and for the women, babies, and facility workers, we have no control over the situations that led so many to show up for an abortion. We don't know their stories, where they come from, or where they've been. But we do know they are part of the human family and part of the family of God. And we, unlike some of them and unlike all the unborn babies, have a choice. We can choose to show up and trust God with our small effort to be there. We can grasp hold of the truth that he loves these women, their children, and the abortion workers more than we ever can. We can choose what we do with our time, whether it's an hour or a few minutes. In all of these things, we can make a choice and trust that God will use it.

In this story from England, God used strangers to heal a broken family in which one member felt she had to sprint and jump fences to bring another family member into the world. God used those faithful volunteers to tear down the falsehood that abortion represents a choice and a freedom. He used his love and mercy to point to this mother's love for her child. This was a close call, but close calls can happen when we place our faith in God in a hurting and divided world.

~

Be always on the watch, and pray
that you may be able to escape
all that is about to happen,
and that you may be able to stand
before the Son of Man.
LUKE 21:36

Father, we rejoice in this amazing story of a mother's determination to save her child against all opposition. I pray that today I will be determined to follow you, to be faithful, and to pray for these mothers, drivers, babies, and facility workers, no matter what the opposition. Amen.

Round the World in 40 Days

~

*Be who God meant you to be
and you will set the world on fire.*
—CATHERINE OF SIENNA

*IF I AM THIS IMPRESSED WITH THIS GUY, OTHERS WILL BE TOO. WE
need to hire him,* I thought as I read another report from the 40 Days
for Life leader in England—Robert Colquhoun.

Robert was well read, a good speaker, and a hard worker. He was
also a gentleman who, like a typical Brit, was never rattled by the
media, drama, or my complaints that there was no statue of General George Washington outside Buckingham Palace with the other
statues.

He is English to the core.

Starting in 2011, the number of requests to launch 40 Days for
Life campaigns in new cities across the globe was constantly growing, so I traveled to England and met Robert. I must confess that he
fulfilled all the stereotypes we Americans have of our friends across
the pond. He crammed three of us into a car built to hold 1.5 people
and sped off.

That was the beginning of a great and busy trip to England. Robert worked me to the bone in just a few days. Afterwards I knew we
needed to bring him on board. Robert and I began regular calls, and
he went to work to spread and manage the international growth of
40 Days for Life.

Since then, 40 Days for Life has had campaigns in nearly fifty countries—campaigns that are growing bigger and saving more lives every year. I could write an entire book on the international growth of 40 Days for Life, but today I invite you to do what I have done many times—jump into Robert's tiny car as he speeds through London, telling you about just a few campaigns around the world. You'll need your imagination, but hearing it straight from his mouth will help.

∼

Bringing 40 Days for Life to my beloved England has taken me to places I never would have imagined—including Texas, where it seems to be the law that everyone must drive a truck. I have met selfless leaders, witnessed babies saved from abortion, and been introduced to new mission territories vastly different from America and the United Kingdom. Let's take a tour of just a few of them.

Nigeria

Kelechi Anyaghara is a young leader in the administrative capital of Nigeria. Abortion is illegal in Nigeria, with a prison sentence of fourteen years. However, there is a widespread practice of illegal abortions, and it is rare for the law to be enforced. Kelechi is the cofounder and president of Save the Unborn Babies Pro-life Initiative (with NGO status) in Nigeria. She started the group in February 2013 in response to the alarming rate of abortions. Her vision is to eradicate abortion through sensitizing society to the humanity of the unborn child, teaching natural family planning, and supporting women in crisis pregnancies to have their children. She also promotes the virtue of chastity and provides counseling to women experiencing post-abortion trauma. I had the privilege of meeting one of the mothers she was helping and a baby saved from abortion. She reports that twelve babies in Nigeria have been saved from abortion through her efforts. At the time, Marie Stopes, the large

London-based abortion provider, was present in nine of the thirty-six states of Nigeria. Marie Stopes publicly claims not to provide abortions, although in some places Kelechi has learned of suspicions that they secretly provide access.

Kelechi wrote after the visit, "It has not been easy fasting and praying for 40 days. Sometimes, I am so hungry I am tempted to excuse myself. However the results have been very encouraging. We have not only experienced spiritual growth, but many Nigerians have been enlightened on the humanity of the unborn child, two babies were recorded saved, and we have witnessed unmerited favors in our personal lives and Save the Unborn Babies Nigeria. Thank you God for the 40 Days for Life project."

South Africa

Colette Thomas has been the campaign leader of the Cape Town, South Africa, 40 Days for Life effort for many years now. Babies have been saved through her efforts in a country where abortion is available without restriction or reason. South Africa is more analogous to a Western nation than to most African countries with regards to abortion legislation.

Colette came to the United Kingdom for several months to participate in 40 Days for Life and to help the local pregnancy center. She then took the campaign back to her home city. She said the current campaign has been conducted with particular restraint so as not to jeopardize current efforts by representatives of various pro-life groups to get the City of Cape Town to lift restrictions that require groups of more than fourteen people to assemble fifty meters away from the Marie Stopes facility. She says people participating in the vigil do gather right in front of the facility because there are usually only a few people at a time. "Even if we change one person's mind [about going ahead with an abortion], we are making a difference saving a soul, saving a baby, saving a mother, saving a family. You can save a community and a nation like that," she says.

Melbourne, Australia

Fons Jannsen, of Dutch descent, has organized over ten 40 Days for Life campaigns in Melbourne. He commits himself wholeheartedly to the campaigns. In each campaign, he has seen one to three "turnarounds" outside the Fertility Control Centre. He travels a tremendous distance to the vigil every day—approximately a four-hour round trip or more. He wears his 40 Days for Life T-shirt on the train to help elicit conversations. In Australia, abortion law is determined at the local level, but at-large abortion is available culturally without restriction or reason. In Tasmania in 2104, a "bubble zone" law prohibits pro-life witness within hundreds of meters of any abortuary.

Today a security guard occasionally guards the building and escorts women to enter it. Over a ten-year period, a volunteer named Richard Grant had seen three hundred women choose life for their babies. One Muslim girl sent him a text on March 15, 2014, stating,

> *I am so happy today because I am a graduate. I want to thank u n everyone who supported me because without u people, I would not be able to complete my studies. Your financial help and moral support means a lot to me. Honestly, I have no words to express what I feel about u. You seriously deserve the words, "The Giant Heart." Thank u for being there for me in my hard time. May God shower his blessing on u and your family.*

By 2014, the Fertility Control Centre had conducted around 300,000 abortions in twenty-two years. In more recent years, the "sex party" in Melbourne has introduced a "buffer zone" around the Fertility Control Centre, and now Fons is praying 150 meters from the abortion center. During the last campaign, a jogging woman was repulsed by his presence there and returned to cover him in tomato ketchup. Fons's humility was to reply, "And she didn't even ask if I wanted fries."

El Puerto de Santa Maria, Spain

William Haag, an American expat, is leading the first-ever 40 Days for Life in El Puerto de Santa Maria, on the south coast of Spain, close to Cadiz, Gibraltar, and the African coast of Morocco, just thirteen kilometers from the Spanish coast.

La Clinica PoliPlanning is an abortion facility in the middle of town where, on Mondays and Fridays, the local abortionist does around twenty to twenty-five abortions a week. William has galvanized the local community by recruiting seven-day captains who, after a slightly rocky start, have done an exemplary job in filling the vigil. Even the siesta spot is full!

The number of abortions has dropped considerably during the campaign. There are reports of five saves from their vigil and two confirmed abortion days without abortions (which would mean fifteen to twenty fewer abortions, based on average numbers) by day twenty-seven. The number of participants praying in front of the clinic has grown to well over one hundred, including sixty dedicated to a weekly hour. Approximately 97 percent of hours have been covered since day seven of the vigil.

Numerous pro-life groups from around Spain (Barcelona, Seville, Algecrias, Granada, Pamplona) are considering 40 Days for Life vigils of their own. The participants from the vigil report tremendous spiritual growth and are actually sad that the vigil will end in a week. 40 Days for Life has grown so much in El Puerto de Santa Maria that they now have plans for a crisis pregnancy center in town.

Nairobi, Kenya

I traveled to Nairobi with Haywood Robinson and his wife, both former abortionists. Haywood writes,

Wow! Where do I start? We arrived in Nairobi only an hour late on Thursday. We were met by Ann Kioko's assistant and transported to our hotel. Ann is awesome! She is totally "sold out" and highly

capable of leading pro-life efforts in Kenya. She is very unassuming but powerful and no nonsense.

Dr. Robinson and his wife, Noreen, addressed a conference on population control and sustainable development. The attendees were interfaith. There were Hindus and Muslims. However, we made it clear that our greatest resource to be sustained is our children. We later addressed Catholic youth and encouraged them to "stay the course."

The 40 Days for Life in Nairobi began in front of the London-based abortion organization Marie Stopes Center. Supposedly education occurs there, but suspicions abound that they perform abortions also, which are illegal in Kenya.

Rome, Italy

Abortion was legalized in 1978 in Italy up to twelve weeks. Many doctors refuse to perform abortions in Italy, and the rate of conscientious objection among doctors is high.

Believe it or not, it took years to finally get a 40 Days for Life campaign in the Eternal City until Chiara stepped up to lead in her home country. The vigil was held outside the San Giovanni Hospital, where one thousand abortions are performed a year. There are hardly any groups in Italy doing public prayer vigils at present.

Chiara is a university student who has started her own student organization and also attended the March for Life in Washington, DC. There will be a pro-life concert for one thousand people later this year with a testimony from a former abortion doctor.

Frankfurt, Germany

Tomislav has run a good campaign in Frankfurt with the Croatian community in the city. They are praying outside Pro Familia—a referral center for abortions. Abortion counseling is mandatory in Germany.

They have been attacked verbally by feminists and Satanists during this time, but they have built a strong community feeling around the campaign and also a sense of solidarity, despite being attacked. God has given them plenty of results. Tomislav has been amazed at the number of people who have come to pray.

When I was there, during the evening event we prayed how we could spread this initiative all around Germany and also recruit more German Christians to participate. The prayers are clearly having an impact at the vigil, and their presence has generated a huge response. They are keen to build stronger and more impactful campaigns in the future to add on to their current successes.

Tomislav is a lawyer and has lived in Germany all his life. Besides Frankfurt, there are another eighty Croatian communities in Germany.

Dublin, Ireland

Carolyn O'Meara (great Irish name!) is the director and cofounder of Gianna Care, a crisis pregnancy center, and she leads the 40 Days for Life campaign. The vigil takes place outside a Marie Stopes referral center. Sadly, Ireland voted to legalize abortion in 2018, so now abortions will be done, not just referred, in Ireland. Carolyn was proud that her pregnancy center offered many different services, including ultrasound, and their presence is even more important now that abortion has been legalized.

Whilst I was at the prayer vigil, some of the volunteers mentioned a Kenyan woman who had given birth the day before and who had been a previous turnaround. During this current campaign, three women have changed their minds and have received help. There have been vigils outside the referral centers here for at least ten years. Marie Stopes is open just three or four days a week, and they do scans but don't show the pictures to the girls.

Carolyn O'Meara has been credited for many saved babies through her leadership. Carolyn said, "I just want you to know how blessed we are to be a part of this life-changing campaign. Thank you so much for all your hard work and efforts. Keep praying for us, and although we are far away, we are united in Christ. God bless you all."

Romania

Dan and Julia are the campaign directors for a first campaign in Romania in Cluj-Napoca (one of the largest cities in the country). Recently Dan met with the hospital director outside where they are praying, and the director offered him a room inside the building to counsel women.

A small number of pro-abortion activists had sprayed the hospital with pro-abortion graffiti, and Dan and his team have agreed to paint the hospital for them. (The paint has been donated).

The March for Life in Cluj attracted four to five thousand people and was a stunning event. All the different denominations participated, not an easy thing to accomplish.

Around six hundred volunteers have participated so far in 40 Day campaigns in Romania, and inquiries have been received from ten additional cities about running their own campaign.

The leader of the pro-life movement in Romania visited Dan and Julia and was astonished that they had achieved so much—and wanted to know how they did it! There are many shy Christians in Romania—so 40 Days is certainly countercultural for them. There are no large, private abortion providers making large financial profits. Both Dan and Julia are highly entrepreneurial, and running a 40 Days campaign for them has been a massive blessing, and they have been overwhelmingly surprised by the results.

ROBERT COLQUHOUN

～

Whether visiting campaigns in other countries or sitting at my desk in Texas, I have been asked many times by media outlets in other countries the same question: "The 40 Days for Life campaign is an American effort. Why is something from Texas coming to our country? Things are different here. Why do you feel you should bring an American effort to our country?"

My answer is simple: "We were invited by the great people of your country because abortion is not an American issue. I know of no Americans being aborted in your abortion facilities, but Americans care about humanity, and if some in our country continue to spread abortion to other nations when they *don't* ask for it, then we can certainly advance pro-life efforts in countries that do ask for it."

I never imagined, when we did the first campaign, that 40 Days for Life would be done in Africa or Hong Kong or Latin America. But the world came knocking. Courage is not limited by geography, and many courageous souls in other countries love their fellow citizens enough to take a leap of faith on something that started in Texas. They did so because abortion is an evil that breaks their heart and that they know breaks the heart of God. Through their courage and by the grace of God, seeds are being planted and growing. Robert has seen it. I have seen it. The abortion industry has seen it. And you have read about it. It is a global movement that happens in your neighborhood. It's not just something you hear about—it is something you can engage in. You can join your brothers and sisters around the world in solidarity as you pray and stand vigil. The world has sent a clear message to the entire pro-life movement in America for many years: Offering hope to a woman considering abortion should not be merely an American effort—it should spread around the world.

~

Consequently,
you are no longer foreigners and strangers,
but fellow citizens with God's people
and also members of his household.
EPHESIANS 2:19

Almighty God, I stand in awe of the global work you are doing through 40 Days for Life. I pray for all the campaign leaders and volunteers in each of these cities and the many more I haven't heard about. Give them the courage and wisdom to stand strong for life in each of their cultures and to rise to the challenges they face. Thank you for raising up leaders all across the globe. Amen.

Pray for Your Own Sins

∼

Have confidence in Christ
and trust in his mercy.
When you think he is far away,
he is often closest to you.
—THOMAS À KEMPIS

THIS IS THE GUY THAT THE UNIVERSITY OF WISCONSIN HOSPITAL *fears?* I thought as Steve Karlen picked me up at the frigid Madison, Wisconsin, airport. Steve had a pleasant demeanor, a friendly face, and an approachable persona. There was nothing intimidating about him.

Steve had helped lead a 40 Days for Life campaign in Madison, Wisconsin, which can culturally feel like San Francisco—except frozen. He was a great local leader and led the effort to stop his alma mater, the University of Wisconsin, from doing late-term abortions at their hospital medical science center. He had flown former abortion provider, Dr. Haywood Robinson, and me to Madison for the event that turned the tide in what had been a long battle. After many prayers had been offered on behalf of life, the hospital finally decided not to go through with their abortion plans. Steve's efforts were successful. It was a dramatic story that I wrote about in *40 Days for Life.*

Steve is a good husband to his wife, Laura, a good father, a good speaker, and a man of his word. My only beef with Steve is something I can never change. He loves the Green Bay Packers and views my Dallas Cowboys as an evil empire. Fortunately, we find this an easy problem to overlook, especially in the offseason.

Steve has seen and faced it all, so as 40 Days for Life grew, I hired Steve to assist local campaign leaders, knowing there was no one better to do it for the real heart of Steve's effectiveness is the same as that of so many of the local leaders he knows and serves for 40 Days for Life: he knows the power of simply spending one hour at a vigil praying.

∼

On a rare warm Wisconsin morning, Steve narrowly made it to Planned Parenthood in time for his 8:00 a.m. shift on the sidewalk. One of his prayer partners that morning was Julie, an excellent and experienced sidewalk counselor. As Julie took a position—just a few feet from a used condom discarded on the sidewalk—Steve found a place to kneel and pray.

As the clock struck 8:00, a Planned Parenthood employee, smiling brightly, came to unlock the door and welcome the morning's clients. In unison, eight to ten women dressed in loose-fitting sweatpants emerged from cars along with their support people. They scurried to the door of the facility as quickly as they could, hoping to avoid any interaction with Julie and Steve. The empty, glazed look in their eyes contrasted sharply with the cheery Planned Parenthood employee who welcomed them inside.

Only a few minutes later, a man in a car in the parking lot began heckling Steve. "Go pray for your own sins!" he shouted. Steve assured him that he would, and he meant it.

The man continued to hassle Steve, insisting that life is about choices. He quoted Scripture, then said, "Listen, nobody came to save Jesus from the cross! Whatever you think you're doing here, you won't change anybody's mind."

Steve said, "We're not here to accuse anyone of anything. We're here to offer a better alternative. And actually, people do sometimes change their minds when they hear what their alternatives are. This campaign in Madison has been averaging one changed mind a week. Maybe today someone will change her mind, and if so, that will be another life saved from abortion."

Steve moved down the sidewalk and knelt closer to the man's vehicle so he could hear him better. As they spoke, the man grew more vulnerable, explaining that he wasn't the baby's father. He had driven his friend, who wanted to sever all ties with the baby's father and felt that abortion was necessary for that to happen. The man said that, personally, he didn't like abortion. Encouraged, Steve and Julie (who had joined him by this time) told the man several times that he needed to encourage his friend to seek a healthy alternative at the Women's Care Center across the street. Each time, he replied, "No way will she change her mind—I've already tried."

Knowing that a life hung in the balance, Steve tried to think of just the right words to say. But like all of us in tense situations, we often don't think of the best lines until later. So Steve just kept kneeling and listening, sensing that this man needed someone to listen to him. And listen Steve did! The man went on for forty-five minutes, with words and emotions pouring out like a flood. Sometimes Steve would chime in, answer a question, or make a gentle correction, but mostly he just listened.

Sitting in his car in the parking lot of this Planned Parenthood abortion facility as a cold wind blew, the man talked about growing up black in a broken home in a segregated part of Dallas. "If I hadn't come from a broken family, I'd be in the NBA, NFL—I could have been *something!*" he said.

Steve listened as the man talked about the children he himself had lost to abortion—children he hadn't even known about until after the abortions had already taken place. He talked about saving a child from drowning and seeing a person shot to death right in front of him. The man said he was homeless but that he has a job he loves.

Steve couldn't do much to help this man's situation, so he focused on what he *could* do—validate this man as a person by acknowledging him and simply hearing him out.

As they spoke, the man's heart softened. He praised Julie and Steve for being there. He asked Steve if he had kids and said he appreciated Steve's being out there because it meant time away from family.

When a passerby shouted, "Quit harassing people!" the man defended Steve.

The man took a long pause, staring into the distance, thinking quietly. Then he looked at Steve and said, "I'm gonna pray with you."

The two bowed their heads and prayed for his abortion-bound friend inside Planned Parenthood just yards away.

After the prayer the man said, "I'll call her and try to change her mind." A few feet away, Julie got down on her knees and prayed, tears streaming down her face.

Steve turned away and tried not to listen to the conversation, but he couldn't help hearing the man say twice, "I will raise this baby. I will!" In the best way he knew how, this man was trying to answer the call he heard as a man to protect women and children.

But it wasn't enough. His friend didn't change her mind. She would have the abortion.

"Are you crying?" the man asked Julie when he delivered the woman's decision.

"Well, yes. I had thought this might work out," she said.

"I know. I'm crying a little bit too," he said.

By this point, the man had developed a sense of purpose. He walked around the parking lot, speaking to other Planned Parenthood clients arriving for their abortion appointments and pleading with them not to do it.

Steve realized that 40 Days basically had an impromptu sidewalk counselor roaming the parking lot of the abortion facility—a first! The man even approached the security guard and questioned why he was working for an abortion facility.

After speaking to the guard, the man came back to Steve and said, "That man is confused. He's confused. Keep praying, Steve. Maybe God will shut the power off and they won't be able to do abortions."

Meanwhile, the sister of an abortion client came out to smoke a cigarette. She lectured Steve and Julie about how children are better off aborted than being raised in abusive homes. Although she wasn't there for an abortion herself, she said she would absolutely get one if the need arose because, "It isn't fair to put kids through that."

Another heckler drove by. The wind seemed to be picking up.

Then a woman in blue jeans exited Planned Parenthood and, with her boyfriend, sat at a picnic table across the parking lot. She buried her head in her hands; the two of them sat and talked for some time. There's no way to know exactly what was happening. Perhaps she had just received a positive pregnancy test and was trying to decide what to do about it.

Steve and Julie hoped to speak with her, but after about twenty minutes, she went back inside the facility. *At least,* Steve thought, *she isn't likely to have the abortion today—not wearing blue jeans.* There might be an opportunity to counsel her when she left—and they could maybe reach her when she came back for the abortion next week.

Those hopeful thoughts were dashed when her boyfriend came back from their car to the abortion center door and handed her a pair of pink sweatpants.

It was now two hours into Steve's one-hour shift. He needed to get home. Time to play with his boys and to help his wife. Steve called over his new friend and said, "Can I give you some information to give your friend inside?" Steve handed him a Rachel's Vineyard brochure and some general information on Planned Parenthood and abortion. Then he shook the man's hand and thanked him for trying to save his friend's baby.

The man said, "God be with you."

Just then the woman the man had driven there for her abortion emerged; the procedure was over. She got into his car. It's very rare that a post-abortive woman says anything to a vigil participant, but she glared at Steve out her window. "You jerks!" she said. "We pray too!"

This would be a good time to wrap this chapter up with a dramatic story of a last-minute success—maybe a saved baby or a post-abortive woman who came forward to seek healing. But God doesn't always affirm us like that—at least not on the timeline we'd like him to. And this had been a day empty of what all that Steve and Julie had prayed for.

So why did I choose this day, out of all days at 40 Days for Life vigils over the past few years, to include in this book? After all, maybe showing a day like this isn't the best advertisement for encouraging people to get involved in pro-life activities. Believe me, it's much more rewarding to be present when the good stuff happens. But this is the spiritual beauty of a 40-day campaign of prayer, fasting, and vigil. It really is a spiritual journey, not a guarantee of results or affirmation. It's an opportunity for us to be faithful, to love the God of gifts more than the gifts of God.

Steve believed, as all local campaign leaders do, that God had put him and Julie there that morning. Maybe their Christian witness would help turn around a life someday down the line. It's not for us to know. What is for us to know is this: that morning Steve Karlen and Julie gave God what they had. Driving there that morning, they hadn't known what the day would look like, but they also knew it wasn't up to them. They just had to be obedient. That day, part of their role was affirming the dignity of a man raised in a broken home. It was turning the other cheek in the face of insults. It was being there for women who had no man present. And it was being there in solidarity with babies who weren't loved by a single person during their all-too-short life on earth.

This is all we can do when we offer Jesus what we have in the abortion crisis. The rest is in God's hands. When we accept that reality, we are ready to be part of the beginning of the end of abortion.

∾

When Jesus looked up and saw a great crowd coming toward him, said to Philip, "Where shall we buy bread for these people to eat?" He asked this only to test him, for he already had in mind what he was going to do. Philip answered him, "It would take more than half a year's wages to buy enough bread for each one to have a bite!" Another of his disciples, Andrew, Simon Peter's brother, spoke up, "Here is a boy with five small barley loaves and two small fish, but how far will they go among so many?"

JOHN 6:5–9

God, we desire to put the outcome of this day into your hands. We ask that you help us to remain obedient, even if it looks as though our efforts are insignificant or fruitless. You ask us to be available, not successful. You ask us to pray, knowing the outcome is yours. Thy will be done through our prayers today. Amen.

A Picture Is Worth
a Thousand Prayers

~

We must accept finite disappointment,
but never lose infinite hope.
—REVEREND MARTIN LUTHER KING JR.

OHIO IS A UNIQUE PLACE. I HAVE BEEN THERE TWENTY-NINE times, and it has rained twenty-eight of them.

Farmers will tell you that although their state is considered fly-over country, they are proud to call it home. Executives in Cincinnati will tell you their city is experiencing an industrial boom, great for jobs. Cleveland is home to the Rock and Roll Hall of Fame, and the Pro Football Hall of Fame is located in Canton. Then there's Columbus, where everything is all about football and hating Michigan.

I have been to all the major cities in Ohio many times and have loved going to small towns across that great state as well. I'll always remember speaking at a pregnancy banquet—in a barn of all places—in 2009. Of course, the food was awesome.

But for as much as you do or don't know, or do or don't care, about Ohio, there are two Ohio cities that reflect the climate of our culture—Kettering and Sharonville. Those are where the notorious Dr. Martin Haskell's late-term abortion facilities are located. Dr. Haskell helped pioneer the partial-birth abortion procedure, presenting the barbaric surgery to the 1992 National Abortion Federation Risk Management Seminar in Dallas.

Most Americans—including many who support abortion—are against late-term abortion or are at least uncomfortable with it. Martin Haskell is not in either category. He is an advocate, defender, and practitioner of this heinous act. Without shame he says, "I've always been kind of a poster child, if you will. I think I've become something of a poster child for their rhetoric simply because of the procedure itself."[23]

The Washington Post reports that in an *American Medical News* interview Haskell was asked, "Is the baby already dead when the abortionist partly removes her from the uterus?" His response was, "No it's not.... I would think probably about a third of those are definitely dead before I actually start to remove the fetus. And probably the other two-thirds are not."[24]

In an interview with *American Medical News*, Dr. Haskell was asked, "Does it bother you that a second trimester fetus so closely resembles a baby?"

Haskell responded, "I really don't think about it. I don't have a problem with believing the fetus is a fertilized egg. Sure, it becomes more physically developed but it lacks emotional development. It doesn't have the mental capacity for self-awareness. It's never been an ethical dilemma for me."[25]

Dr. Anthony Levantino knows the Intact D&E abortion procedure all too well. As a former abortion doctor, he has worked to raise awareness about the brutal nature of abortion. He himself used the Intact D&E procedure of Dr. Martin Haskell. He describes the process, with abortion supporters wearing Planned Parenthood T-shirts behind him, in his testimony before the Subcommittee on the Constitution and Civil Justice in the United States Congress:

> The first task is remove the laminaria that had earlier been
> placed in the cervix to dilate it sufficiently to allow the procedure
> you are about to perform. With that accomplished, direct your
> attention to the surgical instruments arranged on a small table

to your right. The first instrument you reach for is a 14-French suction catheter. It is clear plastic and about nine inches long. It has a bore through the center approximately ¾ of an inch in diameter.

Picture yourself introducing this catheter through the cervix and instructing the circulating nurse to turn on the suction machine which is connected through clear plastic tubing to the catheter. What you will see is a pale-yellow fluid that looks a lot like urine coming through the catheter into a glass bottle on the suction machine. This is the amniotic fluid that surrounded the baby to protect her.

With suction complete, look for your Sopher clamp. This instrument is about thirteen inches long and made of stainless steel. At the end are located jaws about 2 ½ inches long and about ¾ of an inch wide with rows of sharp ridges or teeth. This instrument is for grasping and crushing tissue. When it gets hold of something, it does not let go. A second trimester D&E abortion is a blind procedure. The baby can be in any orientation or position inside the uterus. Picture yourself reaching in with the Sopher clamp and grasping anything you can.

At twenty-four weeks gestation, the uterus is thin and soft so be careful not to perforate or puncture the walls. Once you have grasped something inside, squeeze on the clamp to set the jaws and pull hard—hard. You feel something let go and out pops a fully formed leg about six inches long. Reach in again and grasp whatever you can. Set the jaw and pull hard once again and out pops an arm about the same length. Reach in again and again with that clamp and tear out the spine, intestines, heart and lungs.

The toughest part of a D&E abortion is extracting the baby's head. The head of a baby that age is about the size of a large plum and is now free floating inside the uterine cavity. You can be pretty sure you have hold of it if the Sopher clamp is spread about as far as your fingers will allow. You will know you have it right when you crush down on the clamp and see white gelatinous material coming through the cervix. That was the baby's brains. You can then extract the skull pieces.[26]

Haskell's two abortion facilities in Kettering and Sharonville have been the sites of 40 Days for Life campaigns, and I have visited both. Even Haskell has taken notice of the peaceful presence outside. "They are not as in your face as what we've seen maybe 15 or 20 years ago, but the picketing is constant and every day."[27]

The presence *has* been constant, and that is due to Mary Jo and Leslie, who have led campaigns outside of Haskell's facility in Sharonville, and to Holly, who leads the campaign in Kettering.

There is also another woman who has done so much to save lives from this barbaric practice—Vivian Koob. Vivian runs a network of pregnancy resource centers across Ohio. She is well-known and highly regarded by many pregnancy center directors across America. Her centers—Elizabeth New Life Centers—have locations across the street from both of Martin Haskell's facilities.

Vivian and her husband, Steve, have fourteen children, including five adopted African American children. They have a beautiful—and growing—family with twenty grandchildren and one great grandchild. Vivian has poured her life into this work. She also has a great sense of humor, which I have enjoyed during the many miles she has driven me across Ohio during a few of my trips there.

Today I want to take you to the pregnancy center across the street from Martin Haskell's late-term abortion facility in Kettering, for it has something I have never seen before.

Elizabeth New Life Centers are some of the most well-operated pregnancy resource clinics in the country. They provide ultrasounds, pregnancy tests, and many printed materials and other types of support for women. Their success is clear—just look at the walls, covered with pictures of babies who came close to being aborted just across the street in the late-term abortion facility. There is nothing like looking into the eyes of a child who was saved from abortion. It's so easy to be tempted to despair in the face of the enormity and devastation of abortion, especially when you contemplate the over three thousand per day that happen in the United States. Yet when I see a picture of a baby who was so close to becoming one of those abortion statistics—forgotten by the world as a "choice"—I see beyond any discouragement. I think, *What about this one baby I am looking at?* Surely we can consider seeking to be a voice for just *one* child.

Vivian showed me the baby photos as she strolled through the office and greeted the staff. She's a pro at what she does, having helped women in crisis pregnancies longer than I've been alive. And yet after all these years, she is still enthusiastically sharing the stories behind each photo as if it were her first week on the job.

After we'd seen each photo, her tone softened. "Come this way. Let me show you another room."

Inside the room a wall was filled with even more beautiful pictures—only these were ultrasounds! Ultrasound photos always remind me of my own children—there is nothing like getting that first ultrasound or hearing your new son or daughter's heartbeat for the first time. These pictures bring excitement, anticipation, and hope. They make you think about the future, the possibilities—birthdays parties, graduations, and weddings. They inspire us to treasure life at its earliest stages.

"Look at all of these!" I said. "It's so beautiful that you kept the ultrasounds of the saved babies as well as the pictures of them after they are born."

"Well," Vivian said, her voice still soft. "We don't have pictures of these babies after they are born." She turned and looked at me. "By the grace of God we have helped save thousands of babies over the years, but not all of them. These are the ultrasounds of the babies we know were aborted across the street after their mothers visited here. These images are the only record or memory of them. We don't want to forget them."

I stared out the window and across the street, then back at the wall with those beautiful ultrasound pictures—pictures that were now the only memory, not of statistics, but of beautiful children made in the image and likeness of God. Thanks to Vivian and Elizabeth New Life Center, these children are not forgotten.

Standing in that room in silence, I thought, *This is why we pray. This is why we show up.* Those beautiful pictures put a face on those babies. You could see their feet and arms, and a few of them were sucking their thumbs in the womb. As I looked at one, I noted the date and the size of the baby and realized that the child would have been in elementary school by now.

～

My first trip to one of Haskell's abortion facilities was to Sharonville, years ago. When I walked up, I saw young men and women in school uniforms kneeling in prayer outside—kids from a local Catholic school. It was very moving. On one hand, inside the facility was an abortion doctor in his seventies calmly performing a barbaric surgery that no one would wish on their greatest enemy; on the other hand, just a few feet away from his murderous activity were these children defending other children.

I doubt any of those kids had been in the room at Elizabeth's New Life Center to see the ultrasound pictures of the babies who had been lost, but they still wanted to do what they could to save the unborn.

Their prayers, combined with the prayers of others, were heard. Dr. Martin Haskell's notorious Sharonville abortion facility, after eleven 40 Days for Life vigils, closed completely during the spring 2018 campaign. Mary Jo, the local leader, summed up everything when they closed: "God is good."

Whatever fears or hesitation or weariness you have today, know that a picture is worth a thousand prayers. Each of those photos on the walls of Elizabeth's New Life Center merits an abundance of our prayers and efforts on behalf of the unborn. Prayer is the solution.

If we get on our knees and trust God, who is Father to all children, known and forgotten, he will heed our prayer.

Vivian had not forgotten these babies on the wall who didn't make it. Their simple memory remains in a room in that Kettering pregnancy center. Their presence reminds us today and every day that each of those babies belongs to God. He made them, he doesn't forget them, and they are worth it. A picture is worth a thousand prayers, inconveniences, rejections, and discomforts. A picture can remind us that no one is forgotten by our Father in heaven.

∼

For you created my inmost being;
you knit me together in my mother's womb.
I praise you because I am fearfully and wonderfully made;
your works are wonderful,
I know that full well.
My frame was not hidden from you
when I was made in the secret place,
when I was woven together in the depths of the earth.
PSALM 139:13–15

Holy Father, I thank you that you never forget these babies. You know and love each one by name. I pray you would help me to remember the babies at risk of losing their lives, even when I am not on a sidewalk in front of an abortion facility. Each time I see or hear of an ultrasound, let me pray. Each time I hug my own kids or grandkids or nieces or nephews, let me pray. Help me to not lose heart, but to remember you are the God above all gods, with more power than we can imagine. Amen.

It's Personal

~

*Our Constitution was made only
for a moral and religious People.
It is wholly inadequate to the
government of any other.*
—PRESIDENT JOHN ADAMS

I LOVE AMERICA. I BELIEVE IT'S THE GREATEST COUNTRY IN THE world, offering its citizens great freedom, and with that freedom, great responsibility. Now that 40 Days for Life is in over fifty countries, I have seen that when Americans use our rights to stand up to cultural evils, the world comes knocking, wanting our help.

We do many things right in America, but we also do many things wrong. Great evils thrive within our borders, and abortion is at the top of the list. However, because of the freedoms we have, we are able to save lives from abortion and help other countries do the same. It is up to us to either use our rights for good, seeking to end abortion, or instead misuse our freedom to perpetuate the wrong, waiting for another "greatest generation" to come along and preserve our future generations.

Sadly, many in the United States have used our freedom not to curb abortion but rather to spread abortion around the world. No American entity has done that more than Planned Parenthood. The International Planned Parenthood Federation operates in every Latin American country and the Caribbean. I cannot think of a more condescending message to other countries and cultures than to infiltrate their culture with abortion services. Telling cultures that traditionally love and value family that they should instead kill their unborn is about as offensive as it gets.

Steve Karlen, campaign director, helped get 40 Days for Life campaigns started in Mexico. But things still seemed to be happening slowly for the rest of Latin America. We shouldn't have been concerned, though. We should have known that God had just the person—someone very unexpected—in line for the job.

In high school, Katharine O'Brien had gone on mission trips with her church youth group to the Dominican Republic and Peru. Back home, she participated in 40 Days for Life campaigns. While attending college she went on mission trips to Nicaragua and Chile and, at the University of Virginia, she volunteered for us and soon became an intern.

As 40 Days for Life grew globally, Katharine noticed a huge gap in one section of the world that loves family and is under constant attack from the abortion industry—Latin America. So Katharine volunteered to do something about it.

I thought it was a decent idea that might bear some fruit. Since I had little personal knowledge and experience with that part of the world, I certainly needed someone else to lead. But Katharine? Sure, she spoke Spanish, had a heart for Latin America, and had been there a few times, but she was a college student living in Virginia. How would she be able to recruit campaign leaders thousands of miles away? I had my doubts about the whole setup—but then, I had also foolishly thought 40 Days for Life would only ever be one campaign in one city, one time.

So in 2015, based on Katharine's enthusiasm and confidence that Latin America would be the next explosion for 40 Days for Life campaigns, we gave her an email address and a phone, and she got to work. I didn't share her confidence. I had to keep reminding myself:

If 40 Days for Life could come this far, why couldn't a college intern help light part of the world on fire for life?

No reason at all.

In just a few years, Katharine turned a simple experimental internship into a mandatory full-time job as 40 Days for Life Latin America went from one city campaign in 2014 to eighty-three in 2018.

One of those cities is Bogotá, Colombia. Over eight million people live there in Colombia's capital city, nesting over 8,600 feet above sea level. In Colombia, International Planned Parenthood calls itself *Profamilia*. (They are not the only ones in Colombia offering reproductive services. *Oriéntame*, another organization with several abortion facilities throughout Colombia, also serves many women in pregnancy and performs a large number of abortions in Colombia each year.)

It's difficult to know the exact number of abortions that take place in Colombia, since many of them might be illegal. Also, these facilities don't have the same requirements for reporting as in the United States. The Guttmacher Institute estimates about 400,000 abortions occur each year in Colombia—legal and illegal—which is a much higher number than the official Ministry of Health reports.

Profamilia was founded in 1965 as a private nonprofit with the mission to provide reproductive health services for the women of Colombia. They provided most of the sterilizations and contraceptive services throughout the nineteen sixties, seventies, and eighties. Profamilia helped to usher in legal abortion, then became a major abortion provider. They have centers in twenty-seven cities in Colombia, operating sixty-six clinics and mobile health units, which account for nearly three quarters of the country's family-planning capacity. All of this leads us to believe that Colombia was the perfect place to host the first-ever Latin American Leader Conference. So in 2017, 40 Days for Life did just that.

I wouldn't have planned to attend, but I had met the 40 Days for Life national leader from Colombia, Pamela Delgado, at a 40 Days for Life conference in America the year before. Right away she offered a persistent invitation to come and visit her country. It became quite obvious that she was not going to stop asking until I accepted. Being a native Texan, I had taken fourteen years of Spanish from kindergarten to college. Yet as I planned my trip south, I deeply regretted not remembering any Spanish that wasn't related to food or "La Bamba." I decided to solve that problem by joining forces with Katharine and a team member named Bobby, who also speaks Spanish, on their trip to Bogotá. While we waited to board the plane, I turned to Katharine and asked, "What is Colombia known for besides coffee and drug lords?"

In all seriousness she said, "They have amazing fruit."

I was aghast. "Fruit? Who cares about fruit? How's their hot sauce?"

When we landed at Bogotá, I realized what Colombians *should* be known for—their hospitality. A group of 40 Days for Life supporters greeted us at the airport—at midnight, no less—with balloons, singing, and flowers. I didn't understand a word in the excited conversation surrounding me, but I instantly knew this trip was going to be special.

The next day Pamela took me around to meet many of our 40 Days for Life leaders in person—nineteen leaders from seventeen cities in Mexico and Colombia. She knew everyone and they knew her. And in spite of the language barrier, the Colombians couldn't have been more gracious. They love life, they love family, and they all have a great sense of humor. It was like being in Ireland—without the sarcasm.

The Colombians treated me as they treat everyone—like family. Family shares with each other from the heart. The good, the bad, the highs, the lows. They share hope and heartache. They laugh together and cry together. They stumble over obstacles, then help each other back up again. Nowhere has this been more evident to me than in Colombia.

As I met one after another of these passionate and dedicated people, I couldn't help but think of the doubts I'd had about Katharine and her readiness for the job. I hadn't just underestimated her, I'd underestimated God. Fortunately, God had given her the vision I lacked.

It is easy to have our vision of what God can do obscured by the sheer size of the global problem of abortion. In this work, we can fall prey to questions that seem to have no answers. Can we, humankind, really abort nearly 56 million[28] babies per year in the world and act as if things are going to work out? Can we ignore, forget, and neglect God so we can kill our own for an endless period of time? Can we really make a dent in this tragic global problem? Can we, personally, make a difference? We pray and fast and talk with women and men, locally, one at a time, and often we don't see any results of our efforts.

How easy it is to forget that God is working even when we can't see any results.

And there is a reason we often don't witness the results: Abortion is *personal*. It's hard to grasp the impact of your efforts until you meet those you're trying to reach or those who have had an abortion. In fact, that's often one of the reasons people get involved in pro-life activities. *We make a difference when fighting abortion becomes personal.*

That's also one of the reasons for this book. We share in it the personal stories of women and men affected by abortion and those transformed by our efforts to end abortion one life at a time. By sharing these stories, we hope that fighting abortion becomes personal for the reader.

And that leads to what I took away from the conference in Colombia—a conference that never would have happened were it not for a young intern who had a heart for Latin America. I wouldn't fully grasp for myself the truth that abortion is personal until I witnessed what happened in the next chapter.

~

Now faith is confidence in
what we hope for and assurance
about what we do not see.
HEBREWS 11:1

Jesus, sometimes it's hard to have faith that you're at work in our lives when we don't see results from our prayers. I pray that this day I will have the assurance that you will, in your power, bring about the end of abortion. If not in our city today, please bring it about in the life of at least one woman. Help me hold fast to that faith. Amen.

Good Fruit

~

God loves each of us as
if there were only one of us.
—AUGUSTINE OF HIPPO

THE BOGOTÁ LEADER CONFERENCE WAS ABOUT TO COME TO A close. It had been a good experience for me. The people and the fruit (and the hot sauce!) had all exceeded my expectations. I hadn't realized how much I needed to see the passion of the people and the results of 40 Days for Life in this part of the world.

The numbers and the reports shared at the conference were beautiful, but perhaps because I hadn't been there to actually see all these events take place, the heart of the work still felt distant to me. I felt as though I were missing something.

That all vanished when woman after woman got up at the conference's final event to share their stories. I should mention that, in America, it is difficult to find a woman who has chosen life who wants to share her story. Remember, abortion is very personal. Understandably, many of them are embarrassed to acknowledge that they ever had an abortion appointment to begin with. While they are grateful to 40 Days for Life for helping to save their baby, they usually don't want to publicly explain how that happened. That was the biggest difference I noticed about the Colombians. They were so open and honest about why they ended up there. Each of the women spoke as they held their baby. I was glued to every translated word.

Andrea

I got pregnant and already had three kids. I told the father of my unborn child, and he said, "Just do what you have to do." Then I got fired from my job, and my mother said, "You need to do what you need to do."

When I parked at the abortion clinic, I saw the 40 Days for Life volunteers. One of them said that abortion was not easy and told me to ask to see the ultrasound [in the clinic]. When I did, they [the clinic staff] told me that I was not allowed to see my baby on the screen. So I left and went back to the 40 Days for Life volunteers and spoke to Sophie, who told me, "We can help you. You are not alone."

I felt like such a bad woman. But they took me to a pregnancy center and got me help. It was very difficult. My father rejected me. I told my boyfriend, and he said, "That's good for you, but it's not my plan." I had my baby girl and would do anything for her.

Vivian

I told my boyfriend I was pregnant, and he left me. My father is a good, strong man, and I was worried about his reaction. I called the abortion facility late at night and was surprised they answered so late. I thought about my faith, but that good thought went away. I didn't have any money, so I called friends and asked. I took my friend with me for the abortion. I asked to see the ultrasound, and my friend and I both stared at the screen. My friend looked at me and said, "Don't do it!" I cried a river and went outside and saw the 40 Days for Life volunteers. My friend told me everything would be okay as we walked over to them. A volunteer gave me a hug, and from there things got better. They helped me find a job and gave financial assistance.

I knew I had to face my family. When I told my mom, she said, "Calm down, we love you, we are here for you."

I was very worried about telling my father and wanted to tell him myself. When I said I wanted to talk to him, he said, "What's up? What's wrong?"

I said, "I'm pregnant."

He responded abruptly. "Why? How? You are my princess. How did this happen?" He left. I was crushed. Then out of nowhere he called me. When I answered, he said, "How's my grandson?" He then told me he knew he had to accept it because he knew this child was a blessing from God.

Carla

I used to make fun of 40 Days for Life because my mom would participate. Then I got pregnant, and my boyfriend left. I wanted an abortion and decided to have a chemical abortion and use the abortion pills. I took the pills and bled a lot.

Then I went for a walk in our neighborhood with my mom. We saw the 40 Days for Life campaign and my mom wanted to stop and pray. I prayed too. I also looked at a 40 Days for Life flyer and saw the baby on the flyer. I felt guilty for my abortion.

I talked to a friend about taking the abortion pills and she said, "You could still be pregnant." So I went to the doctor and had an ultrasound—there was my baby! It was a twenty-one-week-old boy and he was sick from the abortion pills. I started taking care of myself and he recovered. I'm in college now. Having a baby did not make me cancel my plans. It has been hard but worth it. So many people in college don't know God's love, and I want them to know that he loves them. Society says you can do anything you want with your body, but that's not true. In the end I'm thankful for my mother's prayers. She never lost hope the entire time.

Diana

I was raped. When I found out I was pregnant, I was determined to get an abortion. My mom told me there was no way I could have an abortion. She pleaded with me not to do it, but I was numb to her comments. In desperation, as I was leaving the house, my mom said to me "What about God?" The way she said it made me stop even though I didn't care about God anymore.

I never made the abortion appointment, but I didn't take care of myself. I finally went to the doctors, and they said the baby had a heart condition and could die. The baby came a month early, and she was fine. I looked at her the first time and fell in love. What about God? I know God is getting me through this, and I know God loves me and my baby girl.

Angela

I already had two children. When I was four months pregnant, I had an ultrasound, and the baby had hydrocephalus. The doctors said he didn't have part of his brain and would only live a few days. I kept asking if there was an option besides abortion. The doctor said, "No, he will die anyway."

Then my baby started having heart problems. I went back to the doctor at six months and he told me the baby was not moving, that he would not be normal, and that I needed to abort. I discussed it with my husband, and we made the abortion appointment. When I arrived at the abortion facility, I saw 40 Days for Life and knew that was the option I'd hoped for. I met Madeline and told her the doctors said that if I deliver, my baby will have a heart attack on the table and die in front of me. I told her that, even so, I just could not abort my baby.

The delivery was very painful because of the size of his head, caused by the fluid going to his brain. I named him Emmanuel. Emmanuel has turned out to be much different than the doctors said he would be. He has no heart condition at all, and he can eat. They say he will never walk, but I am hoping and praying that he walks one day. Either way, I don't care. He is alive. I joked with the doctors that because of his condition he cannot make noises, so he never cries and is really quiet. That makes him an easy baby. They are working on getting his head size down, and I pray he will walk one day. I quit my job to stay home and take care of him. He is my life.

～

When Angela had finished telling her story, she walked over to me without another word, plunged Emmanuel into my arms, and smiled. As I looked at this beautiful boy whom everyone had wanted aborted, my heart was filled with gratitude for two people—Katharine and Pamela. Without Katharine's enthusiasm, and without Pamela's bringing 40 Days for Life to Colombia, Emmanuel would not have had a fighting chance.

That night at the closing dinner, I was sitting next to a professor from one of the major universities in Colombia. He asked me what most Americans think of when they think of Colombia. Through a translator I said, "Coffee and drug lords."

He laughed and replied, "So do we!"

I said, "But for me, that changed after hearing those testimonies today and meeting and holding Emmanuel. Colombia for me will now always be a reminder that God is indeed with us."

How often do we forget that God truly is with us? Not only in this work but in every area of our lives. His gifts abound, moment by moment. And just as I needed to hear the stories of these women in order to fully connect with God's work, there are others who need to hear your story of how God has guided and provided for you.

～

Thanks be to God
for his indescribable gift!
2 CORINTHIANS 9:15

God, thank you for the indescribable gift of your son Jesus. Because of that gift, we can praise you and thank you for the lives of each of these Colombian children as well as the lives of the children whose stories we do not know. We ask that you expand the work of 40 Days for Life to all corners of Latin America, reaching into the mountains, the valleys, the cities, and the villages to encourage the mothers to choose life. Amen.

Milagros, Miracle, was saved at a 40 Days for Life vigil in California even though doctors encouraged her mother to have an abortion because her baby would be born with no legs.

Former abortion doctor Haywood Robinson debates an abortion doctor on Premiere Christian Radio in England.

Dr. Ernie Cyr and his family outside the abortion facility in Pensacola, Florida.

Hundreds of volunteers pray in Bedford Square in London despite a large, noisy counter demonstration. This abortion facility, the site of multiple vigils, went out of business in 2014.

Volunteer stands vigil in a snowstorm in Anchorage, Alaska.

Philadelphia abortion doctor Kermit Gosnell was arrested and convicted of three counts of first-degree murder.

Angela holding her baby boy Emmanuel after she chose life for him at a 40 Days for Life vigil in Colombia. He was diagnosed with hydrocephalus and doctors told her he would die at birth. Here he is with the author (left), Angela, Pamela Delgado, Katharine O'Brien, and Lourdes Varela.

40 Days for Life leaders in Africa gather in Nigeria for training.

Joseph (middle), an American missionary, brought 40 Days for Life to Hong Kong.

Susie Calvey participated in the first-ever 40 Days for Life in College Station, Texas, and continued to pray in front of abortion facilities after she was diagnosed with cancer.

Chris Davis, a 40 Days for Life leader in Shreveport/Bossier City, at the celebration of the closure of the local abortion facility which did over ten thousand abortions before closing.

Ante Caljkušić, 40 Days for Life leader in Croatia, introduces a mom who chose life and her baby to Pope Francis at the Vatican.

The Sisters of Life, who help mothers in need in New York City, tour the headquarters of 40 Days for Life, the former Planned Parenthood abortion facility in Texas where 40 Days for Life first began. Dr. Haywood Robinson, a former abortion provider, acts as tour guide.

Local heroes from around the world gather at the Leader Symposium for training to save lives and end abortion in their community.

Get a Life!

~

Do not worry about why problems
exist in the world
—just respond to people's needs.

~

We ourselves feel that what
we are doing is just a drop in the ocean.
But the ocean would be less
because of that missing drop.

—MOTHER TERESA

"GET A LIFE!"

If I've heard it once, I've heard it a thousand times. It's the most common phrase shouted from cars as people drive past a 40 Days for Life vigil. And isn't that ironic? Life is the very reason we stand vigil!

You don't need to wonder what it means. I can translate its many meanings for you based on the conversations I've had with the folks who yell it and then stop to share their thoughts. I have learned that *get a life* when yelled at those standing in front of an abortion facility can mean many things.

"Go home."

"Stop judging."

"Take care of the kids that are *already* born."

"Bring the troops home."

"Quit being a prude."

"I hate George W. Bush."

"I hate Donald Trump."

"I hate you."

"I hate Christians."

"I hate your church."

"I hate everyone."

"I hate myself."

"Solve a real problem."

"Fight poverty."

"Leave them alone."

"Leave me alone."

"God is dead."

"My father left us."

"I'm on drugs."

"I had an abortion."

"I paid for an abortion."

"I made my daughter have an abortion."

"My relative came here for an abortion."

"You're a sexist."

"You're a racist."

"Then *you* adopt them."

"Religion is evil."

"I'm bored."

"You don't care about animals."

I admit it took me years to learn these many meanings. But the original phrase never changes: "Get a life."

We can respond in many different ways, but often the best response is not to speak, but rather to live our lives for God and help others do the same. There is a group of people who have done this for years. These are the heroes of 40 Days for Life. They are the local campaign leaders. And guess what? They have a life.

You have met many of them in this book and in the book *40 Days for Life*, but there are so many more. We have people of all kinds leading 40 Days for Life campaigns, from stay-at-home moms to retired colonels to airline pilots to college students to business owners to those who just lost a job or a spouse or a child. Only ten percent of them work for a pro-life organization. Over twenty-five percent of them have an abortion in their past. Most of them have never done a media interview. The majority say they have never had any kind of leadership role in the pro-life movement before 40 Days for Life. Some of them have large families; others are unable to have children. Some have adopted children; some were personally saved from abortion. Whoever they are, they have all led campaigns and have sacrificed to save children.

In this chapter I would like to honor three of those mighty heroes who have run the race and have gone home before us: Gene Villinski of San Marcos, California; Mike Stack of Southfield, Michigan; and Tom Kurtz of Brighton, Michigan.

Mike Stack

Mike Stack was in his fifties when he picked me up in his SUV and drove me to two abortion facilities less than a mile from each other just outside Detroit. I quickly learned that he was an engineer, a devout Catholic, and a hard worker. He had brought 40 Days for Life to Detroit and helped spread it throughout the area.

A gentle-hearted man, Mike took abortion seriously. In one of his first interviews in 2009, he told a reporter, "We've embarked on something that seems impossible—a forty-day campaign, in the winter, outside, in Michigan." His intellect and engineering background brought new perspective to 40 Days for Life, especially in those early days.

Mike said, "I did a check with the state—there are 7.3 million cars that will pass by us in those forty days, so our people are preaching the gospel to millions."

When it came to responding to those who are hostile, Mike's calm demeanor and faith in God were unwavering. "Occasionally we'll get someone who's angry with us," he said. "Most are people who have had abortions or whose [family members] were involved in abortions, and they see us as being judgmental. We frequently have been able to talk with them and share God's mercy and forgiveness with them and have them leave with a totally different heart."

Woman Care, the abortion facility where Mike held his vigils, is notorious. It has been in business for thirty years, and Mike was determined to be there no matter what the weather—cold, rain, or sleet, and he saw all three. The abortion doctors there had seen four women die from abortions, including one woman who had complications after an abortion in her twenty-third week.

Mike brought 40 Days for Life to Woman Care and led multiple campaigns there for years. Then he was diagnosed with cancer and given a final timeline for his own life.

On August 14, 2014, Mike Stack went home to the Lord.

Mike once said in an interview, "God calls us to be of service, but he blesses us when we respond."

He responded indeed, and so did God. In the summer of 2017, Woman Care, after thirty years and thousands of abortions, closed their doors. The community gave praise to God and honored Mike by holding a prayer gathering outside the closed facility in his honor.

Gene Villinski

Gene Villinski was a funny man who loved to make people laugh. On my fifth visit to his campaign in San Diego it was raining. "This is your fault, Shawn," he said with a wry grin when he picked me up from the airport. "It never rains here."

Originally from cold, wet Chicago, Gene retired and settled with his wife in sunny San Diego. Most people who retire there spend their time picking out golf course memberships and boats. But not Gene. He looked for and found the large abortion facility operated by notorious abortion doctor George Kung. Then Gene invested himself in leading 40 Days for Life campaigns there.

Full of energy, Gene moved fast. His conversation always overflowed with ideas for new projects, and he often asked for my feedback. On my last trip to visit Gene's campaign, when he blamed me for the rain, we attended his kickoff event at his local church. The event buzzed with pastors and volunteers, and of course everyone knew Gene. As we walked in, I was thinking of how many times I had seen Gene, talked to him on the phone, and exchanged emails. He was one of the leaders who had been with 40 Days for Life for some time, and yet his energy never seemed to diminish—rather, it increased.

Just before the event started, I said, "Gene, I know we joke a lot, but seriously, I want to thank you for your leadership. You're doing a great job. You're an inspiration to me and so many other leaders."

His eyes filled with tears and he said, "This has been the greatest honor of service I have ever been part of."

In 2014, Gene got very sick very quickly. He passed away on July 11 of that year.

The San Diego pro-life community dedicated the next 40 Days for Life campaign to Gene, calling it "Gene's Campaign." Gene's Campaign ended up being a lot like Gene—hopeful. And in the following year, 2015, Dr. Kung's abortion facility, where Gene had led campaigns for years, closed its doors.

I will always remember Gene Villinski as I saw him that night at the kickoff event. He'd spent his retirement, his golden years, selflessly reaching mothers and saving babies from abortion. He didn't get to celebrate the closing of Dr. Kung's facility alongside the hundreds of people he'd recruited over the years. But when I heard the news that it was closing, I heard Gene's voice: "This has been the greatest honor of service I have ever been part of."

Tom Kurtz

Early in 2017, Steve Karlen, the North American campaign director, forwarded me an email from Tom Kurtz saying that the end of his life was near, and he was stepping aside as the 40 Days for Life leader in Brighton, Michigan, where he'd followed in the footsteps of Mike Stack.

Steve knew Tom well and had been keeping our team updated on his battle with cancer. "During Tom Kurtz's five-year run as leader of the Brighton, Michigan, 40 Days for Life campaign," Steve said, reminiscing, "I made a personal resolution to never call him unless I knew I had at least thirty uninterrupted minutes to chat. Whether it was Tom's enthusiasm for a just-completed campaign, prayer requests for friends and family, gratitude for a volunteer who would pray at his vigil for an entire day, or the new pro-life inroads he was making, we just had too much to discuss."

Most of us had no idea that in choosing a vigil site in Brighton, Tom didn't have much to work with. The Planned Parenthood referral center didn't even have a viable sidewalk for a 40 Days vigil. To pray outside the center, Tom and his volunteers stood in the mud and snow that often lingers into April in Michigan.

"The difficult vigil site surprised me when I finally found out about it," Steve said, "because Tom had never mentioned it. He was always too busy praising God."

Under Tom's leadership, the Brighton 40 Days for Life team celebrated the closure of the local Planned Parenthood office in April of 2016. Although his prayers and labor were answered, Tom's heart was too big to stop at that. Without an abortion business in town, he led one last campaign in a public park to make sure that "any abortion-minded women considering traveling out of town for an abortion would know they had options available."

Tom continued to lead even after being diagnosed with cancer. Early in 2017, Tom announced that the end was approaching. Knowing it would be their final conversation, Steve called Tom to thank him for his service, to share our gratitude for the opportunity to partner with him in the pro-life mission field, and to say goodbye. Though Steve fought back emotion in that conversation, Tom was unmistakably filled with the peace of Christ. When Steve asked how he was doing, Tom responded with his trademark joy: "How could I be anything other than great? My trust is in the Lord!"

In addition to his leadership roles with 40 Days for Life and Pregnancy Helpline, Tom served as an elder and deacon at First Presbyterian Church, advocated for his church's men's ministry, and participated in missions to Eastern Europe and Latin America.

Tom's life can be summed up in an email written just before he passed:

> Because of the last conference with our doctors my expected life span is someplace between a couple of weeks and a couple of months. After family discussion, we determined the best thing to do was to seek hospice and palliative care during my remaining days and enjoy my family. God opens doors that no one can open, and he shuts doors that should not be opened, and we trust totally in His saving Grace and His promises throughout scripture. I have often said, and I even have a tie that says, "This world is not my home." I am ready to be totally His and I praise God from whom all blessings flow. See you on the flip side.

Tom went to his home on May 31, 2017.

At every training session or speech I have given to local 40 Days for Life leaders, I start the same way: "Leading a 40 Days for Life is hard."

Some leaders laugh, but most are relieved to hear me say it. This is difficult work, but it's worth it. The difficulty forces us to focus on God and not on our own strength. This is the common thread of these heroes who raised a hand, faced rejection, and recruited volunteers to pray in front of places that take the lives of nearly 56 million children per year around the world. They relied on God for their campaigns. I'm asked all the time what the traits are for a great 40 Days for Life campaign, and my answer is simple—a leader who trusts God.

These leaders trusted God, and like all leaders, some of them saw the results on this side of heaven and some didn't. But we are not in this to see results; we are here to serve God—and, as Tom said, to go home and be totally his.

Local leaders for 40 Days for Life are sometimes told to "get a life." But they have a life indeed—a life they spend defending the lives of others, while remembering that this life is not their final home.

∾

"His master replied, 'Well done,
good and faithful servant!
You have been faithful with a few things;
I will put you in charge of many things.
Come and share your master's happiness!'"
MATTHEW 25:23

Gracious God, I thank you for the service of 40 Days for Life campaign leaders all over the world. Help me to more clearly understand the role you would have me play in saving the unborn and reaching out to women in crisis with alternatives and practical help. I too want to live a life that makes a lasting difference in this world. Today I pray for the encouragement and strength of every campaign leader. May those who are following their example be emboldened to stand firm for life. Amen.

A Mother's Plea

~

If there is no God,
everything is permitted.
—FYODOR DOSTOYEVSKY

BRITTANY SAT IN THE COURTROOM WEEPING, HER FACE HIDDEN IN her hands. How had it come to this? She looked up as the bailiff took her boyfriend, Harold, away to serve a life sentence in prison. For murder. She was only seventeen; he was nineteen.

"Please send me to jail too! Send me to jail too!" she cried, pleading with the judge. After all—what they had done, they had done together.

Brittany and Harold,[29] like many teens, had believed they were in love and happy. As time passed, they grew closer first emotionally and then physically. Eventually they began having sex, believing that, since they were in love, everything was okay.

Then Brittany got pregnant. And what happened after that, which became a national media story, showed just how cold our view of a human life can be.

Brittany and Harold decided they didn't want to have the baby. They didn't want the responsibility or the embarrassment, and they wanted to protect their future. The best plan of action, they decided, was to have Harold apply pressure to Brittany's stomach, thereby inducing premature labor. After several days of Harold pushing on Brittany's abdomen—with his foot—the inevitable happened. In the middle of the night, at twenty-one weeks pregnant, Brittany started having contractions and delivered not one baby but two—into the toilet.

Harold was charged with double homicide. Brittany faced no charges; a pregnant woman cannot be prosecuted for causing the deaths of her own fetuses for any reason, according to a Texas state law that went into effect Sept. 1, 2003.[30] Brittany testified in Harold's defense, explaining that they had done this together. But the law that protected Brittany did not protect Harold, and it treated the babies as what they are—human beings. Harold was charged and convicted on two counts of homicide and sentenced to life in prison.

The apostle Peter tells us that "the devil prowls around like a roaring lion looking for someone to devour" (1 Peter 5:8). He begins by influencing us in small choices, but he doesn't stop there. Little mistakes lead to bigger ones, gradually enticing us to be more and more under his influence.

The image of being devoured by a lion isn't the most uplifting image in the world, but Peter uses it to warn us and instill a healthy fear that will help keep us focused on eternity. Psalm 103 tells that a certain type of fear is good—"The LORD has compassion on those who fear him." In Psalm 111 we learn that "fear of the LORD is the beginning of wisdom" because it leads to humility. There is a God, and we are not him. That realization protects us and enables us to love others as God does, in a way that is much stronger and wiser than we would if left to our own devices. However, we are not to walk around frightened or afraid; quite the opposite. We should have faith and confidence in Christ, for he overcame the world. What Peter warns us of is a good fear—a fear of sin.

Our culture has lost its sense of sin. When we forget about sin, we forget that God loved us so much he sent his Son to die for that sin. When we don't acknowledge sin, we reject God's gift of mercy and lose respect for ourselves and other human beings. We are capable —no matter our age—of hurting ourselves, our neighbors, and our children by what we do or don't do. That reality overwhelmed Brittany as she sat in the courtroom.

No one grows up wanting to get pregnant out of wedlock or have an abortion. If these things happen, they originate in the small steps we don't realize are leading us in a direction we may not be able to come back from. The "roaring lions" don't come to us out in the open. They hide and plot and scheme before they viciously attack. This is exactly what Brittany and Harold faced in that courtroom. What had started off (or at least so it seemed to them) as a harmless and typical relationship was now devouring them. Not only had their decisions led to the death of two beautiful babies, but Harold had lost his freedom for the rest of his life by the time he was nineteen.

Harold and Brittany had fallen for the lie that they could do whatever they wanted, then take extreme action to protect their future.

When this story hit the media, the CEO of Planned Parenthood Gulf Coast, Peter Durkin, told the media the case was evidence of the government trying to give fetuses the same status as adult human beings. He didn't talk about the tragedy of these two babies losing their lives; he discussed instead the possibility that the government might use the case to try to ascribe humanity to the twins.

He also said, "Clearly for a woman in Lufkin, she has to have resources to seek those services out.... Abortion is getting less accessible."[31]

His comments reveal the cold and insensitive mindset required to justify abortion rights. A mentality that doesn't want to recognize this "choice" for what it is or treat the root of the problem. A mentality that mentions "abortion getting less accessible" after twins have died at home. A mentality that doesn't want to right the wrong—that just wants to call it by a different name. A mentality that wants to keep the wrong but make it sound better.

This is why nobody likes Sméagol from Lord of the Rings—his

exterior appearance matches what he really is on the inside. He's hard to look at and even harder to listen to. I have friends who do great Sméagol impressions, and they creep me out. He is a sad, hurting, cold, calculating little weasel. His exterior accurately represents his interior. But in our culture, Sméagol dresses well, has good talking points, and affirms our choices even if they're morally wrong.

Harold's attorney was interviewed on Fox News, and the reporter asked him, "Why didn't she just go for an abortion? Why do this grisly thing?"[32] The reporter's question implies that abortion is *not* grisly. The worst part of this tragedy is not that it was grisly, or even that it was illegal, but that two babies lost their lives.

It's as if we have learned to approve of evil as long as it seems clean or professional or is portrayed as a right. When we think like this, not only are we not fearing being devoured by the lion but we are like the proverbial frog around whom the cool water has slowly been heated to boiling and he doesn't realize it.

Yet nothing escapes our deepest human nature. When Brittany saw what she had done to these two beautiful babies, she didn't feel relief from being pregnant; rather, she was heartbroken. She was reminded, in a very difficult way, that those twins weren't problems that needed a solution—they were her children. That realization showed on her face in the courtroom as she wept for her children and asked to be sent to prison for their deaths. It is also evident in the fact that she still visits their graves. Abortion doesn't go away, no matter how grisly or clean we are told it is.

Brittany will carry the pain of this tragedy forever. Her reaction was appropriate for a mother—she wept and repented. She was honest enough to allow her sin to break her. The reaction from the CEO of Planned Parenthood was to accuse the government of trying to give fetuses the same rights as adult human beings. Whether you support abortion or not, using this situation to reaffirm the societal need for Planned Parenthood is an all-new level of disconnect. We should regret our sins not because we were unable to cover them up, but because we are sorry for them. Brittany's response was appropriate; Planned Parenthood's was disturbing.

But they didn't stop at that. Planned Parenthood also offered help to defend Harold and keep him out of prison. You may ask why. The answer: because his conviction acknowledged that the unborn should be defended under the law.

This story is powerful and disturbing because it's true. But there is one last episode in it that was not covered in the media and that shows the power of prayer. Brittany was not alone, and she did have options—and not the cold alternatives offered by Planned Parenthood. Rather, she had the faithful volunteers praying outside of the Planned Parenthood abortion facility near where she lived.

Even if society had "educated" her on abortion, she would have had an option at the very last moment to choose life for those twins. And if she had, there would have been no trial or bailiff or national news frenzy or cold comments from Planned Parenthood executives.

Those volunteers would have given her one last chance for a life full of matching outfits, double strollers, and dual birthday parties. A life of twice the blessing instead of twice the heartache.

That's why your prayers and presence matter. It could have mattered to Brittany, and it did matter to many other women in her town who turned around at the last moment and chose life for their babies. In fact, after a few more years of 40 Days for Life campaigns, Planned Parenthood Gulf Coast closed that abortion facility near where Brittany lived.

All of Planned Parenthood's sterile talking points are no match for the hope offered on a sidewalk. When we trust Christ's victory over death and stand up to the roaring lion, Christ's love prevails. We need to know the evil reality of abortion, but we need not be intimated by it.

There are hearts, minds, and souls at stake. That is our focus no matter where we live. There are women considering abortion right now in your community. You cannot stop them from having an abortion, but you can help them to stop themselves.

Your presence can show them that they are not alone and that they are loved. That is the real duty of a just society, and it will overcome the emptiness of abortion and end it where you live.

～

Finally, be strong in the Lord and in his mighty power. Put on the full armor of God, so that you can take your stand against the devil's schemes. For our struggle is not against flesh and blood, but against the rulers, against the authorities, against the powers of this dark world and against the spiritual forces of evil in the heavenly realms. Therefore put on the full armor of God, so that when the day of evil comes, you may be able to stand your ground, and after you have done everything, to stand.

EPHESIANS 6:10–13

Lord, please help me to be aware of the lion looking to devour me. Keep me safe and secure in your love and protection. Help me put on the full armor of God daily that I might be aware of the tricks of the devil and be prepared for the battle that lies ahead of me this day. Amen.

The Cajun Factor

~

The peculiar virtue of New Orleans
is a talent for everyday life
rather than a heroic deed.
—WALKER PERCY

CARLA LAY ON THE PROCEDURE TABLE AT THE ABORTION FACILITY looking up at the bright light. The only thing that stood between her and her abortion was an IV.

Over the past weeks, she had spent a lot of time thinking about this abortion and talking about it with her friends. She had convinced herself that it was the right decision, banishing any hesitancy by telling herself that of course she needed an abortion. After all, she was the victim of a sexual assault that resulted in this pregnancy.

Lying on the table, she went over all of her conversations, thoughts, and arguments about why this was necessary. She had made the appointment, arrived on time, and now braced herself for something that, on paper, made complete sense. But despite the logic, she had no peace.

"Ow!" she said as the nurse failed in her first attempt to slide a needle into Carla's vein for the IV.

She thought of the people she had seen praying on the sidewalk as she had driven into the parking lot. She'd briefly shared with them why she was there. They had offered to help, their concern plain on their faces. They had even teared up as she'd told them her experience. She was glad the people on the sidewalk were there for other women, but her situation was different. She was someone who needed an abortion.

She watched the nurse preparing her for the surgery that would alter her life forever. "Ow, ow!" Carla cried as the nurse made yet another attempt to set the IV.

"I'm sorry, ma'am," the nurse said, patting the inside of her elbow to bring up a useful vein. "We're having trouble finding a vein. Wait a moment."

The nurse left, and another came in. Wondering why she had no peace about the abortion, Carla watched the second nurse make attempt after attempt to find a vein. She thought of what would take place when the nurse *did* find a vein. She thought of those people outside who had wept for her and had offered help . . .

"Stop!" she yelled. "I can't do this. I can't do it."

She got off the table, dressed, walked out of the abortion facility, and stopped at the fence surrounding the facility to talk with the people she'd shared with on the way in. "This was a sign from God. I just can't do it," she explained.

～

Of the thousands of babies God has saved during a 40 Days for Life campaign, I have only heard of two where he decided to use an elusive blood vein to stop the abortion. The first time was in Baton Rouge, Louisiana.

A woman pulled up at the abortion facility and, over a period of time, entered and exited the building three times. Each time she left she would get into her car and get on her mobile phone and then go back in. After the third time, one of the long-time sidewalk counselors asked her, "Honey, what's going on?"

The woman replied, "I've been in three times and they tried to draw my blood all three times, but the needle won't go through my skin. After the third time, the phlebotomist said, 'Well, I guess your baby wants to live today.'"

Knowing that she was witnessing a miracle, the sidewalk counselor asked, "Do you want to see your baby, ma'am?"

"Yes, I do."

They went across the parking lot to the pregnancy center next door, a former bank that had been bought and renovated by a pro-lifer. There the woman saw her baby on the ultrasound monitor and chose life.

What would have happened if that counselor hadn't been there on the sidewalk that day?

~

In Louisiana, it feels as if the pro-life community has used every moment of time and sought every lifesaving resource to end abortion at the local level.

Let me tell you about the state. I know quite a bit from personal experience. My mom grew up in New Orleans, and my stepdad is from Shreveport, so we grew up going to Louisiana often, and my travels there since have been frequent. One thing I can tell you for certain is that I really feel sorry for people who have never eaten fried alligator. It's delicious. And there's something satisfying about eating a creature that could've eaten you.

Louisiana is different, and many inside and outside the state want to keep it that way. It is one of those states where their state pride seems to come before anything else. They love crawfish, alligator, boudin, football, fishing, and jokes about Louisiana. The state has a large population, major college campuses, and all the fun and spice that come with New Orleans.

After Hurricane Katrina hit in 2005, Planned Parenthood of Houston merged with Planned Parenthood of New Orleans to form Planned Parenthood Gulf Coast, which is now the fourth-largest Planned Parenthood affiliate in America. To oppose a system that large may sound daunting to most, but Louisiana also has great pro-life leadership.

I'll introduce you to two such leaders.

One is a young man named Ben Clapper, who went to work in a state that needed a pro-life jolt. He first brought 40 Days for Life to Louisiana in 2008 and planted seeds that would bear great fruit for years. Not only did Ben, a husband and father of four girls, lead the 40 Days for Life campaign that helped close one abortion facility, but he eventually founded Students for Life in Louisiana and became the director of Louisiana Right to Life. From there he helped spread 40 Days for Life at every level throughout the state. From the sidewalk to the high school to the state capitol, Ben has been instrumental in making Louisiana one of the most pro-life states in America.

Louisiana is also fortunate to have Chris Davis. Chris brought 40 Days for Life to Shreveport-Bossier City. After I spoke at the Ark-La-Tex Pregnancy Center banquet in 2011, I went to Chris's vigil. All the pregnancy center directors knew and respected Chris and had seen many women come into their centers year after year thanks to his work. I listened as many people that night told me that Chris had led many campaigns, worked with an organization called Sidewalk Advocates to offer alternatives, and worked with pregnancy centers to help women for many years.

Chris is an easy guy to like, but hidden beneath his easygoing nature is great fortitude. After the 2016 fall campaign, Chris said he needed a break and would skip the spring campaign. We understood completely. But Chris's version of taking time off was different from most people's. We were surprised to see that he applied to lead the spring Bossier City campaign after all. He was going to "give one more go."

One more was what Chris wanted to give, and one more is all Chris got. In the spring of 2017 the Bossier City Medical Suite abortion center, a facility that had done over ten thousand abortions, was closing for good, becoming the eighty-fifth abortion facility to go out of business.

"It all starts on the sidewalk," Chris said. 40 Days for Life "is peaceful, and that's why it changes hearts. These 40 Days for Life folks are on the ground with us, getting their boots dirty. That's why this works."

I went back to Louisiana for the celebration event (yes, we had alligator afterwards) on a beautiful spring day. We prayed and celebrated outside a cold building with no front windows and a sterile sign on the door that read "Enter in the back." Only an abortion facility could be so unwelcoming. And now, thanks to Chris's fortitude, they wouldn't welcome anyone else through the front *or* back door.

Chris had gone to work in the state he loves and the city he lives in; he kept it local and focused. He told the crowd, "You may not meet anyone on the Supreme Court in your lifetime, but I guarantee you can help stop abortion when, on the sidewalk, you meet the women and men before they enter these places. You will meet women in need, and that is what will change our country."

The Bossier City closing represents yet another closing in a state that has seen a number of them. And as those abortion facilities closed, Planned Parenthood announced plans to build an abortion facility in New Orleans. They expected a flooded market with many women driving to New Orleans for abortions. What they didn't expect was the response from Archbishop Gregory Aymond. Archbishop Aymond strongly opposed the building of the new facility. The archbishop publicly stated he would "boycott every person or organization" involved in the construction of the 7,000-square-foot facility. Archbishop Aymond was clear: "We cannot cooperate with evil."[33]

His courageous effort and leadership delayed the opening as subcontractors started to bail on helping Planned Parenthood. Nothing is worse for business in New Orleans than having the archbishop take a stand against you.

The Planned Parenthood megacenter did eventually open in New Orleans, but so did the Woman's New Life Center, which provides abortion-vulnerable women a real choice. They report that when a 40 Days for Life campaign is going on, visits to the pregnancy help center increase significantly.

It seems laughable now, but in the first few years of 40 Days for Life's existence, we couldn't get anything going in Louisiana. The campaign was growing from California to New Jersey but not in Louisiana. It took local leaders stepping up and focusing on the most important level—the local level. Every moment matters at the local level. The local level is where you meet people being directed to the back door of a windowless abortion facility that has done ten thousand abortions. The local level is where you meet the best of people. People who eat alligator, take care of their neighbors, and refuse to believe that abortion is here to stay. The local level is where you can represent Christ when a nurse can't find a vein. The local level is where you have a hands-on chance to save a life. Abortion isn't measured by decades or court cases; it's measured by the number of abortions done daily. When the local level is your focus, and you're willing to show up, God can and does change hearts. As Chris said in his great Louisianan drawl, "It all starts on the sidewalks."

∾

Now listen, you who say, "Today or tomorrow we will go to this or that city, spend a year there, carry on business and make money." Why, you do not even know what will happen tomorrow. What is your life? You are a mist that appears for a little while and then vanishes. Instead, you ought to say, "If it is the Lord's will, we will live and do this or that."

JAMES 4:13–17

God, I pray that I would not look at the big picture and be discouraged. Help me to concentrate on the local opportunities to show up, to lead, to pray. To focus on what I can do here in my own town, my own city. I thank you that you don't require me to do great big things, but that you help me see that small things can make a great big difference. Amen.

Saving England

~

All the greatest things are simple,
and many can be expressed in a single word:
freedom; justice; honour; duty; mercy; hope.
—SIR WINSTON CHURCHILL

IT WAS FUNNY YET SO DISAPPOINTING, AND I THOUGHT ROBERT Colquhoun's head was going to explode.

During one of my visits to 40 Days for Life events in England, we had just enough time for a whirlwind trip to Buckingham Palace before my flight left. Robert, the international campaign director, drove his small car seventy miles (I mean kilometers) per hour to get me there. We jumped out of the car and, lo and behold, there were the iconic Queen's Guards, standing attentive.

As Robert took my picture in front of the guards, I said something to him and one of the guards heard my American accent. "From across the pond, eh, chap?" he said.

Automatically I said, "Yes." Then I realized what had just happened. The guard had broken his legendary silence. Pointing at the guard, who was now looking straight forward as if nothing had happened, I said to Robert, "Wait—he's not supposed to talk. That's the whole point, right?"

Robert couldn't believe it either. "Extremely unprofessional," he said. "Should never have happened." He spoke as if the guard had desecrated a church. Personally, I thought it was a great moment in American-British relations.

It was also another sign of how much Robert loves his country and wants to preserve it. Robert has also inspired thousands of his fellow countrymen and women to try to preserve British values. And they need it. The British are following a road that isn't very British. They have implemented buffer zones around abortion facilities—where no pro-life opinion can be expressed publicly. This is an attack on the free-speech ideal that Western democracies are built upon. Similar laws have been proposed and unanimously rejected by the Supreme Court of the United States. But in both England and Canada, these free-speech limitations—targeting only pro-life speech in public—now exist.

Robert has never been intimidated. He has that iron will and stiff upper lip that we all love in the British. He also knows how to laugh, and he loves his family dearly. He met his wife at the closing party when he first brought 40 Days for Life to England. There have been a few "40 Days for Life marriages" in London resulting from people beginning a relationship during a campaign and then deciding to tie the knot. Trying to save babies from abortion and getting married to have more children is a great way to change the culture.

And Robert is changing the culture. As you'll see when you read his reports below from the front lines in the United Kingdom. The rest of the chapter is written by Robert in his own words.

~

Ealing

During one campaign in Ealing, West London, at a location where 8,353 abortions (174 over twenty-weeks gestation) were performed in 2014, twenty-three women have changed their minds and kept their babies. Astonishingly, the building where these abortions took place used to be a Christian house of healing where a plaque honouring Michael the Archangel is still attached to the wall.

In 1929, Miss Dorothy Kerin, whose motto was, "Where God guides, God provides," opened the house as a place of spiritual healing, calling it Chapel House. She held weekly healing services where many were reportedly healed. She adopted nine children after the war and kept the house until 1948.

The fact that Chapel House was founded as a house of prayer and healing and is now home to an abortion provider is a tragic betrayal of the life and mission of Dorothy Kerin. A place of healing and the restoration of life has become a place where life is destroyed.

Scotland

Rose, our leader in Scotland, confided to me, "This is a breakthrough for the pro-life movement in Scotland." She said that people are buzzing with the excitement of it all. It is utterly mind-blowing.

Rose started praying outside the National Health Service Queen Elizabeth II super hospital in Glasgow, where two midwives, Mary Doogan and Connie Wood, refused to supervise staff involved in abortions. They were subject to a high-profile legal case of conscientious objection, and eventually the midwives lost.[34]

Today 40 Days for Life has spread all over Scotland, supported by Bishops. University students complained in Aberdeen about pro-life posters in the chaplaincy, but the Bishop of Aberdeen defended 40 Days for Life, saying that vigils are "peaceful, yet poignant reminders of the tragic reality of abortion."

A Scottish trade union congress general secretary, Grahame Smith, said 40 Days for Life must not "intimidate" abortion patients or "harass" hospital staff, citing support from government leaders. A shame nobody managed to tell poor Grahame that 40 Days for Life only organises peaceful and prayerful vigils. In Edinburgh, volunteers reported that a lot of healing was happening at the vigil and many passersby were sharing their stories and experiences with past abortions.

Persecution

Some students in England have a strong attachment to abortion. At first, the students would play jokes pretending to be God asking prayer volunteers to go away. They would then pretend they were giving up their pro-life protest for Lent. Later, they would pour buckets of water over volunteers as a prank—which only helped to get people more involved in pro-life work. After that, they would start organisations to ridicule, troll, and send death threats towards pro-lifers involved in this work. On one evening they decided to troll an event with glasses of urine to pour over volunteers.

Some abortion providers also played a hand in ridiculing and trying to discredit pro-life activism. Marie Stopes sent letters threatening legal action to pro-life groups. Later, some abortion groups started campaigns to ban any pro-life activity outside abortion centres on spurious grounds of harassment and intimidation. Abortion providers have cleverly framed the abortion debate and will happily play the victim without the slightest of provocations. The British Pregnancy Advisory Service (BPAS), the largest British abortion charity, ran a buffer zone campaign for many years, publicly campaigning to ban pro-life prayer vigils—stunning testimony of 40 Days for Life effectiveness.

I have learnt that the reason abortion providers have been so vehemently opposed to prayer vigils is that they are detrimental to the business of abortion. One BPAS employee walked up to prayer volunteers to tell them, "Your prayers are obviously working because the girls aren't keeping the appointments."

The ultimate sign of flattery is imitation. When pro-abortion activists started to copy pro-life activists by organising a "40 Days of Choice" campaign, we took it as a compliment. As part of the charade, pro-abortion activists would bring along cakes to give to the abortion centres as a sign of their appreciation for their work. A few jokers would bring Jelly Babies as a cheeky gesture.

Some abortion providers were willing to use their friends in the media to write all kinds of obscenities against pro-lifers. With lies and allegations of harassment and intimidation in the public sphere, the ridicule and harassment of pro-lifers only intensified. Pro-abortion activists would throw horse dung at pro-lifers as their sign of appreciation to their witness.

Some individuals claimed that the 'rights my mother fought for are being attacked.' I didn't have the heart to tell them what would have happened if her mother had exercised those rights. The greatest irony was that while pro-abortion groups continue to cry harassment and intimidation, the only groups on the receiving end of such behaviour were the pro-life groups. This was made manifest when a group of three hundred people shouted at the top of their voices, "Stop harassing women!" How ironic that half the audience they were speaking to was women.

Ann Furedi, the CEO of the abortion provider BPAS, challenged one of the pro-lifers present who had brought her children to the prayer vigil. She suggested that because the weather was so cold, this could be a cruel act towards the children. The pro-lifer replied, "Yes. But these children are alive." The children who enter the abortion centre do not come out alive.

Of all the campaigns in the United Kingdom, Cardiff received perhaps the highest amount of abuse. A pro-abortion group organised a permanent protest of the vigil, inciting religious hatred on a regular basis. The abortion centre is on a busy street with lots of shops, night clubs, cafes and offices.

However, the volunteers in Cardiff had a delightful encounter that instilled great hope. A few weeks into their campaign the volunteers were approached by a young man who calmly asked what they were doing. They replied they were praying for an end to abortion. The man told them that his girlfriend was inside the clinic, discussing and planning her abortion. He told them that she had aborted a previous baby and that they also had other children. They were living in temporary accommodations and were being pressured by social services to abort the baby that his girlfriend was carrying, though they wanted the baby.

The volunteers offered the couple support. Weeks later the organisers received an email that the couple had visited the crisis pregnancy centre and were keeping the baby.

Saving England

Maria was a lady who continued to vacillate between the idea of aborting or planning how to keep her baby. The baby was unplanned. Her relationship, though it had lasted for years, had ended a month before she found out she was pregnant. Now her ex had come back to make sure she had the abortion. Maria had grown up in a single-parent home and didn't want the same for her child. But she hated the idea of abortion. Maria was also in the probation period of her new job and could not survive financially if she lost that job.

The abortion facility was closed when she tried to book her appointment, but as she approached twenty weeks she panicked and tried again to book an abortion, only to find that the operating theatre had suffered an accidental fire and was unusable. She was delighted when she passed the twenty-four week limit as she believed she would no longer feel under pressure to abort. BPAS offered her an abortion and 'pro-choice' groups offered to defend her right to abortion. But pro-lifers offered her unconditional help. Maria chose life for her baby. Eventually the ex came to see an ultrasound of the child and is now supporting her to bring up their child. She has now got a permanent position with her firm and is delighted with her child.

～

I had the privilege of meeting Tyson, a baby spared from abortion, thanks to God's grace and the work of 40 Days for Life volunteers in London. It was life transforming to know that had help not been offered to the mother, Gloria, she would have gone ahead with an abortion. Sometimes it seems rare to see the fruits of pro-life work, but this was my best pro-life experience ever.

Gloria is from France and moved to London looking for work. She found herself pregnant after a relationship broke up, and she felt that, with no help available, she had no choice but to have an abortion. She booked an appointment with Marie Stopes in Central London. On the day of her appointment, she met Siobhan outside the Marie Stopes centre, who explained that there were Christians available to offer help, counseling, financial support, housing, encouragement and friendship. In short, if there was any tangible need that she had, she would be supported.

Gloria made a tremendous and courageous decision to keep her baby. She went for the appointment with Marie Stopes, and the only thing they were able to offer was an abortion. She was booked to have the abortion but never turned up to the appointment on the day.

There is no doubt that it was a very hard decision for her to keep her baby. But it is clear that today she is happy that she made the right decision. No matter how hard things become, she has a joy that cannot be taken away. She continues to be supported today. Thanks to her bravery, God's grace, and the work of 40 Days for Life, Tyson is alive today.

Ten Years

As we approach ten years of 40 Days for Life in England, there is hope for the first time in a long time. After three thousand hours of public prayer, BPAS closed its central London abortion facility without explanation. Never in our wildest imagination did we think that in a secularised country such as the United Kingdom, an abortion facility would close.

For years, counterdemonstrations protesting our prayer vigils had taken place there. Yet on April 26, 2014, the day after the lease of the abortion doctor expired, a prayer service was held inside the building. All the noise that had taken place outside that building was silenced with the peace of the Prince of Peace.

I can't emphasize enough how these small and large victories did not seem possible in my beloved England. But alongside our friends across the pond in America, and in nearly fifty countries around the world, we have no doubt that the worldwide prayer and fasting is helping nations take part in the beginning of the end of abortion.

ROBERT COLQUHOUN

∽

As for me, I watch in hope for the LORD,
I wait for God my Savior; my God will hear me.
MICAH 7:7

Holy God, I pray for my brothers and sisters in England who are on the front lines of the struggle for life. Thank you for the victories I just read about. Now I pray for the needs. Lord, help strike down the buffer zones that restrict the freedom of speech of my pro-life colleagues. Encourage the 40 Days for Life volunteers as they endure persecution. Let their godly responses shine your light into the darkness. Continue to strengthen and embolden Robert and all involved in pro-life work in England. Amen.

A "D" in Speech Class

~

Act, and God will act.
—JOAN OF ARC

THE FIRST TIME I SPOKE AT A CHURCH TO ASK PEOPLE TO PRAY AT
an abortion facility was a total disaster. I was twenty-two years old.
Marilisa was with me, sitting behind a table, waiting for the droves
of new volunteers I knew were sure to overwhelm her with sign-
ups after my impressive performance as an orator. After all, I knew
exactly what I was going to say and how I was going to say it. I had
two minutes to share our local abortion situation, our mission, and
then build up to my big finish. "Have no fear! You can do this! With
God we will end abortion in Bryan/College Station, Texas."

Well, at least that's how I'd rehearsed it. But that's not what came
out. Instead, my tone got very stern and I blurted, "You can do this!
You *will* do this!" Instead of correcting myself, I walked offstage. It
sounded bad, it looked bad, it *was* bad. As I took my seat, I realized
I had just yelled at the people in this church—most of whom were
over seventy.

I was upset with myself. We had worked hard to get those two
minutes, and I had completely blown it. When I looked at Marilisa, she was laughing. "What was that ending?" she asked when I
reached her.

Embarrassed, I wasn't laughing. "I don't know. That's just what
came out." As we sat there waiting for volunteers to sign up (none

did—shocker!), Marilisa giggled and I slumped in humiliation. For the rest of that night (and many days since) Marilisa has looked at me and said, "You can do this! You *will* do this!"

In the years since, I've given thousands of speeches and talks across the United States and internationally, and I've made sure to never again end any of them sounding like a prison warden reprimanding his inmates. However, I still sometimes experience that feeling of nervousness before speaking about something that is sure to hit a nerve, no matter what church or event is being addressed.

That's how Kathy Forck felt in 2009 as she got ready to speak at St. Peter Catholic Church in Jefferson City, where she would ask people to pray with her at the Planned Parenthood abortion facility in Columbia, Missouri.

"I am the shyest person you've ever met," Kathy explains. "I never wanted to speak in front of people. Although I was always an A or B student, I took a 'D' in my speech class because I refused to speak in front of people," Kathy said.

That morning as she waited to be introduced in church, she offered her weakness and fear to God. *Okay, God,* she prayed silently, *if this is what you want me to do, I'll get up there.*

∾

When Kathy had moved to Missouri just a couple of years earlier, she had asked God the best question anyone can ask: "What would you like me to do?"

Abortion came to mind. Kathy wasn't sure why. She'd been involved in pro-life activities in the past, but only in minor ways. Still, she and her husband, Mike, went to the Columbia Planned Parenthood and stood outside the ugly building. Kathy says, "It just came to me that we could pray." And so they did.

Not knowing what else she could do, she continued to faithfully pray in front of the facility on abortion days. Soon she met other like-minded people, and they started meeting there to pray together. This was before Kathy had even heard of 40 Days for Life.

One hot August day, a young woman emerged from the facility, sat on the curb, and cried.

Kathy gently called her over and handed her a bottle of water. "Hey, what's wrong?"

The woman said through her tears, "I don't really want to have this abortion."

"Then don't," Kathy said gently. "Where's the dad? What does he say?"

"He was here earlier, but he left," she said, looking back at the facility. "He says it's up to me."

"Well, there's your answer. You don't want to do it."

"But you don't understand. I'm not married. This would kill my mother." The woman went on in some detail about the short- and long-term problems an abortion would create for her mother.

Just then the boyfriend strode up, and Kathy feared things might go south. "Shannon, what's going on?" he demanded. "Who's this crazy lady?"

Kathy said casually, "Hey, congratulations!" She tossed the young man a bottle of water. "Have a drink. You're going to have a baby!"

Rather than the argument she expected, Kathy watched as the couple looked at each other with that beautiful look that a woman gives when she tells her husband, "We're going to have a baby." Crisis averted.

Through Shannon's remaining months of pregnancy, Kathy kept in touch with them. When the baby was born, she asked, "What did you name him?"

"We named him Luke. I don't know where that name came from, because I don't know anybody named Luke."

Kathy's heart went still. She congratulated Shannon and went to see the baby. Then she called her mother-in-law, Lori. "Mom, guess what? That young girl Shannon I told you about had her baby. She named him Luke." Lori started to cry.

In August, when Kathy had first met Shannon, Lori had spiritually adopted an unborn baby at risk of abortion. She prayed for this baby daily, and she even named the baby after her husband who had died a couple years before: Luke.

It was a key moment for Kathy. "That experience made me feel that I had to be doing more. So my heart was ripe when I saw a media story about 40 days for Life." She told six friends about the campaign, and they said that if Kathy would lead it, they would fill all the hours. So Kathy signed up and got ready to start her first campaign, just a few weeks away.

Those six friends committed to bring 40 Days for Life to Columbia, working under their now-fearless, D-in-speech-class leader. As promised, they covered all the hours themselves, unconcerned that they didn't fill the sidewalk with people. "We felt that, if we had somebody there during all the hours, then we were doing what we were supposed to do," Kathy said.

It was their presence that alerted the public to the quiet fact that abortions were being performed in Columbia. Before Kathy Forck and 40 Days for Life came along, Planned Parenthood in Columbia was aborting about eight hundred babies every year. Kathy and her team began the forty-day campaign armed with information about abortion, pregnancy centers, adoption options, and doctors who would help. Soon babies were being saved, and Planned Parenthood's abortion business was in trouble.

The nationwide abortion doctor shortage was hitting Columbia hard. Abortions require licensed physicians, and often those physicians don't want to travel to wherever the abortion numbers are down. They need to make a minimum amount of income per trip to make the trip financially worthwhile.[35] Many such "circuit rider" abortion doctors want easy trips with no one praying outside, and Kathy had created quite the opposite in Columbia. By this time her campaigns were drawing fifteen, twenty, twenty-five participants at a time, faithfully praying outside the building. As a result, Planned Parenthood struggled to get a doctor to commit time to Columbia.

Kathy said, "When they lost the first doctor, we thought, *Oh! We've done our job!* But they found another doctor." In the first three and a half years of Kathy's campaigns, Planned Parenthood lost seven abortion doctors. One of them lasted one day. Others were there for three or four months, then quit.

Then Columbia went three years with no abortion doctor at all.

Although that Planned Parenthood facility had stopped doing abortions, they were still open, and Kathy knew what so many refuse to believe—if you have a Planned Parenthood in town, there is a good chance they will begin doing abortions, either chemical or surgical. Unfortunately, she was right. Planned Parenthood finally found an abortion doctor to come to Columbia. But Kathy didn't get discouraged, nor did she slow down. She still had volunteers out there praying every day the facility was open—year-round, not just during the two annual 40 Days for Life campaigns!

Kathy says, "I thank God for our people. They have perseverance. They have faith. They trust God for what's going to happen. They are there in the heat, the snow, the rain, the sleet—everything. Nothing deters them. Even when passersby yell at us, 'Get a job!' or give us the one-finger salute, we know that God is working and that babies are going to be saved."

The prayer volunteers never know what's going to prompt a person to turn around at the last moment and choose life for their baby. It could be a word, a prayer, a volunteer who resembles an important person in their life, or any number of things.

Once, a young woman spoke briefly with Kathy about options before going inside the building to get her abortion. Kathy immediately began to pray that she would change her mind.

After a bit, the woman came out. Crossing the parking lot, she told Kathy, "I decided I'm going to keep my baby."

Ecstatic, Kathy said, "Do you mind if I ask you what changed your mind?"

She said, "You see that priest over there?"

"Yeah."

"When I saw him, I realized this wasn't right. You see that little boy with the beads in his hand?"

"Yeah."

"When I saw that little boy, I thought, *You know what? There are good men out here and I'm going to find one.* It gave me hope. So I'm keeping my baby."

The priest and the little boy didn't know their presence would save a baby that day, but they gave God a chance to use them as a sign of his hope in front of a facility that thrives on despair.

Many times people have stopped Kathy in church to tell her that because of the volunteers' presence, they now have a grandchild. Twice fathers have told her that a daughter planned to get an abortion and nothing the parents said would deter her. Yet the daughter came home, still pregnant, because of the prayer warriors in front of the building.

There are far more stories than Kathy is aware of. But she does know that, because people took a chance and said, "I can pray," there are no longer eight hundred babies dying every year at that facility. "Look what God has done," she says in awe. "He has carried me in this and sent me faithful followers like Mary Hoffmeyer, Bonnie Lee, Judy Bax, and two men who are always praying on their knees—Jim Imhoff and Leo Steck. These are the saints of God."

∽

One day, after years of leading the campaign, Kathy paid a visit to her proud father. As she shared the victories and trials happening in Columbia, he looked at her soberly and said something that stunned her: "You were almost aborted."

Kathy couldn't believe it. "What do you mean? We're Catholic."

Her dad said, "When Mom was pregnant with you, there was an Rh incompatibility, which can be harmful to the mother and the baby. The doctor said, 'Isabelle, think of it this way—you're not really pregnant. I'm going to remove some tissue and you'll be fine.'

"Your mother told him, 'Yes, I *am* pregnant.' Then she walked out of his office and got another doctor. You were born seven months later."

Kathy said, "I always knew Mom was the most intelligent woman in the world. I just didn't realize that I owe her my life in more ways than one."

Then her dad told her something even more shocking. "When your mom was sixteen, she was sexually assaulted. She became pregnant, and her parents forced her to have an abortion. She suffered greatly from that. She dropped out of church. She dropped out of school. She never forgot that child. She has cried for that baby all our married life. So when that doctor said, 'I'm just going to remove some tissue,' your mother knew exactly what he meant."

Kathy sat in amazement. Abortion had impacted her own family in profound ways, and she was just now discovering it after she had worked so hard to save hundreds of babies.

Her father smiled. "When Mom and I got married, we said to each other, 'We want to have as many children as God will send us.'" And they did. Kathy is the third of their ten children.

∼

When, in 2009, Kathy stood before that congregation at St. Peter Catholic Church, she couldn't help but think of her D in speech class. Though she was terribly nervous to speak that night, she offered her best to God and walked up to the microphone.

After her talk, a young man came up to her and said, "Are you going to be at Columbia Planned Parenthood this Thursday?"

She said, "Yes, we always go."

"My girlfriend is going to have an abortion," he said, clearly in distress. "I can't get her to change her mind. Can you help me?"

Kathy said, "We can pray. We can try to talk to her. We'll do everything we can."

Kathy reached out to her friend Mary in St. Louis, giving her the woman's phone number. Mary called her, and the woman chose life.

Kathy's response was to praise God and ask, *What if we hadn't given that talk at church that day?*

When we offer our weaknesses and frailties to Jesus Christ, he can change us and our world. He chose simple fishermen and sinners, asking them to hand him their weaknesses so that he could draw the world to himself. He didn't conquer death through the elites, or the wealthy, or the intellectuals. He conquered death with suffering, sweat, and blood.

Kathy is a servant, and a humble one. When I told her I was putting her story into this book, her response was, "I'm so glad to hear there will be another book! I can't wait to read about my fellow leaders. They are the heroes, the selfless people who give so much. They are an inspiration to me."

They are indeed. And she just happens to be one of them without realizing it.

∿

Whenever you are arrested and brought to trial,
do not worry beforehand about what to say.
Just say whatever is given you at the time,
for it is not you speaking, but the Holy Spirit.
MARK 13:11

Jesus, I am weak and afraid. But I want to serve you as you ask. Please take my fears and change them to trust. Remind me that your power is found in my weakness, and my failures are not obstacles to you fulfilling your work. Thank you that all you ask is that I be willing to listen and obey, and in that you can do great work. Amen.

Birthdays Are Full of Drama

~

Mountaintops are for views and inspiration,
but fruit is grown in the valleys.
—REVEREND BILLY GRAHAM

"SHAWN, WILL YOU EVER VISIT OUR CAMPAIGN?" PATTI FLORES wrote me in an email. "How about if the abortion facility where we campaign shuts down? Surely you'll come then, yes? I'm not going to cut you any slack. After all, this is my nineteenth campaign." Patti doesn't mince words. She says what's on her mind, and that's what I love about her.

During the many years Patti ran campaigns in California's San Fernando Valley, she wondered why I had never visited despite continued invitations. She pointed out that Steve Karlen had visited her, and so had Dr. Haywood Robinson. She was right. I really had no excuse. I had visited 450 campaign locations, but Patti's was not one of them. I had visited most campaigns in California, many of them near Patti's. But Patti kept getting missed, despite the fact that she ran one of the best 40 Days for Life campaigns in the world and had helped start other campaign locations as well.

Patti is dedicated and, thankfully, she has a great sense of humor. When I would see her at other 40 Days for Life events, she would always remind me of my absence at her vigil and joke that I was avoiding her. One day I said, "You're right, I actually really don't like you and am doing everything possible to not come to your vigil."

She only laughed. But I knew her feistiness was justified, so after that email I scheduled a trip.

Patti is a remarkable advocate for the unborn. She is a single mom who works full time, yet pours every ounce of her energy into pro-life activities. If there is anything pro-life going on within five hundred miles, Patti is there. As a result, nearly everyone in the California pro-life community knows and respects her. She may participate in many pro-life events, but the 40 Days for Life campaign in the San Fernando Valley is her baby. She often prays all day on the sidewalks during her campaigns but still finds time to return every call and email. Her campaigns routinely involve hundreds of people, including a dedicated group of sidewalk counselors, and enjoy great support from local clergy.

With all these resources and dedicated help, I don't understand why, after twenty-one campaigns, with a pregnancy center conveniently located across the street from the abortion facility, that the abortion facility is still open. Many times I've hoped God would close the facility—if for nothing else, to reward hard-working Patti. But he is clearly not yet done with her at that location.

It's often said that the devil has two office locations—hell and Los Angeles. In spite of that, Patti jokes with me about her campaign's "lack of drama." According to her, nothing big ever happens. There has never been an abortion worker who had a conversion and walked out of a facility, or a sign that went up announcing the abortion facility was closing the next day.

But I think Patti is wrong. I think she's overlooking the drama of every campaign she has ever run—the drama of saving lives. She has worked tirelessly to get people out to the sidewalks. And those people's prayers have saved lives. Her campaigns save babies—often.

Here are a few examples of what Patti does not consider drama.

Pastor Erik from First Lutheran Church joins many other pro-lifers every week to pray and counsel in front of Planned Parenthood in Van Nuys. One day his prayer partner, Mike, was there when a man pulled up and said, "Keep standing out here." The man got out of his car and told his story. "Four years ago, I insisted that my girlfriend abort our child. I took her to the clinic at Sepulveda (Patti's 40 Days for Life vigil location). There are often prayer volunteers there. I spat at the prayer volunteer, then took my girlfriend inside for her abortion." The man stopped to gain his composure, "But once we were inside, I started to shake. I couldn't go through with it. I changed my mind, and I have to show you people the result."

This proud and repentant father cried as he took his phone from his pocket and showed Mike the picture of his "princess," a beautiful four-year-old girl named Hayden. The man hugged Mike and thanked him, and Mike responded, "Praise God!" After the father returned to his car, he looked back at these men and said intensely, "Guys, don't ever stop doing what you do."

Don't you love stories like that? They can keep you going for a lifetime in the pro-life movement. If we save just one baby, it's worth all the long hours and difficulties involved in standing vigil. And Patti is full of these stories. Here's another.

"While several of us were praying at the abortion facility, a woman drove up next to us. She told us that the previous year she had been very distraught and confused about her pregnancy. She made three separate appointments to have an abortion here. She changed her mind every time she came, saying she couldn't do it—and it was because she always saw people praying on the corner in front of the abortion facility.

"She rolled down her back window to show us her beautiful baby boy, Matthew. I asked how old he was. 'One! He turns one tomorrow! He's the best thing that ever happened to me!' She looked up at us and said, 'Keep doing what you're doing.'"

And another.

"A woman named Gabriela walked up to the prayer volunteers and said that ten years before, she had been very far from God. She had two children and had also already had two abortions when she came to the facility to have another abortion. She changed her clothes and lay on the procedure table, bracing herself for her third abortion. As she lay there, she remembered the people outside praying on the corner and realized they were praying for *her*. She couldn't go through with the abortion. And now she has a ten-year-old girl.

"A lot had happened to her in those ten years, she told us. Now she feels close to God. She turned to walk away, then looked back at us and said, 'I am very grateful to all of you who stand out here—keep going.'"

∽

In the fall of 2017, I flew to LA and landed, for what seems like the thousandth time, at LAX. Except this time I was going to speak at a huge event Patti had planned for her 40 Days for Life campaign. The bishop and almost two hundred people were expected to attend a pizza party at the pregnancy center across the street from her abortion facility.

I rented a car and drove toward the Valley. As I approached the pregnancy center, I realized I had a few minutes to spare—time to use a restroom and grab some coffee. I pulled into a small, jam-packed coffee shop. I didn't want to risk being late to Patti's vigil, so I left. I drove around the back of the coffee shop, expecting to find an exit to pull back onto the street, but the only way out was through a slim alley lined with fences and trash cans. This wasn't the greatest part of Los Angeles, but I wasn't concerned. I've traveled around the world and have been to hundreds of cities. I am a well-seasoned traveler and, on this day, I was too comfortable. I drove down the alley.

Halfway through it, a massive German shepherd sprinted in front of my car. There was nowhere to swerve, and it was too late to stop. I ran over the dog. I felt terrible. And here came the man I assumed was the owner, coming out of his backyard.

I got out of the car. "I'm sorry, sir. I didn't see—" Then I noticed that his body language didn't exactly match mine.

"You hit my dog, you—" he yelled. (Use your imagination to fill in the blanks.) He gathered the injured dog into his arms.

I jumped into the car and locked the doors. Immediately, three more men came out with another German shepherd. The dog barked viciously as the men surrounded my car and pounded on the windows demanding I get out.

This ain't good, I thought as they pounded and screamed through the window. There would be no reasoning with these folks.

Then I realized, *No one knows where I am. Not Marilisa, not Patti, not a staff member.* I had gone off the beaten path and was paying for it. I called Matt Britton for a three-second conversation. He told me to call 911, which I did. The 911 dispatcher could hear the men beating the windows of my car and told me that they were sending an officer and to hang on the line and not to get out of the car under any circumstances.

In the meantime, Matt had called a friend of his who is the sheriff of Los Angeles County. He told Matt to tell me not to get out no matter what. Now I was going back and forth on the phone between Matt and 911, who was unable to tell me how close the officer was. Matt was on the line when I looked in my rearview mirror and said, "Oh no."

"What?" Matt said.

"They went and got three more guys. I gotta get out of here."

"Yes, you do! Get back on with dispatch and tell them you're leaving. You can't wait any longer."

However, there were three guys in front of the car blocking my way.

The dispatcher told me to stay on the line, crack the window, and ask the men in front of the car to come to the window. There was little chance the dispatcher's suggestion was going to work, but I was encouraged to try it anyway.

I calmly cracked the window and called to them. When the men ran to my window, I sped off down the alley.

The dispatcher told me to come to the police station to describe the men who had surrounded my car. "I can't," I said. "I'm late for an event where I'm speaking." I pleaded until it was agreed that I could come by after the event.

I called Steve Karlen, explained, and then asked him to call Patti and tell her I would be late. "Well, this is a first for 40 Days for Life," Steve said.

"Yes, it is. But I don't want to run for my life from a back alley in LA only to have Patti kill me when I arrive late to her vigil."

We laughed.

The event went great. However, it was the first time I've spoken and announced that I had to go to the police station afterwards.

∽

In the spring of 2018, Steve Karlen returned to Patti's campaign and then went to Yvonne Viramontes's neighboring campaign. (I wrote about Yvonne in *40 Days for Life*.) Yvonne got involved years ago thanks to Patti and eventually saw her location's abortion facility close. But the need continued, so she moved to a new location. Steve went there to speak.

Afterward, Steve met a woman who had been forced into an abortion at age fourteen to cover up incest and abuse. She was now pregnant with her second child. She said she had been planning to have an abortion because of strong pressure from her mother. She and her boyfriend had been at a restaurant near the abortion facility during a 40 Days vigil, and he had run out to beg the vigil participants to help them. He didn't want his girlfriend to abort their baby. The prayer warriors responded immediately, promising to help.

The pregnant woman chose life that day. And the prayer warriors honored their promises to her. They helped the couple get their own place to live so they could escape the pressure from the baby's grandmother to end that little life.

The day Steve was there, the team was loading up bags of groceries and taking a cash offering for the couple. The team also asked who among the crowd praying there could donate furniture and other furnishings for the couple's home, and hands started going up.

After Steve spoke, the young pregnant woman said to him, "My baby only ever kicks at night but was kicking up a storm during your talk."

And then Steve heard the young woman say those words that have been spoken by so many to Patti and many of her volunteers and leaders she's inspired. The mom looked at Steve and said, "I think my baby was saying thank you. Keep doing what you're doing."

∼

I have to laugh today at the thought of Patti's desire for drama. I certainly had my fill of it in that back alley on the way to her campaign. But one thing is for sure—Patti's campaigns save lives, and the saving of those lives is no easy feat and is far from lacking in drama. Each of those lives saved is a dramatic story.

In southern California as elsewhere, many babies came so close to their lives ending before they'd even been greeted by the world. They came close to becoming a statistic rather than a life. That's certainly not lacking in drama. But in her effort to keep that from happening, Patti Flores kept going. That may not be dramatic in the world's eyes or even in her own, but every birthday of a saved child is a miracle, and every miracle is a drama filled with wonder.

~

Simon answered,
"Master, we've worked hard all night
and haven't caught anything.
But because you say so,
I will let down the nets."
LUKE 5:5

Jesus, I pray that you use my story for your glory. Whether or not I see the drama is not important. What is important is that I remain faithful to you and to the work you have called me to do. Wherever my story leads, wherever the drama falls, I pray that I would continue trusting that you will take what little I have to offer and multiply it for your glory. Amen.

Abortion to the Rescue

~

Being Irish, he had an abiding sense of tragedy,
which sustained him through temporary periods of joy.
—WILLIAM BUTLER YEATS

I HUNG UP THE PHONE WITH MARILISA, GRABBED MY KEYS, AND headed out to fill up my truck with gas. Marilisa and I had both just seen the latest weather reports, and it was time to grab the kids, leave Houston, and go to her parents. The hurricane forecasted to hit our area in about ten hours was expected to be bad—but none of us had any idea just how bad it would turn out to be.

Category 4 Hurricane Harvey dumped fifty-two inches of rain on Houston in four days in August of 2017—three times as much as Hurricane Katrina poured on New Orleans in 2005. And Harvey simply would not go away. It remained stationary, continuously pulling water out of the Gulf of Mexico and dumping it on Houston.

We left our home in Houston that day and drove eighty miles north to College Station, where we could stay at Marilisa's parents' home and I could work at the 40 Days for Life office.

When the storm finally moved on, we discovered that the floods had come within two feet of our home. Our house and the houses of a few neighbors had been literally on an island. But many of our friends and neighbors had not been so fortunate. In all, nearly forty thousand homes were destroyed. Harvey was indeed a thousand-year flood.

As a society, we can be defined in part by how we respond to tragedy. It's a good time to take our culture's pulse, reflecting on what we actually value. For the most part, Harvey brought out the best of Texas and of America as a whole, exposing our true heroes. We saw the best of humanity as citizens patrolling in private boats rescued thousands. The renowned "Cajun Navy" from Louisiana hauled their boats into Texas behind trucks and set out to rescue those still stranded.

Powerful forces of nature turn our focus back to the supernatural and remind us how precious—and fragile—human life can be. Harvey was no different. Life became precious again, neighbors had faces, and it was acceptable to mention God during a media interview.

But not all the true colors exposed by Harvey were positive. Kathy Kleinfeld, the director of Houston Women's Clinic, one of the city's prominent abortion facilities, proclaimed, "Pregnancy doesn't stop because of a hurricane."[36] Her facility was one of a few abortion providers in Texas to offer free abortions in the wake of Hurricane Harvey. Compared with the self-sacrificial actions of so many heroes *saving* lives, the abortion industry's empty view of humanity was on full display.

"We did it after Hurricane Katrina in August 2005," Amy Hagstrom Miller, founder and CEO of Whole Woman's Health said. "We did it for Hurricane Rita in September 2005, and we did it for Hurricane Ike in September 2008. Until the end of September, we'll be doing it again for those affected by Harvey. This is who we are, and this is what we do."[37]

This is who we are, this is what we do.

Truer words, I'm sure, Amy has never spoken.

It seems that for those in the abortion business, the answer to the world's problems is to kill our offspring. The abortion industry offered free abortions when tragedy struck. I cannot think of a more unnatural approach to overcoming disaster than to eliminate children.

Amy didn't stop her speech there. She proclaimed the right to abortion as the highest duty of a just and free society: "But it [abortion] is also an integral part of economic justice, racial justice, and true reproductive justice for all. Our care model is rooted in the belief that access to quality abortion care is not only vital to women's autonomy and self-determination, it is essential to our ability to function in society with true equality."[38]

If she is expecting us to look up at her in awe and wonder as she spills this twisted ideology, then I'm afraid it didn't work with me. In reality, her ideals are confusing, inappropriate, and condescending to women. The strongest women in human history, starting with the one who sat at the foot of the cross and continuing to our daughters today, do not need abortion in order for them to "function in society."

During or after natural disasters, volunteers and shelters provide blankets, food, medicine, and water. These things are needed to save life, to enhance life, to protect life. No one has to justify the use of these resources. Yet abortion requires constant justification. It seems the abortion business wants to use tragedy to justify the nature of abortion without acknowledging what abortion does.

No one motoring in on a raft or dropping from a helicopter to rescue someone was concerned about "true reproductive justice" or worried about abortion giving anyone "autonomy" and "self-determination." At that moment, they were preserving life and didn't care about the race or religion of the person they were helping.

This constant attempt to justify abortion in the most insensitive of moments may make your head spin, but it should actually give you hope—it's a sign that we are indeed seeing the beginning of the end of abortion. In the abortion industry there is not a day or a time when abortion is inappropriate—not even when thousands are fighting for their lives against nature gone wild. To suggest such a thing would suggest there is something *wrong* with abortion itself.

Planned Parenthood's response to Harvey was similar: "Because of the devastation brought on by Harvey and Irma ... women who need abortions might be blocked from getting help. What's more, these women could be forced to travel in sometimes dangerous conditions to access the care they need, if they can at all."[39]

A week after Harvey hit, I went to the largest abortion facility in the western hemisphere, the 78,000 square foot Planned Parenthood in Houston, where a 40 Days for Life campaign was about to kick off, our eleventh year at that location. There, just after the hurricane, I saw hope.

The campaign in Houston is run by two wonderful women— Christine Melchor and Theresa Camara. They have a presence year-round through their work with the Houston Coalition for Life. They also operate two medical buses that sit outside the massive Planned Parenthood and offer free ultrasounds, pregnancy tests, and medical care by nurses and doctors. On average, about ten women per day leave Planned Parenthood and then go to the bus.

The Houston Coalition for Life office was flooded during Harvey. That didn't deter Christine and Theresa. "The office was flooded but the buses were fine," Christine said, "so we went right out there knowing Planned Parenthood would be marketing to hurricane victims."

Despite the rhetoric from the abortion industry, Christine and Theresa showed that neither natural disasters nor an industry that offers free abortions can deter the love of life and love of God. A week after Harvey, they sent this report:

> We have an urgent need to help save the tiniest victims of Hurricane Harvey, the unborn. Abortion groups are now collecting donations to offer Harvey victims free abortions. We see that more lives are now at stake; the abortion facilities have been

busier than usual. Thanks be to God we also have been very busy. In the last seven days, we have seen 74 women, one pregnant with twins!... So far, we can boast 100% success with the 74 women that we have seen. Usually, more than 90% of the women that are exposed to our message of love opt for life.[40]

True heroes see dignity in people. They sacrifice, they offer help, and they offer hope. They don't degrade them, talk down to them, or tell them bad weather is yet another reason they shouldn't have children. The abortion industry, by its nature, survives on hopelessness and despair. Tragedies often give them an opportunity to use the subtle, degrading philosophy behind every abortion: "You wouldn't want to bring a child into this circumstance, would you?"

The hope, courage, and joy of Christine and Theresa illustrate the character that will end abortion. They would not let a disaster like Harvey end in despair. Instead, they allowed God to use them to shape the ending. Now, for many women, memories of Harvey won't bring painful reminders of an abortion performed in the aftermath, but rather an image of hope. Making that difference required faith and self-sacrifice from Christine and Theresa.

This is who they are. This is what they do.

In times of difficulty, how we treat the most vulnerable among us will determine what kind of world we will live in when the storm clears.

～

Then they cried out to the LORD in their trouble,
and he brought them out of their distress.
He stilled the storm to a whisper;
the waves of the sea were hushed.
PSALM 107:28–29

Father, in times of disaster, help me to be a light and a hope. Help me to rescue and care and always seek that which is good and perfect. Don't let anything deter me from serving you and standing up for life. Amen.

Homemade Italian Fortitude

~

God has not called me to be successful;
he has called me to be faithful.

—MOTHER TERESA

WHEN DR. JOHN PISCIOTTA ANSWERED HIS PHONE IN THE SPRING of 2017, the voice on the other end said, "I hope you're sitting down."

A knot formed in his gut. He hoped this wasn't his worst fear coming true. But it was.

The voice said, "They're back. Planned Parenthood in Waco, Texas, has filed for an abortion license."

Waco is home to Baylor University, and college towns are hot markets for the abortion industry. Because of this, Planned Parenthood was welcomed by many with open arms—and much financial support. The nation's largest abortion provider, viewed by some as real healthcare, wasted no time getting into the public schools' sex education program. Then they started doing abortions in the backyard of one of the best-known Baptist universities in America.

John didn't just sit back and watch. He went to work.

John is Italian, passionate, a great chef, and a fighter. This economics professor at Baylor University had taken on Planned Parenthood when they'd first started doing abortions in Waco in 1994. He had created Pro-Life Waco, pulled churches together, trained sidewalk counselors, and then brought 40 Days for Life to Waco in 2007. When Planned Parenthood stopped doing abortions in

2013, John—along with the large pro-life community of Waco—celebrated. That celebration had been years in the making, sustained by prayer, perseverance, and John's popular Pro-Life Sunday gatherings, featuring his homemade meatballs—his grandmother's recipe. Not only did John's work contribute to Planned Parenthood ceasing to do abortions in Waco, but Planned Parenthood was thrown out of the public schools and out of the Chamber of Commerce!

But that was 2013. Now they were back.

At the meeting where John shared the news that Planned Parenthood was returning to Waco to do abortions, he looked defeated and sounded tired. Wearing his Italian hair slicked back and sporting trademark suspenders, he shared that he didn't have the energy to fight this battle again. This was not cowardice; it was exhaustion.

Those of us who have known John for a long time knew what he had been through. He had done in Waco what very few thought anyone could do and what no one else would have taken on.

I looked at John across the table, smiled, and said, "I don't really believe you. Right now you're frustrated, and you should be. But I believe there is still fuel in the tank."

John smiled at my expression of confidence. But he still insisted that I needed to act now to find someone to lead this effort against Planned Parenthood returning to Waco.

I shared John's concern about the return of Planned Parenthood. From a business standpoint, the plan to begin abortions again was a smart move for Planned Parenthood. So many abortion facilities in Texas had closed that putting a new one in Waco would draw women from a large part of the state. Their planned location on a main interstate between Austin and Dallas-Fort Worth was nearly a hundred miles from the nearest abortion center. "Waco could become an abortion magnet for women in dozens of counties east and west of Interstate 35," John said.

It wouldn't be difficult for them to schedule enough abortions to get an abortion doctor to fly in. The shortage of abortion doctors in America—and especially Texas—forces Planned Parenthood to fly in doctors from out of state, and this was sure to happen in Waco. The abortion industry, despite what they say, is a business. It needs to make a profit. They are not running ministries or charitable health clinics. They are selling abortion, and Waco seemed ripe after being abortion-free for four years. (Waco's Planned Parenthood had never closed completely. They had remained open as an abortion referral center.)

As the meeting wrapped up, I thanked John for leading the depressing part of it, and we all had a painful laugh. But driving home, I knew John had a big problem on his hands. I also knew that if Planned Parenthood was successful in restarting abortions in Waco, they would also return to College Station—the city where 40 Days for Life first began, just ninety minutes from Waco.

After the news that Planned Parenthood would begin providing abortions in Waco once again, John tasked his Pro-Life Waco colleague, Aine, with organizing that fall's 40 Days for Life campaign. Originally from Ireland, Aine is a gentle but tough soul. Her beautiful accent can disarm people and get them motivated and moving. Together, the Italian professor and Irish activist made quite the duo as they hit the ground running to delay the opening of the new abortion facility Planned Parenthood was building.

Within three months, abundant evidence that John's Italian fighting nature had kicked in began showing up on my computer screen: "Never Again!" These two words from his new campaign to combat Planned Parenthood from bringing abortion back to Waco also appeared on yard signs sprouting up in lawns all over Waco. They moved through the city on the side of a large truck.

Most autumn 40 Days for Life launch events take place in late September—right before the vigil starts—but John and Aine wanted to build momentum early. They invited me and Sue Thayer, a former Planned Parenthood manager turned local 40 Days for Life leader, for a mid-June kickoff rally. (You may have read about Sue in *40 Days for Life*.)

The fast start paid off. By day one, one hundred pro-lifers had already pledged to pray on the sidewalk in front of Planned Parenthood. That number increased sharply following an intensive community outreach blitz featuring radio ads, billboards, simple yard signs, 40 Days for Life T-shirts, visits to dozens of Waco-area churches, and a newspaper ad inviting community members to join the vigil. The ad was signed by sixty-four area pastors. Deborah, CEO of Care Net Pregnancy Center in Waco, also joined in, supporting John and providing a medical facility for women to go to once they turned away from abortion.

∼

"Do you know this is abortion day?" Rev. Ronnie Holmes, pastor of Church of the Open Door in Waco, Texas, asked a woman who had just pulled into Planned Parenthood's parking lot. A reporter from the *Waco Tribune Herald* looked on with curiosity.

"Yes, I'm here to get one," the woman replied defiantly, even pumping her fist to demonstrate her enthusiasm.

Holmes, a veteran sidewalk counselor for more than a decade, was undeterred in his efforts to save this mother and baby from abortion. "I urge you to reconsider," he said. "A baby's heartbeat can be heard three weeks after conception."

Her callous response shocked vigil participants and even made front page news in the *Waco Tribune Herald*: "I wouldn't care if it was 5 years old. I'm going to kill it."[41]

Rev. Holmes's heart sank, as did the reporter's. It was a difficult way to begin a 40 Days for Life vigil, to say the least.

But by the end of the day, the brokenhearted prayer warriors found reason to celebrate. An out-of-town woman who'd recently learned she was pregnant arrived at Planned Parenthood with instructions to "take care of it." But that effort to pressure this young mom into an abortion hit a snag when the abortion provider demanded money to perform an ultrasound.

"I didn't have any money," she said later. "I started crying and walked outside, and that's when a man on the sidewalk asked me to come talk to him and to pray. He introduced me to a nurse from Care Net. When I said I didn't have a way to get there, the nurse offered to take me to Care Net to get an ultrasound and to talk about my decision."

Meeting her baby on the ultrasound machine screen changed everything.

"When they did my ultrasound, *my baby was dancing!* Right then I knew I was not going to have an abortion," she said. I couldn't stop laughing and crying all at the same time. I am so happy that I get to have my baby and build a life for us. Thank you to the people on the sidewalk in the 40 Days for Life shirts and signs. You saved my baby!"

Despite the disheartening beginning to the first-day vigil, John and Aine saw God show up in this young woman's life. Their energy renewed, they watched as many on the sidewalk got involved for the first time. By day forty, the number of campaign participants had tripled to more than three hundred. Some volunteers drove more than fifty miles to attend the vigil. Best of all, many babies were saved.

John and his team found out that Planned Parenthood's new $4.3 million, 9,000-square-foot facility would be designed to create obstacles for 40 Days for Life participants and sidewalk counselors. Not only would Planned Parenthood erect an eight-foot fence around the property, it would also remove the public sidewalk.

"I'm not at all discouraged by this," Pisciotta said. He was adamant that babies could be saved even without a sidewalk. "It shows that Planned Parenthood is disoriented, and they don't understand the challenge they face in Central Texas."

John and his team wondered when Planned Parenthood would make the big announcement about *when* they would start building their new facility. But Planned Parenthood had no intention of promoting the opening. And Pro-Life Waco finally found out why Planned Parenthood would announce no grand opening. They had decided to have a quiet opening, starting abortions in their new facility the week of Christmas.

Christmas is about our Lord coming to save the world through the womb, through a family, and abortion insults that on the deepest level. Did Planned Parenthood know this? I've known Planned Parenthood to do abortions on the day before Thanksgiving and Holy Saturday—the Saturday before Easter. Many post-abortive women share that they always remember two dates: their due date (if they were given one) and the date of their abortion. I can't imagine the pain caused by having it so close to a holiday, much less the day the world humbly welcomed the King of Kings into the world. That would cause deep pain every year, a pain that Planned Parenthood apparently couldn't care less about. Abortions are their business. It is that cold attitude that reminds us of the sterile, distant approach that is required in the abortion business.

However, John and Aine weren't going to allow Planned Parenthood's new abortion business to greet Christmas in Waco without attention. They decided to host an event called "Christmas Is for Angels, Not Abortions." Former Planned Parenthood Director Abby Johnson, representing her ministry And Then There Were None, spoke and offered hope to the workers taking part in abortions the week of Christmas.

The event was a huge success. The media coverage allowed the community to see how disconnected Planned Parenthood was from the heartbeat of Waco. And Planned Parenthood's silent grand opening was not silent after all.

As pro-life's peaceful presence and momentum grew in Waco, I remembered how John had looked in that original meeting—a warrior, but a worn and tired one. He had run the good race and then, exhausted, discovered that he hadn't yet finished. He was called to make another run when many said he had given it his all and deserved a rest. But John isn't wired to take the easy way. When it was time to accept that Planned Parenthood was back and doing abortions, he didn't despair. He got back into the race, started saving babies, and gave us an example to follow.

We are here as the hands and feet of Christ to serve him according to his timing, not ours. As Mother Teresa said, "God has not called me to be successful. He has called me to be faithful." And faithful is written on every corner of John Pisciotta's effort in Waco. His fortitude, faith, and courage are an example to us and a reason why that mom could enthusiastically exclaim after leaving Planned Parenthood, "My baby was dancing!"

~

The LORD himself goes before you
and will be with you;
he will never leave you
nor forsake you.
Do not be afraid;
do not be discouraged.
DEUTERONOMY 31:8

God, I thank you that nothing is a surprise to you. That the rise of a facility thought dead does not reflect upon your power, but on the persistence of the enemy. I pray that you will open the eyes of our leaders to the enemy's tactics so that they may guide us in the battle against abortion. Amen.

Music through the Wall

~

Darkness cannot drive out darkness;
only light can do that.
Hate cannot drive out hate;
only love can do that.
—REVEREND MARTIN LUTHER KING JR.

MIKE WAS A CONFIDENT MAN, A PILOT WHO FLEW 777 COMMER-
cial jets around the world for a living. At the moment, however, he
felt anything but confident as he stood in the Seattle rain. *What am
I doing here?*

He stood in front of an abortion facility, praying and feeling self-
conscious. Every so often he looked up, waiting for something to
happen. Surely someone would drive by and yell, gesture, or stop to
say something. *After all,* he thought, *this is Seattle. Not a city known
for its conservatism.*

It was his first time to participate in a 40 Days for Life vigil. He
had liked the idea that the campaign was about prayer and not con-
frontation, so he thought he would give it a shot. Now, as the rain
continued, Mike realized that something was indeed happening—
and that something was nothing.

Nothing, that is, except that he was praying for an end to abortion with fellow believers, and so far, at least, the bottom had not
dropped out. None of the stereotypical behavior that accompanied
abortion center protests in the media had happened—no heated

rhetoric, no fights, no yelling. It was indeed a prayer vigil and nothing else.

Mike was hooked.

Sometime later, Mike's job as a pilot required that he relocate his family from Seattle to Manassas in northern Virginia. He made it a point to find the closest 40 Days for Life campaign.

After participating in a Manassas campaign, Mike felt a call to lead it even though he was still new in the area and didn't know that many people. When he went online to sign up, he was surprised to see that another person had already signed up to lead the campaign. Tim had also felt a call to lead the campaign, and this was definitely a match that God had put together. Mike had more time during the day to organize the campaign, and Tim, who had lived in the area for a number of years, had many contacts and connections.

Mike and Tim had willingly volunteered. In truth, they had no idea what they had gotten themselves into, but whether naïve or in over their heads, they got to work regardless. "I had no idea how hard it would be to fill the hours," Mike said, "but we were determined to make sure that every vigil hour was filled."

"We can't have gaps," Mike told volunteers at their first meeting. "Gaps will send the wrong message about how serious we are about saving babies. We have to be out there every hour we say we are going to be."

Mike and Tim's combined efforts led to a very successful campaign and added quite a number of new participants and a new enthusiasm for the 40 Days for Life campaign. But it came with a cost. At the end of that campaign Tim, a father of eight, discerned that he had to put his family first and his leadership role was putting a strain on the family. This required him to take a role in the campaign that did not require so much time away from his family. The good news was that Mike was now in a position to take on the leadership role himself.

The abortion facility in Manassas was well known. Amethyst

Health Center for Women opened in 1989 in a small business park on one of the busiest roads in this Washington, DC, suburb. When word first got out that an abortion facility was opening in Manassas, a group of people in the community got together and decided they needed to respond. Their answer was to open a pro-life pregnancy resource center called AAA Women for Choice. Providentially, it was located at the opposite end of the same business park as the abortion facility.

Having the pregnancy center in the business park started to cause problems for the abortion facility. People drove by the pregnancy center first, before reaching the abortion facility, and many of them stopped there instead—causing the abortionists to lose potential clients! What happened next is incredible: Amethyst Health Center for Women moved right next door to the pregnancy resource center! I have never heard of this happening anywhere else.

The move was actually an attempt by the abortion facility to stop a loss of clients. The abortion doctor figured that if his facility was directly next door to the pregnancy resource center, then women wanting an abortion would clearly see his office and come to him rather than go to the pregnancy center. What the doctor hadn't counted on was that this created a perfect opportunity for the AAA Women for Choice sidewalk counselors and the 40 Days for Life campaign to go to work right outside his abortion center. Unlike most campaigns, where participants in the campaign need to send women elsewhere to find the help they need to choose life, they could immediately refer women to a place right next door to the abortion center. It only required a few steps to find the resources and support they needed. And the results of that convenience started showing up quickly: Babies were being saved.

One young woman driving past, seeing vigil participants praying with their 40 Days for Life signs, made a U-turn and pulled up in front of AAA Women of Choice. Thinking she was entering an abortion facility, she went inside looking for someone to talk to about having an abortion.

A counselor greeted her and easily saw how discouraged and sad the woman was, facing such a sad choice. The counselor spoke with the woman for an hour and a half—after which the woman walked out relieved, happy, and determined to keep her baby.

Ken, an ardent Manassas pro-life prayer warrior, said, "Praise the Lord! It was an encouragement to keep fighting for these precious babies and their mothers in the name of our Lord Jesus Christ."

One woman came out of the abortion center in tears. As she was about to drive past the prayer volunteers, she stopped the car, got out, and ran toward them, happily shouting that she had decided to keep her baby. The woman embraced the vigil volunteers, and then she surprised everyone by grabbing a sign, holding it up proudly, and praying with her new friends. "Your presence out here is powerful," she told her new friends. "Keep it up! You never know what good might happen."

In the spring of 2015 a snowstorm hit the East Coast, and businesses and government offices closed—but not the abortion facility. So Mike decided to continue the vigil despite the extremely cold weather. "They're not letting up," Ken said, "so neither can we!"

The decision bore fruit. Three babies were saved from abortion during those bitter cold days.

One day, Mike was standing outside the facility praying when a van pulled up. The woman inside motioned a volunteer over and told her story, which Mike relayed to me.

During a previous 40 Days campaign, a woman had decided to get an abortion. On the day she came, although it was raining, the 40 Days for Life participants were out there praying. She felt uneasy going into the abortion facility for an abortion when the 40 Days volunteers were there praying, so she decided to come back later. On the day she returned it was snowing—and the volunteers were still there. She left a second time.

On her third visit, the weather was fine and the volunteers were still there praying. "I felt that your faithful prayers in all kinds of weather were a sign that I was to keep my baby. And I am so thankful for your faithfulness, because now I have a beautiful baby daughter. I'm so happy that I decided against an abortion."

When the abortion center moved next door to the pregnancy center, the odd reality was that the two facilities now shared a wall. It soon became horrifyingly clear that those on the pregnancy center side of the wall could hear the procedures being performed on the other side. The reality of the darkness of the abortion facility rang true with every single abortion.

This situation needed prayer—not only outside where Mike was leading the campaign, but also inside, where the sound of the procedure that was depriving a child his or her life could be heard many times a day.

Because that darkness could be met only with prayer, the pregnancy center turned the room on their side of the shared wall into a chapel. Staff and volunteers prayed, played music, and sat there in solidarity with the babies and the unseen women lying on that exam table just a few feet away.

Just as those in the pregnancy center could hear the abortions, those in the abortion procedure room could hear the prayers and music coming from the other side of the shared wall.

One day as Ken was praying outside Amethyst Health Center for Women, the abortion doctor came out to talk to him. This wasn't uncommon—Ken had felt a call to try to dialogue with the abortion doctors as they came and left. Most of them hardly acknowledged Ken, but this one was very friendly with him. "What was that music I heard today?" asked the abortionist.

Praying silently for wisdom, Ken said, "Oh—that was the 'Divine Mercy Chaplet'. It's a simple prayer where you sing to Jesus, *'For the sake of His Sorrowful Passion, have mercy on us and on the whole world.'* Are you Catholic, Doctor?"

The doctor admitted that he was and even commented that someday he would like to stop doing abortions.

"Well, if you ever want to see a priest, I would be glad to arrange it," offered Ken.

That very next week, on the final weekend of the spring campaign, the abortion doctor came out, finished for the day. Seeing Ken standing alone, he quietly said, "I can't do this anymore. I think I need to see that priest."

Ken, moved with emotion, blurted out, "Oh, doctor, you are going to have the best Easter ever!" Ken fumbled in his pocket for a pen so he could write down the doctor's contact information and give the doctor his cellphone number. No pen. "Do you have a pen?" Ken asked. The doctor checked his pockets. No, he didn't have a pen either.

The scene that followed could only be created by the power of prayer. Ken said, "Let's just run into the crisis pregnancy center and grab a pen so we can get you connected with a priest." So Ken and the abortion doctor walked together into the AAA Women for Choice Pregnancy Center, causing the staff at the pregnancy center to nearly have a collective heart attack. The shock passed quickly and grace intervened. A pen and paper were provided and contact information exchanged so that the abortion doctor could see a priest.

"It was a shock at the moment," Ken said, "but later we had to laugh."

Perhaps God was showing his sense of humor—but more importantly, his mercy. That doctor did meet with a priest and he *never* did another abortion. Incredibly, the day he met with the priest was a day called the Feast of Divine Mercy, when the mercy of Christ is celebrated in a special way by Catholics around the world.

Mike and Ken gave all praise to God for this outcome, but their story had yet another chapter to write. Their years of hard work and a dedicated vigil schedule were about to pay off. In 2015, Mike sent me this email: "I bring you good news of great joy! Our prayers have been heard! After 27 years of abortions, on September 29, 2015, Amethyst Women's Health Center has closed their doors!"

After all the years that volunteers in Manassas had prayed outside the abortion center during fourteen 40 Days for Life campaigns, after hours of snow, sleet, heat, after one repentant abortionist, after countless referrals to the pregnancy center, they were watching the abortion facility close for good. Today the former abortion facility is a free health clinic run by Catholic Charities. The place of darkness, death, and despair is now a source of light, hope, and healing.

God shows us that working through the efforts of so many people, each responding to God's call, great things can be accomplished. Some are called to lead a campaign like Mike, others to be weekly prayer warriors like Ken, others to be sidewalk counselors or run a pregnancy center. We might even be called to step back a bit at times like Tim, and play our parts just for a season.

Mike had come a long way from standing in the rain in Seattle wondering why he was praying in front of an abortion facility. He had responded with a small yes and allowed God to use him to close an abortion business that had been open for twenty-seven years and had performed twenty thousand abortions. When Tim put first things first and took a step back to spend more time with his kids, God raised up Mike to take his place. Both actions required the men to trust, do the right thing, and leave the rest to God.

"This is truly God's work through many, many hands in our community," Mike said. "Light always conquers darkness. This is indeed a great blessing for our Manassas community."

We pray that every abortion doctor will be moved by the praise of the Lord on the lips of his people, and we pray that even the longest-standing abortion facilities will come down through that praise.

~

The light shines in the darkness,
and the darkness has not overcome it.
JOHN 1:5

God, as I read this story, all I can do is sing your praises. Only you could move a place of death to share a wall with a place of life. Thank you for the faithful vigil participants who bathed both facilities with prayer, and thank you for your remarkable answers to those prayers. Lord, move me to pray with such dedication and persistence. Bolster my faith, Lord. Give me fresh confidence that you are a mighty God who delights in surprising your people with your remarkable answers to prayer. Amen.

DAY 31

Are They Still There?

~

*The most merciful thing that the large family
does to one of its infant members is to kill it.*

—MARGARET SANGER,
Founder of Planned Parenthood

KENTUCKY IS KNOWN FOR BASKETBALL, THE KENTUCKY DERBY, and bourbon. And more importantly, Kentucky is on the brink of becoming the first abortion-free state in America. The one remaining abortion facility in Kentucky is in Louisville. There is a pregnancy resource center next to it, and a maternity home, and there are many churches working together to make Louisville abortion free. One of their best resources is a local 40 Days for Life leader named Laura Grijalba.

Laura, originally from New Jersey, is the wife of Adam and the mother of seven kids ranging in age from seven to twenty-six. And Laura, like most moms who often have ninety-three plates spinning at once, knows how to get things done. And get things done she does.

After she and Adam, a combat veteran and bronze star winner who served in the army for twenty-four years, landed in Louisville, they began participating in 40 Days for Life.

The campaign struggled at times. Laura thought it could do better, but she was busy raising her family. Then Adam read *40 Days for Life* and gave it to Laura when he was done. After finishing the book, she said in her New Jersey accent, "That's it! We gotta do more. We gotta go twenty-four hours a day in Louisville!"

Adam smiled. "Yeah, I was afraid of letting you read that book."

"I mean, come on," Laura said. "Are we serious about ending abortion? We've got to go twenty-four hours a day."

In each city that participates in the campaign, a 40 Days for Life leader decides whether, in their forty-day campaign, they will do twelve-hour vigils each day or twenty-four-hour vigils. There are many good reasons for doing twelve hours per day, the main considerations being the abortion facility's location and safety. We work with local leaders and law enforcement to help each leader decide on the best plan for their city. In Louisville, we had the all-clear to go to a twenty-four-hour vigil, and Laura stepped up to take it on.

Laura challenged everyone, especially men, to sign up for the extra hours required to go 24/40. "We need men," Laura said. "Men need to realize they are leaders in the fight for life—and we are seeing that more and more in Louisville."

She shot the campaign in Louisville full of adrenaline and led by example. A man named Joe heard about the switch to a twenty-four-hour vigil and committed to come pray for two hours each day three days a week—six of those hours during the most difficult middle-of-the-night slots. "Joe's the hero of our city," Laura said.

Another man looked at the schedule to find the hardest possible shifts to fill. He took multiple 2:30 a.m.–4:00 a.m. shifts, sacrificing decent nights of sleep for himself while giving other volunteers a chance to get consistent sleep every night of the vigil.

Why is Laura successful at filling vigil hours? I think it's because, as a mother of seven, she takes abortion personally. "We need to be out there for these young women. And we need to teach our own children to sacrifice."

A few years back, I spoke at Laura's kickoff event and met many of the pastors and volunteers she has bragged about for years. But I was most struck by Laura and her ability to lead, direct, and encourage people, all while managing her well-behaved smaller kids who were with her. She has a lot going on, but in the end her fire and her faith can be tied to the fact that she's just a mom of seven from New Jersey, and she must get things done.

You'd be wrong if you assumed Laura is a parent who runs out the door to save the world but neglects her own children in the process. Quite the opposite. She puts first things first. Her children pray right alongside her. As a result, her oldest son, Ray, who is married, will drive in from out of state with his wife to pray during the night shifts to help fill in. He's so proud of his mom for leading 40 Days for Life that he made a YouTube video about her. He says, "My mom is almost like an adopted mother to some of these babies who are saved. One girl who was saved from abortion almost two years ago wanted my mom in the room when she had her braces put on. God has been so good to 40 Days for Life, and we do this freely out of love because Christ loves us freely and we need to do the same. We need to be the hands of Christ, even in the middle of the night."

Another one of her sons, John, who graduated from the University of Kentucky in May 2018, would drive in from Lexington for each fall and spring campaign to fill in on the hard two-hour shifts. He would also pray his regular two-hour shift weekly on Sunday mornings. Then John would get some sleep before getting up early to drive back the eighty miles or so to the university for Monday morning classes.

The fact that there is only one abortion facility left standing in Kentucky has not gone unnoticed by abortion advocates or the media. In 2017, CNN published a story on this abortion facility. The article told the story of Emory, one of the facility's volunteers. His job is to help escort women into the facility. Only thirty-one, he was inspired by the "horror stories" he'd heard about how women who attempted to walk into the facility were harassed by protesters. He wanted to stand up for women by helping them get inside and have an abortion.

"I want to be a voice of reason on the other side," he told the reporter, then went on to say that he was baffled by how often pro-testers invoke religious songs and prayers. "They'll sing the Ave Maria song a lot, and they'll do the Lord's Prayer a lot. I grew up in the church, so I'm familiar with all of it. I just can't imagine … the Jesus I grew up with believing in that. The Jesus I grew up with would be walking with the client. I grew up knowing that Jesus was about compassion and love and understanding. He was always willing to be with those who might be dealing with hardships in life— and being able to always walk beside them.[42]

Sadly, Emory isn't the warrior-hero for women he believes himself to be. He's a well-meaning young man who is mistakenly helping facilitate something evil. The real warrior for women is the mom of seven from New Jersey—an everyday hero, inspiring Louisville to pray and offer hope in front of a dilapidated building housing a nearly forty-year-old abortion practice.

Emory is, however, like many who volunteer or work in the abortion industry. He has his justification intact—because abortion requires constant justification, whether that includes discounting Scripture, or molding Scripture and religion to suit their needs, or ignoring biological science, or all three.

The 40 Days for Life volunteers don't shout "you're going to hell" or curse those who enter the abortion facility. They simply stand and pray. That's what's effective, and that's what drives people like Laura.

In 2016, Laura received the Albert J. Schweitzer Humanitarian of the Year Award (not to be confused with the Albert Schweitzer Humanitarian of the Year Award).[43] In her speech she accepted the award on behalf of the pro-life work her mom began years ago. But Laura isn't interested in getting awards, nor does she want recognition or praise. She simply wants more people out praying on the sidewalks, because that's what saves lives. She wants to honor God and create a better world for her own children. During her acceptance speech, she thanked many faithful supporters of life in the Kentucky-Indiana area, then went on to encourage others to defend life by joining Louisville's efforts on the sidewalk.

I look forward to receiving vigil reports from Laura. Here's a typical one:

> With my mom's funeral, things are a little hectic in Louisville. I heard from our regular daily sidewalk counselor that there were nine babies saved this campaign. Here are five more:
>
> Oct 11: A mother chose LIFE for her twins!!!
> Oct 25: A mother chose LIFE for her baby!!
> Oct 28: A mother chose LIFE for her baby!!
> Oct 31: A mother chose LIFE for her baby!!
>
> Thanks for the beautiful flowers at my mother's wake. I carried them from Florida to New Jersey and then back to Kentucky! May God Bless You!"

She is gracious—even when it took me too many years to come speak at the kickoff of one of her vigils. She had every right to complain, but instead, here's what she wrote:

> Thank you for coming! Everyone said our 40 Days for Life kickoff was awesome! It helped the crowd realize they can do more. Not long after two women chose life! One mom came with a man who tried talking her out of the abortion. She has four kids and didn't think she could handle another child since she was in her 40s, but she chose life.
>
> Another woman went to the pregnancy help center right next door and made an appointment for an ultrasound. It was an ultrasound image that made all the difference in the world. She started crying and chose life.

Laura's husband, Adam, said, "Laura often says we will never really know how many babies we have saved. She's right. Only God knows."

But the night she received that award, God lifted the curtain a little more to show Laura what he had accomplished. At the end of the banquet, a woman came up and congratulated her, then shared that Laura's work had indeed impacted her family.

The woman's daughter called the abortion facility for an appointment. Since she was living with her boyfriend and her mom did not support this decision, she and her mom weren't on speaking terms. When she called, she wanted to make sure none of her mother's friends would be at the center. She was afraid they would recognize her, and she knew she couldn't go through with the abortion if they were there. *I'll find a time when no one is out there and schedule my appointment around that time,* she thought. Then she called again, and the abortion staff member said, "They are out there twenty-four hours every single day."

She decided to call the abortion facility every day and simply ask, "Are they still there?"

The woman explained to Laura that the constant prayer presence prevented her daughter from ever returning; she just couldn't do it. As the hotel staff put away the chairs after the night of celebration, the woman told Laura, "I must thank you. My grandchild is due in October because of you!"

Are they still there? It's a question that will continue to be asked in Kentucky and many other places in America. It's the question that is making people realize what God is doing, whom he is using to do it, and why we are seeing the beginning of the end of abortion.

~

Start children off on the way they should go,
and even when they are old they will not turn from it.
PROVERBS 22:6

God, I pray I will be an example to my children that encourages them to join wholeheartedly in the fight for life. I pray I would challenge them to love you and serve you, no matter what the cost. Thank you that even I can be an everyday hero—simply by showing up and praying faithfully for these hurting women and their babies. Amen.

Might Makes Right

~

Since love and fear can hardly exist together,
if we must choose between them,
it is far safer to be feared than loved.
—NICCOLÒ MACHIAVELLI

I CAN JUST IMAGINE IT. GREG AND ANDREA,[44] A MARRIED COUPLE staring at a positive pregnancy test, elated at the best news any couple could get. Then during their ultrasound, the news got even better—twins! A boy and a girl. We've seen a lot of positive pregnancy tests at our own house, and each one brings us new joy, excitement, and anticipation. And there's something about being pregnant with twins that turns up the excitement to a higher level.

I can visualize Andrea excitedly preparing a nursery to welcome their beautiful babies.

At some point, Andrea and Greg decided to have tests run. They learned that one of their babies, the boy, had Down syndrome. They decided on a "selective abortion"—aborting the baby boy who had Down syndrome and keeping the baby girl. For this, they went to Dr. Matthew Kachinas, an abortion doctor in Sarasota, Florida—although he had never done the procedure before and told them so.[45]

After the abortion of the baby boy, perhaps they felt life was now going the direction they'd planned. They no longer had twins, but they would soon give birth to a healthy baby girl.

A little over a week after the abortion, Greg and Andrea went to their follow-up appointment to check on their baby girl. The ultrasound monitor confirmed that there was only one baby left in Andrea's womb. But the baby was a boy. Their baby girl was nowhere to be found! To everyone's horror, they realized that the doctor had aborted the wrong baby.[46]

∼

Unborn children with disabilities have a target on their back. ABC News reported on a study showing that, after a prenatal test confirms Down syndrome, those children are aborted more than 90 percent of the time.[47]

Once unborn children are diagnosed with a disability, they are stripped of their dignity and humanity and become inconveniences we must get rid of.

Iceland might be leading the way to a new and distressing future. In August of 2017, CBS News reported that Iceland has nearly "eradicated" Down syndrome in their country. Only one or two children with Down syndrome are being born each year. The article read, "Since prenatal screening tests were introduced in Iceland in the early 2000s, the clear majority of women—close to 100 percent—who received a positive test for Down syndrome terminated their pregnancy."[48]

So why isn't the number 100 percent? Icelandic officials explain that a few children born with Down syndrome went undetected. Hulda Hjartardottir, head of the Prenatal Diagnosis Unit at Landspitali University Hospital, where around 70 percent of Icelandic children are born, said, "Some of [the babies born with Down syndrome] were low risk in our screening test, so we didn't find them."[49]

Even after these precious children are born, even though they have done nothing wrong except to exist, their crime of having an extra chromosome is not tolerated by some abortion advocates, journalists, doctors, or sadly, even their own parents.

At Landspitali University Hospital, Helga Sol Olafsdottir counsels women who have a pregnancy with a chromosomal abnormality,

"This is your life—you have the right to choose how your life will look."

When questioned by those who oppose this intention to eradicate Down syndrome, she responds, "We don't look at abortion as a murder. We look at it as a thing that we ended. We ended a possible life that may have had a huge complication … preventing suffering for the child and for the family. And I think that is more right than seeing it as a murder—that's so black and white. Life isn't black and white. Life is grey."[50]

The notion of grey areas in abortion is deceiving. We are told over and over about the suffering a disabled child will endure and that we are being kind in taking life from them before it begins. The reality is that children with disabilities are viewed as a burden—a burden that can be avoided through abortion. It's a viewpoint that reveals much about how we treat the weak and marginalized in our society.

No one would deny the challenges one faces in raising a child with Down syndrome or any other disability. In the book *40 Days for Life,* I wrote about growing up with a stepbrother who had cerebral palsy. But those greater challenges can also bring greater strength, greater character, and yes, greater joy.

Greg and Andrea bought the lie that it is not only acceptable but preferable to end a pregnancy that won't end in a perfectly formed child. They believed that they and their baby boy would be better off if he were aborted. What is even more astonishing is that they wanted so badly to avoid having a child with disabilities that they knowingly went to a doctor who had never before done this delicate procedure, putting their other baby at risk. And that little boy on the ultrasound monitor was still very much alive. The procedure had been unsuccessful.

That's the first irony revealed by this case: Abortion is considered a failure when life results. It's considered a success only when a baby loses his or her life. And Greg and Andrea were determined to have success. They returned to Dr. Kachinas and had the baby boy with Down syndrome aborted.[51] This time there was no mistake; the little boy did not live through the second attempt on his life.

Dr. Kachinas, after a long career of aborting healthy and unhealthy babies, eventually lost his medical license[52] over the ordeal—and apparently, very nearly his mind, since he claimed he was suicidal.[53] I won't speculate on why he told the media he was suicidal, but one thing is clear: he knew that he took the life of a baby who was *wanted*. And he blamed this "mistake" of aborting a perfectly healthy baby girl on faulty ultrasound technology. And that's the second irony: the ultrasound technology was called faulty because it didn't contribute to the death of that baby boy. But ultrasound technology was not developed to assist in death. And that same ultrasound technology saves lives every day as couples, intending to abort, see their healthy baby on the ultrasound and choose life nearly 80 percent of the time.[54]

In our culture, if we *want* a baby, it's considered a *blessing* and we plan baby showers. If we *don't* want the baby, it's a *choice,* and ending the life of that baby is considered a responsible decision. With abortion, *our will* becomes the deciding factor in choosing life or death. We have the power to carry out that decision. It is indeed a case of might makes right.

Might makes right gives no voice to the vulnerable. It didn't in the tragic case of Greg and Andrea's twins, and it doesn't for any of the other children aborted because they are unwanted—no matter the reason. Every abortion forces the will of another onto a weak and defenseless baby.

The power we give ourselves over others weaker than ourselves dictates what our families, schools, churches—what our society as a whole—look like. For Greg and Andrea, instead of bringing home two beautiful babies, these parents came home to an empty house after two abortions, all because they wanted to control what their family would be like.

This case is a revealing one that reaches far beyond the lives of Greg and Andrea. It reveals our flawed, cold mentality that believes we can control life without consequence. It places fear of the unknown and sacrificial challenge of a special-needs child ahead of love. It is the opposite of Good Friday. Our Lord had the power to avoid fear and death but chose to lay down his life. He did so out of love.

Thordis Ingadottir is the mother of one of only three Down syndrome babies born in Iceland in 2009. Her daughter, Agusta, is now seven. Thordis gave birth to Agusta at the age of forty. Her wish for Agusta is that of any mother: "I will hope that she will be fully integrated on her own terms in this society. That's my dream," Ingadottir said. "Isn't that the basic needs of life? What kind of society do you want to live in?"[55]

A beautiful and challenging question by one of only three parents in Iceland that year willing to raise a child with Down syndrome. *What kind of a society do we want to live in?*

∼

The closing event for the Madison, Wisconsin, fall 2012 40 Days for Life campaign was packed as enthusiastic volunteers poured into a church after spending a thousand hours on the frigid Wisconsin sidewalk.

One of those volunteers was Joseph. Joseph was new to 40 Days; he had stumbled on the vigil as he drove past Planned Parenthood one evening. When he learned that dozens of pro-lifers were out in the cold, dark night praying in front of an abortion facility, Joseph shared that his daughter was twenty weeks pregnant, and her baby had been diagnosed with Down syndrome.

Joseph's daughter and her husband were planning on an abortion and were not open to reconsidering. Joseph was heartbroken.

So he did the only thing left to him to do. He prayed.

He joined the volunteers, then came to the closing celebration at the church. There he met new friends as he shared his daughter's story and asked people to pray for a change of heart for his daughter and son-in-law. The Christian charity he experienced among campaign participants touched his heart deeply. Not one but two families he met were so moved by his story about his grandson that they offered, right on the spot, to adopt the boy. The first was Steve and his wife, Laura, and the other family was a couple who had already adopted another child with Down syndrome. After months of fear and frustration with his daughter and son in-law, Joseph was speechless at this outpouring of love.

Joseph had originally joined the vigil as a desperate grandfather without hope. But after participating in 40 Days for Life, he returned to his daughter as a steadfast advocate for his grandson with Down syndrome. He shared with his daughter that it didn't have to be this way. That they didn't need to live in fear of this baby boy. He talked about the Christian charity he'd found at the 40 Days for Life vigil and the celebration event he attended. He talked about *hope*.

His daughter was moved. She chose life for her son, whom she named Thomas. Thomas is now five years old because his grandfather and his parents did not allow fear to overcome love. Thomas, like all children with Down syndrome, is full of joy and a reminder that life is indeed good.

The day after Thomas's birth, Joseph sent an email to the Madison team with photos of the precious little boy. "What a wonderful, beautiful outcome we have from all our prayers," Joseph wrote. "God truly loves and blesses his children." Since then Joseph has put in nearly two hundred hours at the Madison vigil. That family who had previously offered to adopt Thomas ended up adopting another child with Down syndrome who was scheduled to be aborted.

When we look at a child with fear and not love, when we allow that fear to decide whether that child is worthy of life, we reveal that it is we, not the children, who are truly disabled. It is we who are broken.

I have traveled to over 450 cities for 40 Days for Life, and am most moved when I see parents praying at a vigil with their disabled children. These parents are the heroes. They overcome the cold and condescending mentality of our society that some children just aren't worth the effort. They faced fear and overcame it.

Others never even considered fear. They simply loved their child unconditionally the moment they found out they were having a baby. There were no tests or conditions put on their parenting commitment. There was only love, a love that didn't measure sacrifice. Their love is that of the cross, love without condition and without fear. They are examples of how much Jesus Christ loves us and how much we need him in a society that can so easily let fear determine human dignity.

Let us love as these parents love. Let us love as Christ loves. And let us live knowing that true might and power can be found in those we view as weak and disabled.

∾

Jesus said,
"Let the little children come to me,
and do not hinder them,
for the kingdom of heaven belongs
to such as these."
MATTHEW 19:14

Heavenly Father, I pray that I would not fear what is before me. I pray that I would trust in Jesus, who led without fear but with sacrificial love. I pray that I would not be afraid as I go out to pray today. Help me to lean into you when I feel afraid. Help me to remember that you are my God, and I can trust you with all things. Amen.

Heroes Don't Need Fairy Tales

~

*All the pleasures of the world are nothing
compared with the sweetness found
in the gall and vinegar offered to Jesus Christ.*
—IGNATIUS OF LOYOLA

WHEN 40 DAYS FOR LIFE WAS LAUNCHED AS A NATIONAL EFFORT in 2007, we expected certain cities to sign up first—those in Texas and in many of the Bible-touting cities of the Deep South. From that foundation we would build toward our goal of twenty-five cities for that first campaign. How God must have smiled at our naiveté!

When the first city application came through, from Sacramento, California, I should have given thanks and glory to God, but instead I thought it was a computer glitch. I thought, *God is everywhere, but he's not in California.* I never dreamed California, a state that does 350 abortions per day, would become the largest state for 40 Days for Life campaigns.

On my first trip to visit that campaign, I met our new leader, Wynette Sills, outside a huge Planned Parenthood abortion facility in Sacramento. Wynette was standing next to the driveway with sweat on her brow, ready to hand out the informational brochures she held in her hand. It was a great sight, and I instantly sensed that she was a warrior.

Wynette led multiple campaigns in front of that Planned Parenthood and was so effective that Planned Parenthood put up a wooden fence to deter abortive women from speaking to the volunteers, claiming that the 40 Days for Life participants were intimidating and harassing women. They even changed our name to "40 Days for Harassment."

The wooden fence they built was no little decorative picket fence. It was huge and completely surrounded the building. It made Planned Parenthood look like a fortress out of the movie *Braveheart,* but that didn't stop Wynette. Over the years Wynette has led campaigns, watched abortion facilities close due to her efforts, and helped save hundreds of babies.

One of the more challenging locations was a late-term abortion facility in Sacramento in the basement of a multiuse medical office building. Ironically, a well-respected hospital with a very dedicated neonatal intensive care unit was located right across the street from where late-term abortions up to twenty-five weeks were being done.

As I visited, I found it unfathomable that we were praying in a location where, on one side of the street, doctors were using every medical process and resource to preserve and save the most vulnerable lives, while just a few yards away, abortionists were deliberately killing babies of the same age. Doctors working to saves lives; doctors working to end lives; and Wynette and her team praying outside, pointing out the great contradiction. That late-term abortion facility eventually went out of business, praise God.

The Sacramento pro-life team, besides having received amazing media coverage, has been able to create pregnancy centers and has seen a few abortion facilities close due to their efforts. It seems that Wynette and another wonderful Sacramento leader, Susan Money, and the countless volunteers have done everything right.

But doing everything right does not mean everything turns out all right for these families. The truth is, not all children saved by abortion have fairy-tale lives.

Wynette has had the privilege and heartbreak of spending time with some of these families. She tells of being able to love on a six-year-old whose life was saved as an infant during a campaign. She was able to take him, along with his brothers, mother, and grandmother, Christmas shopping. She has been able to spend time with him and talk with him about what he wants to be when he grows up. To be able to see him off to school is something precious. But Mom doesn't always make good and safe choices for her children. And that can be painful to see.

Wynette says, "Sometimes, after changing their mind and deciding to keep their child, the parents go right on with their education, pursue their career goals, and everything turns out like a fairy tale. I have a few of those stories. But sometimes the ending isn't very pleasant, and that's why we need our faith."

Wynette has never been one to shy away from reality, nor from playing her part in personally helping those she encounters. She and her team assisted a homeless family who already had two school-aged children and who then discovered that twins were due. They provided job opportunities, paid for car repairs, and paid for the first few months of rent on an apartment. But the father wouldn't show up for the jobs that were made available to him. Wynette was there when the twin babies were born prematurely with drugs in their system, causing them to be taken by Child Protective Services. By the grace of God, a loving, stable family is now in the process of adopting the twins, and they have a positive, healthy future ahead of them. The biological parents are also receiving the help they desperately need. The time 40 Days volunteers spend at the sidewalk can save a whole family.

One woman, Jessica, met some classmates who were part of the pro-life group Students for Life. She was pregnant, in crisis, and considering abortion. She had already had one abortion and didn't want to go through another.

Students for Life befriended Jessica. They gave her a baby shower and became godmother to the little boy, who was born just before Jessica's graduation. In fact, she walked across the graduation stage with her son in arms. Not only did she graduate—she went on to get her master's degree, got married, and had another baby. Little Stefan is now a six-year-old big brother to a beautiful little addition to Jessica's family.

Wynette recently reconnected with this mom after six years. "To see her succeed, graduate, go on to get her master's degree, get married, have a family, have a home, have furniture, have a car. It is beautiful to see—but that kind of resolution is rare for me."

I've known Wynette a long time and have always considered her a saint in the truest sense of the word—someone who puts aside comfort and convenience for the love of Jesus in every circumstance our Lord presents to her.

During one 40 Days for Life campaign, Wynette was out there twelve hours a day, every day, offering alternatives. Let that sink in. No wonder volunteers were so inspired by her example. But on this particular day Wynette needed a break. So she went to a nearby McDonalds, where she saw a young couple about fifteen or sixteen years old sitting in a booth. She said hi to them. The next day she saw them there again, so she sat down, introduced herself, and told them what she was doing down the street. Wynette discovered that the young couple was homeless. She began bringing them food, sleeping bags, and pillows, trying to at least make their homelessness more comfortable in the short term while also addressing the long-term path to sustainable housing and self-sufficiency.

As their friend, Wynette helped them in many ways. She drove them places. When the young woman got pregnant, Wynette took her to a life-affirming pregnancy clinic where the young woman saw her baby on the ultrasound. Wynette helped her get enrolled in a prestigious program called Women's Empowerment, whose mission is to end homelessness and poverty through employment. The participants attend an extensive six-week class of job readiness, resume writing, GED completion, and practice for job interviews.

Wynette thought things were going well—until one day "I saw

her out on the street soliciting for a few bucks. I rolled down my window and said, 'Just get in my car. You don't have to do this. Our family will take you in.'"

The girl got into Wynette's car with everything she had. Because Wynette's own children are all grown and gone, she was able to set the girl up in one of her children's bedrooms. The young woman had never had a bed before. "She'd always slept on the couch, on the floor, or on an air mattress. She'd been in foster care, on the streets, or a runaway her whole life."

Wynette continued to take her to classes every day. She became a part of their family. She went to church with them, sitting next to them in the pew at mass. She went to family birthday parties.

"I wish I could say, 'And now this young woman has her college degree and everything has worked out.' But that's not what happened." When she came to the end of her six-week course, she didn't meet the program's expectations of progress. And on weekends, rather than stay with Wynette and her husband, she preferred to go back to her friends and her boyfriend. She told Wynette, "I'm addicted to the hood." As much as Wynette's family tried, the young woman eventually moved out. "I thought we would care for her and her baby for the next eighteen years."

Wynette looked at me and said, "It's not a fairy tale. My prayer request is for continued perseverance in situations where we've tried to bring the love of Christ and tried to be the light in the darkness, and it's not accepted. The young woman's baby was saved from abortion, but our love, support, and prayers must continue, even when rejected."

There is nothing wrong with admitting that being faithful in the face of disappointment is easier said than done. Think about it. After the resurrection, things worked out and we all lived happily ever after, right? Of course not. There was division, fear, and persecution. Our culture is in bad shape, and standing outside an abortion facility gives us a front-row seat to observe just how bad it is. This is why

40 Days for Life isn't a protest or a political movement. It's a prayer movement. It requires prayer because of where it happens and what is encountered there, and prayer gives us hope even in the darkest of situations.

Stephanie was certainly not living a fairy tale when she met Wynette. The mother of five had chosen abortion before, even while married, and she was raising her sister's child following her sister's murder. Now Stephanie was pregnant with a child diagnosed with alobar holoprosencephaly, a condition in which the brain is not developing properly. The baby was not expected to survive the pregnancy, and even if it did, doctors predicted that it might live only a few minutes or hours, six months at most. Stephanie was advised by everyone to have an abortion. And when she did, guess who was there to greet her with a smile? Wynette.

Wynette spoke to Stephanie as if she were her own daughter, as if she had known her for years. She listened to Stephanie and learned about her life, her circumstances, and the baby's condition. She cried with Stephanie.

Stephanie saw Wynette as a sign that she was not supposed to have the abortion. She said, "I didn't get any support from my family. After my sister died it tore our family apart. I didn't get any support except from those in the pro-life community." Many would say that Stephanie had every reason to thank Wynette for her time and then have the abortion. But Stephanie had already experienced the pain of abortion as well as the joy of motherhood. She found hope at the most unexpected place—the very doorstep of an abortion facility.

Holding her beautiful baby girl, Stephanie said, "I chose life for Khya as a form of redemption, and to help others understand how wrong abortion is, and also to send a powerful message to my other children, as we all became her caregivers."

Stephanie chose to spend whatever time she had with Khya to comfort and love her, not to "put her out of her misery," as the doctors had said abortion would do. Little Khya was not only a witness to love and life, she was a fighter. She brought joy to her mother and siblings and, against all medical predictions, lived to be two years old before she passed away. Wynette and her team had done much for Khya and her family, including helping with prenatal care, providing a car, being there when Khya was born, and helping with family expenses. Once Khya passed away, the pro-life community of Sacramento provided a funeral, flowers, food, and a gravesite for sweet Khya, who was well loved by everyone.

Stephanie needed help and hope, and God provided that on a sunny sidewalk outside an abortion facility. Stephanie said, "What the world sees as 'imperfect' or a 'mistake,' we see as our much-loved little sister and daughter. Khya has taught us so much about faith, hope, and love. I thank God for picking me to be her mom."

Stephanie went on to nursing school and now helps our friend, Pastor Walter Hoye, raise awareness about the devastating impact abortion is having on the African American community. She stays in contact with her friend Wynette, who was there for her as God's reminder that, ultimately, none of us are alone.

Wynette is a hero and an inspiration, but pro-life work doesn't always have a fairy-tale ending. Rather, it's *better* than a fairy tale. As a mission of the gospel, it is both miraculous and painful. It is freeing even though it comes with many crosses to bear, for it holds the promise of victory through Jesus Christ. Wynette knows better than anyone that we don't write the endings of the stories we encounter. We are just called to be faithful to play our active role in *God's* story. Wynette didn't sign up to lead because she wanted to be in a fairy tale; she signed up because she loves the God who has the final say in every story.

~

*I consider that our present sufferings
are not worth comparing with the glory
that will be revealed in us.*
ROMANS 8:18

Lord, I confess that I sometimes would prefer fairy-tale endings over the messiness of reality in this broken world. Thank you for the example of Wynette, who doesn't let that messiness keep her from doing her best to make a positive difference. I pray you give her the perseverance she asks for. Help me to remember that even though doing my part in the cause for life doesn't mean those whose lives I touch will have happily-ever-after stories, you still want me to play my part. Help me fulfill my calling in the present and trust you for the future. Amen.

Fighting God

~

The cleverest of all, in my opinion,
is the man who calls himself a fool
at least once a month.
—FYODOR DOSTOEVSKY

I INTRODUCED YOU TO STEVE KARLEN IN DAY 18. IN 2012 WE hired Steve to direct North American campaigns. He has now represented 40 Days for Life in forty-six states, four Canadian provinces, and Mexico.

Steve has seen a lot. From screaming abortion advocates, blowing whistles, and clanging noisemakers, to disrupted events, a midnight climb to the top of the 40 Days for Life tour bus alongside a South Dakota interstate to make a repair in forty-mile-per-hour winds, and a trip that took him to Washington, Oregon, California, Alaska, and Hawaii *on consecutive days*. He even had coffee thrown at him in Seattle—which is doubly offensive to a non-coffee drinker.

But on this particular day, Steve Karlen did *not* want to go to an abortion facility to pray.

In 2015, Steve led a workshop in Indianapolis for 40 Days for Life leaders in the region. Before leaving his home in Wisconsin to make the road trip, Steve asked our Indianapolis leader, Eileen, whether she'd like to host a rally at Planned Parenthood the night before the workshop. She replied, "Could we do it at noon instead?"

Without thinking through the logistics, Steve said yes. Then he thought about it and felt the tidal wave of regret when he realized he would need to get up even earlier to make it to the rally by noon. And then he realized he needed to get up even earlier than that because he would cross time zones, losing another hour. And that meant moving through rush hour traffic in Chicago. Make that another hour earlier. Grrrr. Have you been there before? I have, plenty of times. We commit and then we regret it—usually due to selfishness. At those moments, God has used my selfishness to point out how pathetic and weak I am. God can use even such moments as those—and man, do we need him to.

This was one of those moments for Steve. He asked his compassionate and sweet wife, Laura, to suggest a way he could back out. No one was more understanding than she, and Steve could always rely on her for sound advice.

Laura listened and nodded at her tired husband. And when he'd made his case as well as he could, Laura said, "Suck it up! Go do your job. Save some babies."

That sounded like wisdom to Steve, whether he liked it or not, and he made it to Indianapolis on time. He pulled up to the rally scheduled for the day before his workshop and saw a huge crowd. Everyone was glad Steve had made the trip despite the difficult travel, and many volunteers had come out for the first time. Steve tried to tamp down the guilt he felt as he met so many enthusiastic people excited about 40 Days for Life. *Thank God for Laura*, he thought.

Then about halfway through the rally, someone announced, "We just saved a baby!"

The rally was a one-off event—not part of a 40 Days for Life campaign. If it hadn't been for the rally, nobody would have been at Planned Parenthood that day to pray or sidewalk counsel. "I had been willing to cancel the rally so I could get a few extra hours of sleep," Steve said. "If I'd gotten my way, that baby would have been lost. God used me to help save a baby, even though I fought him every step of the way."

But things were just getting started. A half hour later, another attendee shared news of a saved baby.

Steve said, "I know! I heard that about thirty minutes ago. That's great!"

The volunteer said, "No! Another baby. The mother was in the waiting room. She heard the speeches over the PA system and changed her mind!"

When Steve got home to Wisconsin, he thanked Laura for her kick in the rear in response to his complaining. He called Eileen a month later just to check in, and at the end of their conversation Eileen said, "By the way, we learned there was a *third* baby saved that afternoon."

Showing up really is half the battle, and it seemed to Steve that every baby saved that afternoon was God's beautiful version of rubbing it in.

A few months later, motivated and without a complaint in sight, Steve visited the 40 Days for Life campaign in Atlanta, Georgia.

Most of the crowd consisted of students, parents, and teachers from a nearby Christian high school. After addressing vigil participants, Steve met a woman named Leslie, who told him that, as a teenager, she had been the victim of a sexual assault. She became pregnant and had an abortion.

It took Leslie longer to heal from the abortion than from the assault. After the abortion, she went into a tailspin. She became addicted to drugs. She became a prostitute. She had two more abortions.

Through God's grace, Leslie found healing, became a Christian, got married, and had two more children. By the time of Steve's visit to Atlanta, those children were now teenagers and students at the Christian school participating in the rally, and they were the ones who had invited Leslie to attend. It wasn't until the night before the event that she realized she was returning to the very facility where she had had her third and final abortion.

As Leslie shared her story, her eyes filled with tears—tears of regret and sorrow but also tears of joy. You see, her children led praise and worship music that afternoon at the abortion center, and she couldn't have been prouder.

It's an example of why Jesus died on the cross and of the power of his life, passion, death, and resurrection. A drug-addicted prostitute aborted three of her children. But then she met Jesus, who blessed her with two more children. And now those children had brought her back to the abortion center, this time to *protect* life. It is the kind of difference only God can make.

"I can't help but to think of our Lord's words in the book of Revelation," Steve said. "He makes all things new."

He does indeed. He makes us new even when we get tired, lazy, or idle.

Steve's reluctance to get up before dawn to drive for hours to a rally are only human. We can all relate. Who would rather be at a rally at an abortion facility on a Saturday than watching college football or grilling pork ribs? When we *want* to go out and pray at an abortion facility, that's a gift from God. But when we *don't* want to, that is our service to God. To say yes in rain or shine, early morning or dead of night, to mean yes not only on Easter Sunday but also on Good Friday, these are all a part of the daily battle to end abortion. Through whatever challenges we face, these are situations in which God can teach us humility. It is his gift to us, and he uses it to show how he can use even our complaints and weariness to save a life that was scheduled to be aborted. If we let him, God will use our frustration and drowsiness to give hope in what are otherwise lonely parking lots of abortion facilities. It's why he gets the credit and why he's the fuel behind the beginning of the end of abortion.

~

He who was seated on the throne said,
"I am making everything new!"
Then he said, "Write this down,
for these words are trustworthy and true."
REVELATION 21:5

God, please give me the strength to say yes when I want to say
no. Give me the strength to sign up to pray when I would rather
play. Give me the ears to hear when you whisper, "Go," even
when I have other plans. Help me to be faithful, even though
my tendency is to be faithless. Amen.

For God and Country

~

The ultimate test of a moral society
is the kind of world that it leaves to its children.
—DIETRICH BONHOEFFER

I'LL NEVER FORGET HAVING, AT THE IMPRESSIONABLE AGE OF fourteen, my first conversation with a prisoner of war.

The POW was the grandfather of my best friend, Chris. John Yuill served his career as a pilot in the United States Air Force. Everybody loves Grandpa. He seems to do everything right in life, never complains, and has a classic sense of humor. He loves God, his wife, their eight kids, and Cracker Barrel.

I loved hearing his stories about his B-52 bomber being shot down. I will always remember his description of how he felt when, after his bailout and his descent by parachute, he hit the ground and braced himself to be shot and killed. He told us how he went through hell for our country, never knowing if he would ever see his wife and children again. When you're a boy of fourteen, you can listen to those stories all day long.

But after one of those story sessions one day, he changed his tone and said, "I am a single-issue voter."

Okay, I thought. I felt as if I should know what his issue was. Thinking of his time as a POW, I said, "I bet it's national defense, right?"

He said, "No. That is obviously very important, but there is no more crucial issue to the future of our nation than abortion. I vote pro-life first and foremost."

He had had a military career, moving his eight children from place to place as his duty required. He had been on the brink of death in a war prison and had sacrificed many comforts for our nation. But his surprising comment to me that day had been about abortion.

"There are no accidents," he said. "God created us, and he will always look out for us. We just have to trust him."

He of all people knows the importance of trusting God with your life.

∾

What kind of country do we want for our children and grandchildren?

We hear that question so often from politicians that it has become a cliché. They often ask it as a setup for their view on tax reform, healthcare, gun control, war, or infrastructure.

Psalm 90, verse 10, reminds us how short this life is when considering eternity: "Our days may come to seventy years, or eighty, if our strength endures."

We do not determine when we are born or into what family we are born. We are called to respond to the circumstances we are given, and beyond that, to answer the questions behind the ones the politicians ask. Questions such as, *What do I stand for? What do I really cherish? What will I defend?*

The founding fathers of the United States asked themselves these questions. They pondered what was necessary to have a free nation under God. They argued about what would set this new nation apart from all others. What would this country cherish more deeply than would a king in a foreign land? What would the rights of Americans be? What would we, as a nation, put first?

Their answer came in three simple things, in this order: life, liberty, and the pursuit of happiness.

We can adjust taxes, and then another president or Congress messes them up again. We can take away guns or lift all regulations. We can fight for healthcare to keep costs down and make it available to those in need, or we can coast along as we always have. We can start or end wars. We can build new interstate highways or complain about our current ones. We can and must consider and debate all these things.

The question is—then what? What will we do with laws we agree with, taxes we can afford, and roads we can depend on? What guarantees that our country will outlast good or bad policies, presidents, and politicians? There is an undercurrent in America and the entire West that calls us back to the founders of the United States and their first requirement if America would survive—*life*.

All other rights assume that we have a right to life. Without the right to life, any guarantees of other rights are meaningless. What is safe? What is off limits?

You don't need me to tell you that the family, as an institution, has been beaten down in the West the last fifty years, often from within. *Family* used to be the foundation for joy, responsibility, security, and love, but it is now often a source of pain, mistrust, and exhaustion. If you doubt that, look at the parking lots of abortion facilities.

The men and women who enter those facilities for abortions sometimes have good families, but often not. No matter what their family is like, they're all choosing to do what was *not* done to them— ending the life of their own child. There is nothing more unnatural or more painful than that. It is painful for the baby, painful for the mother and father, and whether they admit it or not, my experience with abortion doctors would indicate that it is painful for the doctor as well. Abortion thrives on pain, which is why, in our 40 Days for Life campaigns, we bring the Great Physician to the sidewalk.

It is the Great Physician who is restoring the family. It is he who is closing abortion facilities. It is he who is saving babies and offering hope to those who have been through an abortion. It is he who is changing the cold hearts of abortion doctors. It is he whom the heroes of 40 Days for Life, the local campaign leaders and volunteers, serve.

Over 750,000 people have participated in 40 Days for Life around the world. And it's often hard—just ask them. You're outside in all kinds of weather. You may face persecution. Your intentions may be questioned. Local media may not hold you in high regard. Standing out on a sidewalk praying for an end to abortion is not how most would want to spend an early Monday morning or a Saturday evening or anytime in between. But when we see each life in the womb as one of God's children, all these difficulties become irrelevant. When we view the world through the lens of Christ, we see the intrinsic value of human life that cannot be altered by fads, Hollywood, reporters, or politicians. And so we endure these difficulties for love of God and love of country.

Right now there are men and women around the world fighting to save a baby from abortion, to give hope to a woman, or to reach an abortion worker. We don't do this because we *have* to—we *get* to do this in the United States of America. And this freedom is a gift from God that has been preserved by the many who have laid down their lives for this country.

Every abortion is an attack on the future of America. Every abortion is an attack on the future of the family. And every abortion is an attack on the future of humanity.

The 40 Days for Life campaign is a spiritual journey that is challenging and that is sustained by prayer and fasting. But it is also a patriotic service.

In 2006 I was in a meeting in Houston, helping to shape a plan to oppose the largest abortion facility in the western hemisphere—the 78,000-square-foot Planned Parenthood in Houston. My friend and longtime pro-life leader Eric Scheidler said something I'll never forget: "There would be no first amendment without the pro-life movement. No one uses it more than us. And if we go away, it will too."

But there is a deeper reason for the growth of 40 Days for Life. It's something our culture is losing—a sense of duty.

When you stand up for the rights of the unborn, you are using your rights as an American to serve God even as many others work to remove him from our culture. Your service is a beautiful witness to your love of God and love of country. And there are thousands of women and babies and hundreds of abortion workers grateful for your prayers and sacrifice.

It can be so easy to get stuck in the overwhelming statistics of abortion. There are nearly one million per year in the United States, and every single one of them pierces the heart of God. But God can also use you in ways you would never imagine, to be that last line of defense for that baby and his or her mother. Grandpa was right—life is a gift from God, and he will take care of us if we trust him.

What will we do with our freedom?

The beginning of the end of abortion starts with prayer and ends with you trusting God that in his timing he will end abortion in the United States and beyond.

～

You did not choose me,
but I chose you and appointed you
so that you might go and bear fruit—
fruit that will last—
and so that whatever you ask in my name
the Father will give you.
JOHN 15:16

Lord, I thank you for the freedoms I have, and I thank you for the freedom that is exercised everywhere a prayer volunteer is standing vigil outside an abortion facility. Stir me to exercise my freedoms to speak out and take action on behalf of the unborn, their mothers and extended families, and abortion workers. Help me never to take for granted the freedom you've given me. How would you have me use my freedom, Lord? Amen.

Violence Is No Match for Love

~

Love can accomplish all things.
Things that are most impossible
become easy where love is at work.
—THERESE OF LISIEUX

"ERNIE," SAID MARY BETH CYR TO HER HUSBAND ONE EVENING AS she served dinner to their growing family, "we need to go out to the abortion facility and pray as a family."

They had recently moved from Boston to Pensacola, Florida, for Ernie to take a position as a pharmacist. She was volunteering at a pregnancy resource center and felt called to pray outside one of the two local abortion facilities. "I feel like I could reach more abortion-minded women if our family was with me."

"No way," Ernie said, shaking his head emphatically. "We will *not* go out there as a family. Those people who demonstrate in front of abortion facilities are crazy. They're violent. They do nothing but harm."

At the time, Ernie had no idea how true his words were in describing his community. Because the family was new to Pensacola, they were unaware that in the 1990s, two abortionists and a security escort had been shot to death and one abortion facility bombed in the Pensacola area. As a result, very few people had been willing to publicly oppose abortion in Pensacola for many years.

Early one spring morning, six months after their dinner conversation, Ernie turned on the television as he got ready for work. The Global Catholic Network EWTN was airing a show that I had produced to help launch our first national 40 Days for Life campaign slated for that summer of 2007. We'd already had our first local campaign in 2004, and over the following three years we had helped a few other cities put on campaigns. But launching this campaign nationally was our next big step of faith.

We thought a professionally produced show would help get the word out. An Emmy Award–winning director donated much of his time to create a high-quality show that conveyed the 40 Days for Life philosophy that praying at an abortion facility is a labor of love and never promotes acts of violence. We planned to air the show multiple times on EWTN and then open applications for volunteers who wished to lead a campaign. We just didn't know if people would watch. But Ernie Cyr watched. And he asked his wife to watch with him that evening. When the show was over, they turned to each other at the same time and said, "We have to do this." They submitted an application, went through our training, and were ready to recruit volunteers, still having no idea of Pensacola's past.

But once they started to recruit volunteers, friends, people from their church, and coworkers told them of the bombing and shootings. At first Ernie and Mary Beth were shocked and afraid. Ernie could have easily thought, *You know, this is not the time or place for a campaign like this. We weren't aware of the city's history, and this is not prudent for Pensacola*, and thrown in the towel. But he and Mary Beth decided that 40 Days for Life was different. They weren't holding a protest. They were presenting a movement of prayer, fasting, and love through a peaceful vigil. Love could overcome violence. They would continue.

Not surprisingly, they didn't experience a flood of volunteers. On the first evening, they began their candlelight vigil with ten participants on a very busy highway where the abortion facility was located.

As the days and weeks progressed, Ernie and Mary Beth continued to pray, to care, to speak to women. They developed great relationships with the pregnancy resource centers. Because of Ernie and Mary Beth and their volunteers, women were choosing life, and lives were being saved from abortion at a rapid pace. It didn't matter whether these women knew Pensacola's violent history or not. What did matter is that they knew people were there praying for them and offering hope for them and their babies. And they were responding.

The numbers slowly built over the weeks as people saw that 40 Days for Life was, indeed, a peaceful, prayerful event. By the end of the 40-day campaign, one hundred people attended the evening candlelight events, and a cautious optimism for this new ministry along with an awakening of the spirit in Pensacola was underway.

Women choosing life is bad for the abortion business—facilities don't make money when women choose life. So not even three years after Ernie told Mary Beth they would not be going out to pray because "They're just a bunch of crazy people who do more harm than good," the abortion facility where Ernie and Mary Beth prayed with their six kids and hundreds of volunteers could no longer stay open. Pensacola went from two abortion facilities to one.

Ernie and Mary Beth didn't stop. They moved to the next abortion facility, and it didn't take long to see God saving even more lives.

One day when the family had planned to be on the sidewalk for only a few hours, they ended up staying for twelve. The reason? They couldn't pull themselves away as women kept choosing life. Seven women chose life for their babies that day!

At one point that day, a woman drove up and beckoned Ernie over to her car. She said, "I've talked my sister out of it. She's not going to get an abortion. But she's still inside. She's been there for hours."

Ernie said, "Bring her out here to talk to us. We have resources. We've got a pregnancy center counselor right here."

The woman went inside, retrieved her sister—the last woman to leave the abortion facility that day—and brought her to Ernie and Mary Beth, who were able to get her connected with a great pregnancy resource center. A few days later Mary Beth went with the woman to her OB/GYN appointment. Together they stared at the ultrasound monitor as a beautiful baby boy appeared on the screen. In that moment, all the mother's worry and concern vanished.

When baby Denzel was born via C-section, Mom wanted Mary Beth at her side. And a few months later, Ernie and Mary Beth became Denzel's godparents.

The number of lives saved from abortion continued to be "bad for business" for the abortion industry in Pensacola. Over the nine years of campaigns, according to the Agency for Health Care Administration in Florida, abortions in Pensacola had dropped by 47 percent.

Ernie was ecstatic when he saw the report. "It is an affirmation that the volunteers' efforts, through God's grace, are not in vain. God is healing our land one life at a time. He is hearing our prayers and answering them."

Although Ernie celebrates these numbers, they do not slow him down. There is work yet to be done. "We must continue to reach out to the precious mothers in our community, so that they will never feel the need to abort their child. Someday soon, in God's time, the reported number will be zero!"

During the spring campaign of 2016 one mom, Tia, came from out of state to get an abortion. After meeting Ernie and Mary Beth, she chose life instead. They helped her find local resources in her home state through the 40 days for Life campaign there. Ernie and Mary Beth walked with her all the remaining months of her pregnancy and then surprised her with a baby shower.

Tia named her baby girl Zyliee. She was born just before the fall campaign. Her grandmother and Zyliee made a Skype video to encourage volunteers that their presence makes a difference. Her grandmother's words remind us to trust the love of God. "You can compel someone to make a decision with lovingkindness more than with aggression. My beautiful granddaughter is the result of what God can do when people have a heart for God's people and are willing to take time. You all didn't have to be standing out there. I don't know what would have happened if you hadn't been there." Breaking down in tears, then gathering herself together to continue, this loving grandmother holding her newborn granddaughter said, "I don't even want to think about it."

She closed by encouraging people to continue to go out and pray because it makes a difference. "God has been showing my daughter that she is not alone, and that's because of people like you."

This message was beautiful for everyone but especially for Ernie. That spring campaign when Zyliee was saved had been one that Ernie had originally wanted to take off, and we had encouraged him to do that, feeling that he needed a break. But as the campaign got closer, he decided he was up for it. The result was Zyliee's life.

"I'd say don't worry about what the world's going to say to you," Ernie said. "Worry about what God is asking you to do; what God is calling you to do. It's time for us to trust in God 100 percent and not let people stop us from being part of a movement that is changing the culture. A movement that is asking every Christian to be a part of it. I often tell people, I'm a clinical pharmacist, I have a pretty significant job at a local hospital as a pharmacy administrator. I also coordinate the residency program and am busy raising our six children. But God is calling every one of us to do our part. You don't need a medical degree to save a life. Just by going and being present, lives are saved."

In 2016 our board chair and general counsel, Matt Britton, and I started a leadership award for local campaign leaders. At our leader symposium, we named Ernie Cyr the first recipient of the 40 Days for Life Leader Award.

It was a great moment as Ernie's selfless fellow campaign leaders stood to applaud him. He came on stage and called Mary Beth and their six children to join him. Ernie kissed Mary Beth, then spoke these simple words: "This is how we overcame fear in Pensacola—the family. What is abortion doing? Attacking the family. So how do we win? Through the family. Through love."

Pensacola was known for violent attacks against abortion providers. Yet few understand that abortion is also violent. It is the most violent surgery you can imagine. It's not only destroying innocent and beautiful children but families as well. And it happens millions of times per year worldwide.

We all fear, we all doubt, we all hesitate. But our willingness to trust the love of God is what changes our communities. Ernie and Mary Beth trusted the approach of 40 Days for Life and didn't let the past actions of criminals—who can't be pro-life if they are in fact taking human lives—define the pro-life movement in Pensacola. The Cyrs responded to the injustice of abortion not with the sword but by trusting God, putting their hope in him, prayer, fasting, and action.

The next time you're tempted to be timid or to give in to fear when it comes to defending the unborn and their mothers, think of the pharmacist from New England who was simply getting ready for work one morning when he allowed God to take him on a journey to be part of the beginning of the end of abortion. Ernie and Mary Beth Cyr trusted God. They are living proof that violence is no match for love.

～

"Put your sword back in its place,"
Jesus said to him,
"for all who draw the sword
will die by the sword."
MATTHEW 26:52

Jesus, fill my heart with your sweet Spirit. Fill me with your love and gentleness so that I might not fight fear with fear or violence with violence but would trust in the power of your love to overcome all. I pray that your love through me would permeate the hearts of all the evil and violence that might come before me. Amen.

Where Were You?

~

Love without truth is blind,
truth without love is empty.
—JOSEPH RATZINGER

ONE OF THE LARGEST PLANNED PARENTHOOD LATE-TERM ABORtion facilities on the West Coast is located in Orange, California, where Paula is a dedicated 40 Days for Life volunteer. To set the scene, you might remember that in *40 Days for Life,* my first book, I share the beautiful story of the birth of Milagros—*Miracle.* Milagros was slated for abortion at this facility after her mother was told that her baby was severely handicapped and would be born with no legs. But at the last moment, her mother chose life. Milagros's story has been widely shared in *40 Days for Life,* and she was featured on the cover of our first issue of the quarterly magazine *DAY 41.*

Planned Parenthood, Orange, is a difficult location. Paula is always there praying, always available to give out free information. A soft-spoken woman in her sixties, she is very approachable, exuding grace, so it's no wonder so many women feel comfortable speaking to her about alternatives to abortion. Paula is nonconfrontational and gets nervous when people yell. If you met her, you would understand that she would be a difficult woman to be upset with. But one woman found a reason.

"What are you doing here?" the woman shouted at Paula, walking aggressively toward her. "You have no right to be here judging these women. You have no idea what they're going through. You're a self-righteous know-it-all trying to force your beliefs on strangers. You don't even know the people going in here!"

Paula took a breath and opened her mouth to speak, but before she could get a word out the woman continued her tirade, gesturing wildly. "You need to leave. You shouldn't be here. No one wants you here harassing these women." The woman paused and glared at Paula. "Planned Parenthood saved my life."

In her soft voice, Paula said, "I'd like to hear—how did they save your life?"

With full conviction and a rush of breath, the woman said, "I was a pregnant teenager. I was raped, and I was homeless. I was brought here for an abortion and they gave me one. Otherwise I'd have had a kid all these years. I wouldn't have been able to do all of the things I've done in life. They literally saved my life. Without them, my life would be completely different. You don't know what all these people coming here for help are going through. And you don't know how much help this place provides. They saved my life. I owe everything to them."

Paula had talked to hundreds of women on the sidewalks. She thought she had heard it all. But this was new. Paula had never heard someone claim that Planned Parenthood had saved her life. As the woman continued to vent, Paula prayed about what to say. Clearly the woman's passion, evidenced in her tendency to speak rapidly and repeat the same things over and over, indicated a deep wound regarding her abortion. Paula decided to take a risk. She looked at the woman with compassion and in her sweet, calm voice said, "They didn't save your life. They killed your baby."

The woman was stunned into silence. She stared at Paula in disbelief. Then she gathered herself together and said, "They saved my life. You have some nerve being out here."

They stood on the sidewalk, looking at each other. Paula intended to break the silence by saying that she'd meant no harm in her earlier comment, but the woman spoke first. "No one was here for me," she whispered. She took a deep, ragged breath and let the pain pour out. "I was raped. I was young—just a teenager. I was innocent. I was brought here for the abortion."

As the two women focused on each other, the sounds of the neighborhood and traffic faded.

Tears filled the woman's eyes. "When I was brought here that day, no one was standing where you're standing. No one was here doing what you are doing. No one. No one was here for me. That abortion destroyed my life, and no one was here. I was a child."

She looked closer at Paula. "Where were you? Where were you when I was brought here after being raped? When they told me that an abortion would solve my problem? I see you every week, standing out here for the women who are coming now, but where were you *when I needed you?*"

Paula recalled, "I could still see the scared teenager she once was, who needed someone to help her, not hurt her and her baby. She was about thirty-two to thirty-five years old, so her abortion was over fifteen years in the past. That's when I felt really bad and had to look at myself." Paula again told the woman the truth. "I was too much of a coward. I was too busy. I always said I was pro-life, I said I should come out here, but I never did until a few years ago. Back then I didn't take my faith as seriously as I do now. I was scared. Timid about what others would think." Paula made sure the woman was looking in her eyes before she continued. "I'm sorry that you went through that. I am sorry that I was not here for you. I should have been here for you, but I was weak."

Paula's honest response surprised the woman. Paula later said, "My heart bled in pain for her. I saw a post-abortive woman who had a deep wound that had never healed, and I saw a coward (myself) who should have been on the sidewalk years earlier trying to save women like her from making an irreversible decision." The woman's demeanor completely changed toward Paula, who had been truthful to both the hurting woman and herself. Before the woman drove away, she looked at Paula sadly one last time and said, *"Where were you? Where were you when I needed you most?"*

~

John 1:14 says that Jesus came from the Father "full of grace and truth." The grace and truth (and love) of Christ are what truly saves, and they are what we pin our hope on to end abortion. Grace and truth met the woman at the well, grace and truth were cursed by the Pharisees, grace and truth defended the woman caught in adultery, grace and truth were mocked by soldiers, grace and truth were nailed to a cross on Calvary.

When we pray outside an abortion facility, we join grace and truth at the foot of the cross. At the foot of the cross is where life and death meet, where grace and truth can repair the great evil of pitting mothers and fathers against their own sons and daughters.

The calming reality is that the grace and truth of Jesus didn't end at Calvary but continued on to his resurrection. And if we truly believe that the resurrection of Jesus Christ is a reality, then we know that life can overcome death in all its forms, and we can trust that where sin abounds, grace abounds even more.

We are witnesses to the fact that we are indeed living in the beginning of the end of abortion. We are seeing that no lie can last forever. There is no sanitizer, no truth revealer, like the sunlight. Despite decades of abortion legalization and government funding, abortion tears at us like no other issue. As Mother Teresa sagely said, "Abortion is the greatest destroyer of peace in our world." And it always will be—until it ends.

Even though we often hear differently from the media, the abortion issue is not complex; it is very simple. It is all about the gift of life. If you are reading this book, you are alive, and you did not create yourself. Your life is a gift, and it gives you a chance to make the journey from birth to eternity. Life is full of kids' soccer games, arguments, birthday cake, cancer, college football tailgates, algebra homework, the IRS, snow days, spilt milk, wedding dresses, endless laundry, car accidents, overpriced coffee, new socks, lawsuits, candlelight dinners, annoying people, and smoking brisket. We are not robots; we are pilgrims.

Yet millions of our brothers and sisters have that gift and that journey stripped from them in a most violent surgery. They are completely helpless at stopping it. They have no autonomy; they have no chance; they have only *you*.

If we want to end the injustice of abortion, we must turn to the Author of Life, thank him for our life, and make a commitment to be our brother's keeper. You see, the beginning of the end of abortion does not start on CNN or Wall Street or in Congress. And it doesn't start with you or me deciding we will go end abortion on our own power. It starts with one thing: prayer.

I challenge both myself and you to close this forty-day journey with the question, "Where will I be?" Where will I be when the opportunity to save a life from abortion arrives? Where will I be when abortion ends in my city, my state, my country?

I don't know your role in this fight, and I'm not going to tell you what it is. I don't respond to that kind of brow-beating in books, and I have no intention of writing one like that. We are in different places with different circumstances, and that means that each of us has different limits and opportunities regarding what we can and can't do. It is not pro-life to neglect our duties or our families. We all have our own answer to that woman's question—"Where were you?" We may be content with our answer. Or maybe, like Paula, we feel regret.

But regrets relate to the past, and we cannot live in the past because abortions are happening today. If we live in the past, we will despair. There is no room for despair when you believe in the resurrection.

We began this 40 Days for Life journey by putting first things first. Our world is hurting, and we need not be timid in bringing the joy, grace, truth, and love of Christ to a hurting world.

The pages of this book are full of people who changed the world by doing the ordinary—by just being there. They didn't wait until all their questions about abortion were answered—they just started. They showed up. They asked a question and trusted God with the results:

Where will I be?

∼

"Then the King will say to those on his right, 'Come, you who are blessed by My Father; take your inheritance, the kingdom prepared for you since the creation of the world. For I was hungry and you gave me something to eat, I was thirsty and you gave me something to drink, I was a stranger and you invited me in, I needed clothes and you clothed me, I was sick and you looked after me, I was in prison and you came to visit me.' Then the righteous will answer him, 'Lord, when did we see you hungry and feed you, or thirsty and give you something to drink? When did we see you a stranger and invite you in, or needing clothes and clothe you? When did we see you sick or in prison and go to visit you?' The King will reply, 'Truly I tell you, whatever you did for one of the least of these brothers and sisters of mine, you did for me.'"

MATTHEW 25:34−40

Oh blessed, holy God, I ask for your presence with me today. I ask you to help me answer the questions that should be on my heart: Where will I be? What would you have me do? Where would you have me go? Let me not sit complacent in my life but be willing to go forth in grace and truth to wherever you call me to go. Amen.

Baby A, Baby C, and Baby D

~

The autonomous self can kill unwanted people,
old people, useless people, and unborn people
and do so reasonably, without passion.

—WALKER PERCY

BABY A, BABY C, AND BABY D BROKE THE HEARTS OF AMERICA.

And the man convicted of their murder brought the public's attention to the reality of abortion like no one else in history.

In February of 2010, the FBI raided Dr. Kermit Gosnell's Philadelphia late-term abortion facility after a tip that it operated as an illegal prescription mill.[56]

That raid discovered what law enforcement called a "house of horrors"—the worst conditions of any medical facility in America. To say that the facility had unsanitary conditions was to put it mildly. The FBI found blood stains on beds, nonsterilized instruments in use, and the results of two flea-infested, free-roaming cats that used the stairs as their litterbox. In Gosnell's basement they found freezers that were "full of discarded fetuses." Inside Gosnell's refrigerator they discovered baby feet in jars. On the ground were stacks of bags, jugs, and bottles filled with fetal remains.

Gosnell's laid-back nature and casual approach to his crimes made him downright creepy. For example, as law enforcement officers raided his home, he casually played his piano, clad only in a bathrobe.

A few days after the raid, he lost his medical license and was charged with (among other things) killing babies born alive by snipping their spinal cords with scissors. The gruesome details of what went on within the walls of his clinic, revealed in the Grand Jury report[57] through the evidence and testimony of staff members and women who'd had an abortion there, made America's stomach turn.

One segment of the Grand Jury document reports that Adrienne Moton had worked for Gosnell. She wept as she described the death of Baby A, aborted by Gosnell at twenty-nine weeks (seven months). Ms. Moton was so upset that she took a cellphone photograph of the baby, which was shown in court. She testified that when Gosnell saw Baby A, he joked that the baby was "big enough to walk me to the bus stop."

Testimonies and other evidence presented at Gosnell's trial showed that many more babies at much over the legal limit in Pennsylvania for late-term abortions (twenty-four weeks) had been delivered alive, then killed by either Gosnell or his staff. Many of the women patients suffered brutal, permanent damage to their bodies or contracted venereal diseases from the unsterilized instruments. A Nepalese refugee, forty-one-year-old Karnamaya Mongar, who had just arrived in the United States, suffered a fatal drug overdose while undergoing an abortion performed by Gosnell.

Despite the filth, botched abortions, and deaths, among other crimes, Gosnell's defense attorney, Jack McMahon, insisted the trial was a witch hunt because Gosnell was black. In a Fox News interview, he stated that Gosnell "was a dream client ... nothing but a gentleman ... a soft-spoken man. An intelligent man."[58]

The story of Dr. Kermit Gosnell led to a documentary, books, and a movie starring Dean Cain as the original narcotics investigator who invaded Gosnell's clinic looking for drugs. It was a story that seemed to light up in America for just a moment—then nearly vanished.

My recounting of the multitude of stories of Gosnell's despicable actions against women and their babies isn't the point of this chapter. For me, although those stories are horrific, something else put an additional burden on my heart.

While the criminal case against Dr. Gosnell highlighted the barbaric nature of late-term abortions, it also seemed to highlight our cultural need to bury the truth that every abortion—no matter when it is done—ends a human life. Most everyone on either side of the debate would likely agree that some abortions are more graphic than others. Some use poison, others use surgical instruments, others use a vacuum. But the outcome is always the same. A life is ended, the life of a person the law of our land declares has no rights. We have rights over these lives, including the right to kill them.

In a Fox News interview, Gosnell's attorney, Jack McMahon,[59] defended his client and the right of abortion to the media.

> **McMahon:** There's a big difference between the abortion process and killing.
>
> **O'Reilly:** OK. But abortion is killing the fetus. Abortion is killing the fetus.
>
> **McMahon:** Well, it's legal. It's legal, Bill, and you know that.
>
> **O'Reilly:** It doesn't matter whether it's legal. He still killed them. He killed them. It doesn't matter if it's legal, he killed them.
>
> **McMahon:** Well, it's legal.[60]

After the trial, Jack McMahon spoke to the media, exposing within himself the inconsistencies that often exist in those who defend abortion. He stated that he believes all abortion should be illegal at sixteen weeks, before a baby is viable. Many abortion advocates seem to agree, saying that if the baby can live outside the womb, then abortion should be illegal. The problem with that line of reasoning is that the age of viability is not universally agreed upon and continues to shift. In Sweden viability is twelve weeks; in Romania it is twenty weeks; in Pennsylvania it is twenty-four weeks.

This takes the abortion debate back to the belief that a life is more valuable if the baby is not "dependent" upon the mother for survival. This logic leads to the issue of dependency of children with disabilities—or any newborn who needs to be fed by someone who can offer them a bottle! Viability doesn't give us our humanity; otherwise, I know a few out-of-work forty-year-olds living in their parents' basement who would be in danger.

The argument that life doesn't begin at conception is offensive enough. It denies science. It denies smaller and younger babies their right to life. Planned Parenthood didn't defend Kermit Gosnell, nor did NARAL. Even Jack McMahon—the man who defended a serial killer—thinks we should give the rights of babies sixteen weeks and older precedence over the rights of the women who carry those babies.

The Gosnell case revealed a truth about humans—most of us are offended by *some* abortions, but we differ on when abortion offends us. Our culture's response to Gosnell's actions was limited. Many of us weren't appalled at *all* of the many abortions he did, but rather by only a few, based on the age of the victims.

During his defense of Gosnell, McMahon said, "When they went in they found 47 fetuses there, 45 of them were in the legal limits of 24 weeks for Pennsylvania."[61] Why are we not, as a people, offended by those forty-five? Just because they were aborted legally at a stage of development with which we are comfortable? What does this say about us?

Many in our country—even many who support abortion—were appalled that babies would be aborted by Gosnell after the Pennsylvania legal age of twenty-four weeks—meaning that, at that stage, they were first born and then their spinal cords were cut as they moved with life on the table. Hearing about those babies, nearly everyone saw what abortion is. They saw abortion as murder.

The standards upon which we base our decisions about abortion are both discriminatory and inconsistent. In the Gosnell case, people were passionate about Baby A, Baby C, and Baby D. But what about the babies aborted in their early weeks of gestation? If abortion at that stage is all right, then what's wrong with late-term abortion? What's wrong, morally, with killing a baby at twenty-five weeks if abortion is okay at twenty-four weeks? Or if abortion at twelve weeks is all right, what's wrong with abortion at twenty-two weeks? Why is it okay in some states but not others?

Think about it. Baby A, Baby C, and Baby D, just a few weeks earlier, would have been legal abortions with few to advocate for them. When abortions are "normal," it's easy to discount the humanity of the fetuses.

In his closing arguments of the trial, McMahon said to the jury, "Abortion, as is any surgical procedure, isn't pretty. It's bloody. It's real. But you have to transcend that."[62]

It would have been more accurate if he had ended his comments after he presented the fact that abortion is bloody and real. Period. Like most successful lies, his bore an element of truth. With every medically necessary surgery, those involved must transcend the bloody, messy reality of it in order to save a life, to enhance a life. The bloody, messy reality is part of removing cancer, replacing knees, replacing organs, or putting a torn body back together. Bloodshed is often used to preserve life—with the ultimate example being Christ on Calvary.

But abortions are not like any other surgery. Bodies are not repaired to achieve life, but torn apart to end it. Yet according to McMahon, we need to see abortion as normal and get over it; we need to "transcend" the messy reality.

The impact of the Gosnell case continues as regulations are introduced across the country to make abortion facilities cleaner and safer. But abortion facilities, by their nature, will *never* be clean or safe or secure for one group of people—the unborn. These are not tumors or dysfunctional knee joints. They are human beings, as the Gosnell case reminded us. It served as a bright light that flashed the horror of abortion into the eyes of our culture.

Because Gosnell broke the law, we were given evidence of how appalling and brutal abortion is. Our culture could not be numb to the babies in jars and bags that were aborted (some of them illegally) and kept by Gosnell.

But our culture's full outrage was limited to those specific late-term abortions. There would have been no trial if Dr. Gosnell had performed all of those abortions within the legal time limit in a sanitary facility. No outraged reporters, no problems, not even newsworthy. Just another procedure that occurs over three thousand times a day in America. The outrage was limited to Baby A, Baby C, and Baby D's movements on the table. At his trial, Gosnell was convicted of first-degree murder for Baby A, Baby C, and Baby D. Reporters, politicians, and even abortion advocates lobbied for justice for these three babies. Justice was served, and Gosnell will spend the rest of his life in prison.

Allow the Gosnell case to challenge you. What did Gosnell do that was morally wrong that was different from every other abortion? Morally speaking, Gosnell was at least consistent. He didn't believe babies have rights; instead, he believed he had rights over them, so much so that he was willing to break the law. If we put our faith in the autonomous self to decide when a baby is viable or not and when an abortion is too ugly or not, if we give ourselves that kind of autonomy, then the Kermit Gosnells of the world will have all they need to justify their work. And that, if it happens, will shock us—but that is the price we pay for *not* being shocked and outraged at every abortion. As the saying goes, you cannot practice vice with virtue.

The result of what Gosnell did to twenty-five-week-old babies is the same as the result of what he did to ten-week-old babies. He is consistent in his view of human life. Are we?

~

Jesus turned and said to them,
"Daughters of Jerusalem, do not weep for me;
weep for yourselves and for your children."
LUKE 23:28

Dear Lord, give me the courage to be a voice in our culture that helps others see that every human life is precious and to be protected, from conception until birth and afterward. As disturbing as Dr. Gosnell's story is, may it open the eyes of those who hear it to see that viability is a slippery slope upon which to build an argument for ending the life of a child. Help this tragic story to be remembered and told, challenging fair-minded people to reconsider the value of every human life. Amen.

Joe Knows His Why

~

Men are not born saints with special gifts and privileges.
They fight against the world, the flesh and the devil,
and as they conquer, the spirit of Jesus begins
to shine through with more clarity.
—MOTHER ANGELICA

"Are you a Cracker Barrel man, Shawn?" Joe asked as we sat down in the popular country restaurant.

"I am. I support all establishments that, without passing judgment, encourage eating a chicken fried steak for breakfast," I replied.

That day, Joe had on his classic outfit. I don't think I would recognize him without his 40 Days for Life hat and his 40 Days for Life polo shirt.

He had been leading campaigns in Spring, Texas, outside Houston for years. Now approaching retirement, Joe still spent endless hours outside the Planned Parenthood facility in the spring along with a friend—his faithful prayer warrior, Joyce, who first challenged him to "get out there and make a difference." Joe got hooked, and over time he knew everyone who worked there and they knew him. Joe was not only calm and joyful, he was thankful, and therefore a contagious person to be around. He never complained—ever. Not about the heat, the rain, upset staff members, or angry passersby. Joe was always calm, steady, and ready to hand out information about alternatives to abortion or a 40 Days for Life flyer. He had been featured in the local newspaper many times, and his campaign continued to grow. Joe was known by churches and pastors of every kind. Everyone knew and loved Joe.

Inside Joe and every one of the leaders you have read about in this book is a *why* that drives them. *Why* put in so much time? *Why* are they constantly recruiting volunteers and promoting life? *Why* be the "pro-life lady" or "pro-life guy" at your church or workplace? Sure, half of all Americans consider themselves "pro-life," but why take what you believe so far?

We all have lives apart from pro-life work, and it does no good to go to extremes and throw yourself into saving babies if it means you neglect your own family, job, and other responsibilities. Doing what you can and trusting God with the rest are basics in serving in 40 Days for Life. But there is a smaller group of people like Joe who have the desire and the ability to live and breathe 40 Days for Life. Even though she was ill, Joe's wife, Barbara, enthusiastically supported the time he spent leading the campaigns. Perhaps that was because he never neglected her. Her needs always came first.

I was not the first to hear Joe's *why* the day I met him at the Cracker Barrel in Texas. The first person to hear it had been a hurting woman outside Planned Parenthood. Joe related the story to me that day over a good country breakfast.

That day, like so many others, a car pulled over to the curb where Joe prayed. A woman rolled down her window and shouted at Joe, "What are you doing here? Leave!" Her enraged voice soared over the shopping center on Louetta, where Planned Parenthood was located. The woman continued to shout, her voice full of fury. "You have no right to be here. You don't know what it's like to be a woman! Leave! Take your stuff with you! Why are you even here? Why?"

Joe calmly backed up to show respect and quietly waited, letting her vent. Planned Parenthood staff and volunteers came outside, drawn by the ferocity in the woman's voice echoing through the streets. Joe watched her with his deep-set eyes, waiting until she completed her rant. When it was clear that she was done, he was ready to answer her demand: *Tell me why you're here!*

I know the *whys* of most of our local leaders, but I'll never forget hearing Joe's. It takes us to a dark place that shows the pain of abortion—the very pain we are fighting.

~

Joe's story begins with him sitting in the parking lot of a Houston abortion facility, waiting for his wife and sixteen-year-old stepdaughter. He knew he shouldn't be there. His frustration with himself seeped out along with beads of sweat. *I've said nothing. And now we're here.*

Although Joe and his wife were against abortion, his stepdaughter was too young to have a child. Abortion looked different now that it was *their* daughter who was pregnant. *Their* daughter—only sixteen.

And it was their daughter Joe had driven to have an abortion at the facility where he now sat in his car. Joe felt empty as he battled his conscience, his weakness, and God, waiting anxiously for his wife and stepdaughter to come out. He stared in the rearview mirror until the front doors opened and they appeared.

He watched them as they walked toward him in painful silence, their body language expressing how they felt about the finality of what had just taken place. Joe thought, *This is going to destroy them both—I can already see it.*

Unfortunately, he was right.

That afternoon, Joe's daughter was a different person from the young lady he'd taken to the facility that morning. It wasn't just the end of her baby's life but part of her own as well. Instead of dealing with a baby being born into imperfect circumstances, they had to live with the pain the evil of abortion had released upon them all.

Their daughter was no longer that happy, bubbly, outgoing young teenager who loved life and was contagious with joy. She became strangely more reserved and serious. Her spontaneous laughter and other expressions of unbridled happiness were far less frequent and eventually grew nonexistent.

She married her sweetheart, the father of her aborted baby, at the young age of seventeen. They soon had two beautiful baby boys, and it seemed she had regained some of her joy. But the abortion of her first baby grew into deepest despair and severe depression. Even with professional counseling, medical, and clinical in-patient treatment, the pain grew unbearable. Finally, the fateful morning arrived. Her young husband kissed her and drove off to work. Then Joe's stepdaughter went into their bedroom and took her own life, seven years after her abortion. She was twenty-three.

~

As Joe finished telling his family's story to the woman whose angry diatribe had drawn a crowd, she was no longer in her car. She was standing near to Joe, and her expression had softened in recognition of Joe's humanity.

"My wife nearly lost her mind from the horror of what happened," Joe said. "She still cries when she allows herself to remember our beautiful daughter and the grandchild we could have enjoyed during this life on earth."

The Planned Parenthood employees watched the whole scene unfold. The woman looked at Joe, walked over to him, and hugged him tightly.

Joe has kept in contact with that woman since then. She is now considering joining Joe on the sidewalk during his 40 Days for Life vigil.

In 2018, after years of sickness, Joe's wife, Barbara, passed away. She wanted nothing more than for Joe to continue to be out there and getting others out there to reach women and save babies.

"Shawn," Joe says, "I do this because I did nothing to try to convince a young girl to not get an abortion years ago. I was against abortion even then, but I said nothing. *It was I who drove.*"

There have been nearly one million abortions per year in the United States since 1980. That is nearly one million babies lost forever, one million women, one million men, and one million drives to an abortion facility. Abortion doesn't just kill a single baby. It kills families. That's why it pierces our heart like no other issue.

Some *whys*, like Joe's, come from pain and regret. God uses Joe's pain to save lives from abortion. He's given Joe forgiveness, peace, and a mission.

Emotional pain is just one of the things God might use for our *why*.

Meanwhile, the devil uses distractions to keep us from knowing or living out our *why*. We and our culture don't see abortion as God sees it or as Joe sees it. So many don't see it as something that matters.

Why can't we see how much is at stake in every single abortion? Why are we silent? Are Planned Parenthood and the media right in calling 40 Days for Life "40 Days of Harassment"? (We've been called worse. You have to admit, though, it is kind of catchy.) Should we just mind our own business? Do we need, in fact, to "get a life"?

To mind our own business would be to ignore the pain of abortion for young women like Joe's stepdaughter. It would mean ignoring the woman screaming at Joe, as well as the curious Planned Parenthood workers watching and listening as Joe tells his *why*. Ignoring the men affected by abortion. And those who drive women to their appointments. Minding our own business leads to ignoring the media, the politicians, and the talking heads who make so much noise over the ones who have no voice—the babies.

We often miss the efforts that go into distracting folks from the reality of the baby. The devil started by distracting us from the baby in the manger and continues distracting many from the reality that these are live babies in the womb. These unborn babies are created in God's image and likeness. Their circumstances are not always ideal. They may be born poor or disabled or neglected. They might be considered a minority. These boys or girls or twins may grow up to fail at school or to become president. But no matter what, they are God's, and so are we.

They are worthy of your why.

Joe has a powerful *why* for his involvement in pro-life work. He had to go to hell and back to get it, and he lives with the painful consequences today, but he is allowing God to use that powerful *why*. He is no longer silent. He once drove his stepdaughter to get an abortion, but now he has driven thousands of times to his local abortion facility, his car loaded with "Pray to End Abortion" signs and alternative information. He is now a beacon of hope to those driven by desperation to seek abortion. He is saving babies from abortion and showing the mercy of Christ—a mercy he himself has experienced.

Finding our *why* requires getting out of our distracted culture, finding silence, and praying for wisdom to speak up for those who cannot speak for themselves.

∾

Do not be afraid of them, for there is nothing concealed that will not be disclosed, or hidden that will not be made known. What I tell you in the dark, speak in the daylight; what is whispered in your ear, proclaim from the roofs. Do not be afraid of those who kill the body but cannot kill the soul. Rather, be afraid of the One who can destroy both soul and body in hell. Are not two sparrows sold for a penny? Yet not one of them will fall to the ground outside your Father's care. And even the very hairs of your head are all numbered. So don't be afraid; you are worth more than many sparrows.

MATTHEW 10:26–31

Dear God, I pray that you will meet me and reveal to me my why. Give me clarity in my purpose so that I can play the part you've called me to play in reaching out to hurting, grieving, and frightened women and men who are facing unexpected pregnancies or who are grieving in the aftermath of an abortion. Give me the courage to help save lives. I lift up all the 40 Days for Life volunteers around the globe. Give them the courage to share their whys, and embolden them with the persistence and resilience they need to stand in peaceful, prayerful vigils. Thank you, Lord, for inspiring this movement that has saved and transformed so many lives. Amen.

The Beginning of
the End of Abortion

~

"I am in fact a Hobbit in all but size.
I like gardens, trees, and … farmlands;
I smoke a pipe, and like good plain food …
have a very simple sense of humor …;
I go to bed late and get up late (when possible).
I do not travel much."

—J.R.R. TOLKIEN

ANTHONY ROLLED DOWN THE WINDOWS AND TURNED THE RADIO
up on a beautiful late April day in Pennsylvania.

He had gotten off work earlier than expected and was glad to be
headed home. His night shifts as a cop had ended, and he was enjoying his new schedule. Pulling into his driveway, he was immediately
reminded that he would need to mow the lawn after the kids' baseball game on Saturday morning. He also needed to power wash the
porch. *The list never ends,* he thought as he opened the door.

"Daddy!" The high-pitched screams and parade of little feet
began as his three boys and two girls came to greet him.

"You're home early," his wife, Jen, said.

"Yep. Sarge told me to go home, and I didn't argue," Anthony
said, studying the inside of the fridge. "Why is it that at the end of a
pay period we only have Cheerios and cheese sticks?"

"Chill out, mister. I'm cooking you the dinner you requested three weeks ago," she laughed. "It's your birthday meal. Did you forget?"

"It is?" Anthony asked, smiling. "Well, in that case, I'll smoke the cigar Sarge gave me."

"Not around the kids! We can sit outside later."

Anthony kissed her and headed to the back porch where a football game was breaking out.

"Don't tackle your sisters!" Anthony called as he sat down and saw that the brothers were acting like brothers. "Man, I need to power wash out here too," Anthony muttered as Michael declared himself the full-time QB to his younger siblings. That would definitely not end well.

~

Anthony and Jen have five kids—Michael, Isabel, Gianna, Keith, and Joseph, ranging in age from three to eleven. Little Joseph, the youngest, has cerebral palsy. When he was born, Anthony began the push to get off night shifts. Raising a child with disabilities was getting hard on Jen. She never complained but knew things had to change.

They've been married thirteen years. Jen had promised only one date to the persistent literature major back in college. "What are you actually going to do with a literature degree anyways?" she asked on that first date as they ordered the fish tacos Anthony swore by.

"Lots of things" he said, smiling. "I can read books and then brag about it to those who don't read."

"That's not a real answer," she replied.

"I love books. I just wanted to study something I love. Plus, if we get married and have kids, I can teach our kids about literature, since you're studying—what is it, finance?"

"Accounting," she said as the tacos arrived.

"Accounting! That'll get you jacked up and out of bed in the morning. Who needs Shakespeare when you have accounting?" He took a bite, swallowed, and then said, more seriously, "No, I won't use my degree, actually. I'm just graduating and then going to the police academy."

"Really? You're going to be a cop?"

"You got it. What I've always wanted to do. That and have kids."

Jen said, "My dad's a cop. He's about to retire."

"Sounds like a good father-in-law to me," Anthony smiled.

"There's something wrong with you," Jen said, laughing. "Although you do have good taste in tacos."

Now, years later, Anthony and Jen struggle. They have homework every night, a porch that needs power washing, a yard that needs cutting, and a child with disabilities. Anthony has a stressful job, and Jen stays home with five kids. They go to church, pray, play with their kids, and—locked and loaded with strollers and snacks—make it out to their local 40 Days for Life campaign when they can.

≈

I've been to hundreds of abortion facilities. On the forty-day journey we've shared in the pages of this book, I have taken you to a few. I've spoken with those who are about to have an abortion, those who have had an abortion, those who are paying for an abortion, and those who on their way to do an abortion.

There is a glaring vacancy on the other side of the fence, the side where the abortion facility sits. The beauty that abortion directly attacks—a loving family—is nowhere to be found. There is nothing more unnatural than paying a physician to end the life of your child. There is nothing more natural than a married couple welcoming a baby into their home, and there is also nothing more exciting or rewarding.

"A saint is one who struggles," goes the timeless Christian saying. We are not promised, in this life, a perfect upbringing or healthy kids or a good night's sleep. We *are* promised a struggle, and much of that struggle today, as we stand on the sidewalk praying, is for the family. Abortion is first and foremost an attack on the beauty of the family; for it to happen, there must be an unwanted child. The real heroes of our culture aren't on television. They're raising their children, listening to their children, laughing with their children, and suffering with their children.

Anthony and Jen and those like them are the answer to the great attack on hope in our culture.

Perhaps more than any culture in history, we view children as a burden. The joy of having children and raising them is being lost because of the lie that children are a burden, that they're simply not worth it. This is the hopelessness that fills parking lots of abortion facilities. But it didn't start there. It started in the home—or perhaps because of the lack of one.

There are many ways to help end abortion, and we need to pray and get busy. But more than that, we need the Anthonys and Jens of the world. Yes, they struggle, but not everything has to be picture perfect. It's okay to struggle. Our Lord could have popped out of an acorn and saved us from our sins in a millisecond.

He's God. He can do anything. But he didn't. He entered the world through a family. He was born in a barn, in exile; he cried, he worked, he sweated, he humbled himself, and he learned from his earthly parents. Salvation came through a family. A family of humble means, a family that endured scandal and gossip around a pregnancy, a family that experienced suffering and death.

Abortion facilities are full of anxiety, fear, instability, and loneliness. Compare that with the peace and serenity of a loving family. We need not be anxious about the crisis of abortion. Instead, we need to pray, work, and trust. I hope the previous pages have given you many examples of heroes doing just that.

In the gospels, the highest level of anxiety we see in Jesus' young family concerns what every parent fears most—losing a child. Mary and Joseph didn't know where Jesus was for three days. Imagine not knowing where one of your children is for just ten minutes! Mary and Joseph discovered he was missing when they were already on their journey home from celebrating Passover, and they had to travel back to Jerusalem to find him. Three days of worrying, imagining, and seeking. Only to learn he was in the first place they should have thought to look—his Father's house.

This—the family—is where we place our hope to end abortion. There are many basic and secular reasons to be against abortion. But the physical assault on the baby reflects the greater assault on the family, and therefore an assault on hope. Abortion represents and brings about loss of hope. And yet the stories you've read in this book show that hope is not lost. Hope can be restored, even at the last moment. Hope is present in a loving family that faces struggles together and yet keeps going, together.

~

At the March for Life in Washington, DC, a few years ago, I looked in the distance and saw Anthony, Jen, and their kids. I had first met the family at a campaign vigil years before. I waved. They couldn't see me, but there they were, holding signs, five different snacks spread among the kids, everyone bundled up in the January wind, with little Joseph in a stroller, just his blue eyes showing.

I don't know whether Anthony had to go back to night shifts or if he ever power washed his back porch. But I do know he is a man who loves his wife and his kids. He doesn't resent getting another medical bill for Joseph, and he's overjoyed to dance with his girls in the kitchen on a school night. He prays with them, and yes, reads literature to them.

He and Jen have the usual family problems: boys showing an interest in their girls, college expenses coming, broken-down cars—and on top of that, future medical concerns for Joseph. In short, they have a life. But they pray, and they entrust their family to God. Their house is decent, though it needs some work—but their *home* is magnificent. It has the power to change the world.

They are raising a family.

They are the beginning of the end of abortion.

∾

Every year Jesus' parents went to Jerusalem for the Festival of the Passover. When he was twelve years old, they went up to the festival, according to the custom. After the festival was over, while his parents were returning home, the boy Jesus stayed behind in Jerusalem, but they were unaware of it.

Thinking he was in their company, they traveled on for a day. Then they began looking for him among their relatives and friends. When they did not find him, they went back to Jerusalem to look for him. After three days they found him in the temple courts, sitting among the teachers, listening to them and asking them questions. Everyone who heard him was amazed at his understanding and his answers.

When his parents saw him, they were astonished. His mother said to him, "Son, why have you treated us like this? Your father and I have been anxiously searching for you."

"Why were you searching for me?" he asked. "Didn't you know I had to be in my Father's house?" But they did not understand what he was saying to them.

Then he went down to Nazareth with them and was obedient to them. But his mother treasured all these things in her heart. And Jesus grew in wisdom and stature, and in favor with God and man.

LUKE 2:41–52

Dear Lord, help me to remember that it's okay to struggle.
Use me to be a positive force for family in our broken culture.
Lord, I want to be the beginning of the end of abortion.
Amen.

Acknowledgments

I'M THANKFUL TO GOD AND MY PARENTS FOR THE GIFT OF MY LIFE and the opportunity to serve this greatest cause of my generation.

Writing this book came at one of the busiest times of my life—40 Days for Life had more campaigns around the world than ever before, and we had just launched a new magazine, app, online store, and podcast. Marilisa and I were also awaiting the delivery of our seventh baby. I could not have done this without the support of the 40 Days for Life headquarters team—Steve Karlen, Robert Colquhoun, David Brandao, Katharine O'Brien, Melinda Giambo, Bobby Reynoso, Lourdes Varela, Jill Copeland, Gilbert Gonzales, Nathan Kocmoud, Andrew Kocmoud, Ben Starnes, and Cheryl the Great (Tamez), who has been with us since the very beginning. The contents of this book show what a great team we have.

I am especially grateful for the encouragement of the chairman of the board and general counsel for 40 Days for Life, Matt Britton. His enthusiasm and support allowed me to take the time to complete this project.

Since 2007, 40 Days for Life has grown very quickly, but we have a board of directors—past and present—that has been up to the challenge: Dr. Haywood Robinson, Tibor Baxsy, Carol Siedhoff, Mark Spearman, Matt Britton, and Alfonso Chicharro. They work hard to serve our leaders and have a deep desire to offer hope to women and their babies. I'm thankful for their many sacrifices.

Many thanks to 40 Days for Life's donors, who make the growth and improvement of 40 Days for Life possible. Our donors are not distant from our mission; rather, they are participants, and we never forget that.

This book would not have been possible, nor would it have any point, without the heroes of 40 Days for Life: the local campaign leaders. There just aren't enough pages to share how God has used this courageous group of people who are living their faith and changing our world. Working alongside you is one of the great honors of my life.

To Dave and Cindy Lambert and the entire Somersault Group team: You are so good at what you do and have a wealth of knowledge and experience. I'm thankful you are using your gifts and background for books that point people to the gospel. Cindy, the Irish like to talk and write—sorry for my long-windedness and complete disregard for word count. I'll never learn to write just one chapter at a time.

Thank you, Wes Yoder of Ambassador Agency, for your wisdom in getting this book and 40 Days for Life in the hands of as many people as possible. Your burning passion for the pro-life movement is a blessing to the literary world. I love working with you.

Thank you to my children, Bridget, Bailey, Seamus, Bernadette, Declan, Mary Cate, and Celinda. Your constant asking about how the book was going made me laugh and made me answer the question daily. You kept me going. Mom and I love all of you very much and are blessed that God entrusted you to us.

In thanksgiving for the many holy priests in our life—your joy and faith are contagious.

Finally, thank you to Marilisa, my wife, who first asked me to go pray at a Planned Parenthood abortion facility during my freshman year of college. God was looking out for me when you said yes to our first date. Thank you for your love, support, laughter, and feedback. I love you.